Learning at the Feet of the Savior

Additional Insights from New Testament Background, Culture, and Setting

David J. Ridges
Taylor Halverson, PhD

CFI
An imprint of Cedar Fort, Inc.
Springville, Utah

ISBN 13: 978-1-4621-4596-6

Published by CFI, an imprint of Cedar Fort, Inc.
2373 W. 700 S., Springville, UT 84663
Distributed by Cedar Fort, Inc., www.cedarfort.com

LIBRARY OF CONGRESS CATALOGING-IN-PUBLICATION DATA

Names: Ridges, David J., author. | Halverson, Taylor, author.
Title: Learning at the feet of the Savior / David J. Ridges and Taylor Halverson.
Description: Springville, Utah : CFI, an imprint of Cedar Fort, Inc., [2018] | Includes bibliographical references and index.
Identifiers: LCCN 2018034468 (print) | LCCN 2018039506 (ebook) | ISBN 9781462129423 (epub, pdf, mobi) | ISBN 9781462122820 (hardback : alk. paper)
Subjects: LCSH: Jesus Christ--Mormon interpretations. | Church of Jesus Christ of Latter-day Saints--Doctrines. | Mormon Church--Doctrines.
Classification: LCC BX8643.J4 (ebook) | LCC BX8643.J4 R527 2018 (print) | DDC 232--dc23
LC record available at https://lccn.loc.gov/2018034468

Cover design by Jeff Harvey

Edited by Kathryn Watkins and Allie Bowen
Typeset by Kaitlin Barwick

Printed in the United States of America

10 9 8 7 6 5 4 3 2 1

Printed on acid-free paper

This book is dedicated to my mother, Verla Nelson Ridges, who taught me early in my life to love the scriptures, especially the doctrines of the plan of salvation, and to my wife, Janette, who stands by my side and encourages my writing and makes life pleasant and beautiful.

—David J. Ridges

This book is dedicated to my grandparents Lionel and Anne Halverson, who stoked my flames of curiosity in the New Testament world. They both passed soon before I returned home to share with them the life-changing transformation I experienced during a Fall 1994 semester study abroad at the Brigham Young University Jerusalem Center. I hope they are pleased with my efforts.

—Taylor Halverson

Also by
David J. Ridges

The Gospel Studies Series

Our Savior, Jesus Christ: His Life and Mission to Cleanse and Heal

Mormon Beliefs and Doctrines Made Easier

The Proclamation on the Family: The Word of the Lord on More than 30 Current Issues

65 Signs of the Times and the Second Coming

100 Signs of the Times

Doctrinal Details of the Plan of Salvation: From Premortality to Exaltation

To This End Was I Born : Walking with the Savior in His Final Week

Temples: Sacred Symbolism, Eternal Blessings

Priesthood Power Unlocked

Using the Signs of the Times to Strengthen Your Testimony

The Red Porsche

The Righteous Role of a Father

Gospel Questions, Gospel Answers

A Mother's Perfect Hope

Seasons of a Mother's Love

Born to the Virgin Mary

Also by
Taylor Halverson

Scriptural Insights and Context: The New Testament

Millions Shall Know Brother Joseph Again: Daily Inspiration from the Prophet Joseph Smith

Distance Education Innovations and New Learning Environments: Combining Traditional Teaching Methods and Emerging Technologies

Learning for Eternity: Best BYU Speeches and Articles on Learners and Learning (forthcoming)

Knowing Why: 137 Evidences that the Book of Mormon Is True

History of Creativity in the Arts, Science, & Technology, Pre-History to 1500, 3rd edition

History of Creativity in the Arts, Science, & Technology, 1500 to Present, 3rd edition

"Finding Myself Alone": Positive Thoughts, Insights, & Discoveries of LDS Singles (forthcoming)

Memoirs of the Ward Rumor Control Coordinator: Or, Smile If You Are a Mormon!

Contents

INTRODUCTION

This book is an invitation to come learn anew at the feet of the Savior, to learn additional insights into the New Testament teachings of Jesus, to become better at how to learn, and to become better at learning how to teach.

Jesus is the Master Teacher, and we all aspire to be more like Him. The Gospel narratives (Matthew, Mark, Luke, and John) provide numerous examples for how Jesus created compelling learning experiences. We, as His students, can all benefit not only from what He taught, but also from how He taught. We learn even more when we pay close attention to the settings and culture in which He taught. Teachers and learners can learn from Jesus how to improve teaching and learning and how to better design learning experiences that help others draw closer to God. Being a better learner and teacher of the gospel of Jesus Christ are two ways that we can follow the footsteps of the Master. This book was written to provide guidance and encouragement, based on the New Testament Gospels and the life and example of Jesus for how we can improve our learning and teaching of the principles of the eternal teachings of the Savior.

We have organized each chapter of this book into five separate sections: We quote a scripture episode, provide cultural and historical insights, describe Jesus as the Master Teacher in that episode, explore potential applications of the insights discussed as they pertain to learning and teaching improvement, and conclude with suggestions for teachers.

Scripture Events

In the pages of this book, we select a number of important (and sometimes overlooked) episodes or scriptural blocks from the Gospels to show Jesus as a teacher and learning designer. Each chapter is dedicated to a specific scriptural episode. We identify the scripture block, name the scriptural episode, quote the scriptural block complete with helpful, guiding notes based on David Ridges's *Your Study of the New Testament Made Easier, Part 1* publication, and where relevant, quote the Joseph Smith Translation (abbreviated as JST).

Background, Culture, and Setting

In this section, we provide cultural and historical insights relevant to the quoted scriptures. Some of these sections are lengthy, others shorter. Regardless of the amount of content in each section, our intention is to help bring perspective, relevance, context, and understanding to the New Testament Gospels, especially to the specific scriptural episodes we quote. Roughly two thousand years separate us from the time of Jesus. During that enormous span of time, tremendous changes have occurred between the world of Jesus and the world of today. We hope to clarify what life was like in that time. When we understand the scriptures in their cultural context, the foreignness of some aspects of the scriptures can be replaced with familiarity and new moments of discovery.

The Master Teacher

We seek to look at the scriptures in fresh ways, through the lens of Jesus as Master Teacher. How did Jesus create compelling and inviting learning environments? What did He teach? What conventions did Jesus use to teach? Why did He teach the way He did? Why did He teach what He did? What can we learn from Jesus about how to learn? About how to teach others? These are some of the questions we attempt to answer in this segment of each chapter.

Possible Applications for Learners

As exciting as new scriptural insights are, it is insufficient to have great thoughts without action. This portion of each chapter is dedicated to encouraging learners and teachers to think about how to apply (1) the teaching and learning principles derived from the quoted scripture block, and (2) the gospel principles discussed in the chapter.

Helps for Teachers

We end each chapter with a section that provides helps for teachers. Typically, we provide a list of potential discussion questions a teacher could consider for quickly involving students in classroom discussion, or that a learner could use for increasing the effectiveness of personal study time. These questions may focus on gospel principles or teaching and learning principles.

HOW TO USE THIS BOOK

This book can be used profitably in a variety of ways. You might read the book from beginning to end and find yourself inspired again by the beauty, truth, timelessness, and timeliness of the New Testament teachings of Jesus Christ. Or you might find specific chapters that contribute to your personal scripture study. Perhaps you are a Sunday School teacher. If so, you may find new insights or teaching ideas for specific scripture passages that correlate with Sunday School curriculum. Or if you are teaching family members, or teaching in any other setting, you can seek to learn from the teaching principles Jesus employed. As a learner, you can seek to apply to your own life the learning principles Jesus used in His ministry.

We hope that this book inspires you to read the scriptures with fresh eyes, to ask new questions that lead to learning more about the gospel, learning how to be a better teacher, and learning how to be a better learner. Our hope is that this book encourages you to ask more questions in your scripture study, such as: Why is this story in scripture? What are the details of this scripture and why are they shared the way they are? What can I learn from this scripture story about the gospel? What can I learn about Jesus as Teacher? What can I learn in order to be a better teacher? What can I learn to be a better learner?

As we seek learning, we fulfill the purpose of the plan of salvation to access the Atonement of Jesus Christ and become more like God.

Matthew Gives the Genealogy of Christ

Matthew 1:1–3, 5–6

1 The book of the generation [*genealogy*] of Jesus Christ, the son of [*descendent of*] David, the son of [*who was a descendent of*] Abraham.

> The genealogy of Christ, given here by Matthew, is that of the legal successors to the throne of David, not a strict father-to-son genealogy. It includes living successors such as grandson, nephew, etc. Luke's genealogy of the Savior, as given in Luke 3:23–38, is a strict father-to-son genealogy. Since Joseph and Mary were cousins (see *New Testament Student Manual*, page 22), Joseph's genealogy is essentially Mary's genealogy, and thus, the Savior's.

2 Abraham begat Isaac [*was the father of Isaac*]; and Isaac begat Jacob; and Jacob begat Judas [*Judah; see Genesis 29:35*] and his brethren;

3 And Judas begat Phares and Zara of Thamar; and Phares begat Esrom; and Esrom begat Aram;

4 And Aram begat Aminadab; and Aminadab begat Naasson; and Naasson begat Salmon;

5 And Salmon begat Booz [*Boaz, Ruth's husband; see Ruth 4:13*] of Rachab; and Booz begat Obed of Ruth; and Obed begat Jesse [*King David's father*];

> You've no doubt noticed that some of the names here are spelled differently than you are used to from the Old Testament. What is happening here is that the New Testament is using Greek forms of the names, which sometimes differ from the original Hebrew. Thus, Ruth's husband, Boaz, is listed as "Booz," and Judah is listed as "Judas."

6 And Jesse begat David the king; and David the king begat Solomon of her that had been the wife of Urias [*Bathsheba*].

Background, Culture, and Setting

What do we miss when we skip this genealogy in Matthew 1 that has been carefully documented and preserved for us? Among other valuable information, we miss the beautiful message that all people are redeemable and God will accomplish His work.

In this genealogy, four women are identified: Tamar (Thamar), daughter-in-law to Judah, who had to trick him into fulfilling his obligation to provide her a son; Rahab (Rachab), the prostitute of Jericho who helped Joshua's spies; Ruth, the non-Israelite Moabite; and Bathsheba, the wife of Uriah (Urias) the Hittite, who became involved in an adulterous relationship with King David. What do all these women have in common? Each of these women came from nontraditional, unusual, or unexpected circumstances. They were either gentile non-Israelite women, or they were women who had improper relations with a man.

Why would the genealogy highlight *only* four women and then make such *unusual* choices? Why not choose Hannah or Sarah or Rachel or Rebecca?

THE MASTER TEACHER

How was Mary like the four women mentioned in the genealogy? She too had unusual circumstances of bringing forth a child in unexpected and nontraditional ways. In fact, some, who don't know the true circumstances, might say, "Why, Mary wasn't even married when she got pregnant. That is out of order! Mary's life doesn't conform to the pattern of the gospel we should expect from an upstanding child of God." What this genealogy teaches us is that God can do His work and redeem all of His people. Foreseeing the potential criticism of Mary's nonconforming life circumstances, the scripture writers were inspired to remind readers, using scriptural genealogy, that Jesus Christ's honorable lineage had a number of unexpected twists and turns, which demonstrate that all can ultimately be redeemed and honored by God, including those whose lives don't seem to conform to the gospel standard. God will do His work and fulfill His plan.

POSSIBLE APPLICATIONS FOR LEARNERS

Reading Matthew's genealogy of Christ can show careful readers that the redeeming power of the gospel and Atonement of Christ is available to all. Also, Matthew's genealogy can remind us not to judge others by their background or family origins. For example, Rahab, the harlot of Jericho, helped Joshua's spies so that Israel could conquer Jericho. Even though in her past she had been a harlot, because of her support for God's people, she received divine favors. Or consider Tamar, the daughter-in-law to Judah. By law and convention, she was due a child. When Judah did not fulfill his obligation to provide a new husband for her from his remaining sons after several husbands had died, she played the harlot and tricked him. Though the Bible does not advocate for trickery and harlotry, Tamar still is included in the honored lineage of Jesus. Similarly, Bathsheba, who was fulfilling the law of Moses to ritually purify herself, was taken by king David while she was married to another. She had little agency, because, as king, David could do almost anything he wanted. Of course, Nathan the prophet confronted David over his egregiously erroneous deeds. Bathsheba, too, is part of Jesus's honored lineage, even though her life circumstances were different than the ideal.

HELPS FOR TEACHERS

Well-designed questions can help promote involvement of class members in the discussion. For example:

- How does this scripture block teach that all people are redeemable?
- How can we inspire learners to see God's hand in their lives everywhere?

- How can we help all of us to be less judgmental of those whose lives don't seem to conform to our understanding of the gospel?
- How can we be patient in letting God's plan unfold?
- How can we be more believing that God can redeem any and all of His children?
- What are some other scriptural examples of "unconventional" people that the Lord used for righteous purposes?

Scriptural Event: Wise Men Come from the East

Matthew 2:1–2

1 Now when Jesus was born in Bethlehem of Judaea in the days of Herod the king [*see Bible Dictionary, pages 700–701, for background information on Herod the Great*], behold, there came wise men [*no doubt inspired men of God; perhaps prophets*] from the east to Jerusalem,

2 Saying, Where is he that is born King of the Jews? for we have seen his star in the east, and are come to worship him.

> JST Matthew 3:2
>
> 2 Saying, Where is the child that is born, the Messiah of the Jews? for we have seen his star in the east, and have come to worship him.

Background, Culture, and Setting

The Bible narrative does not dwell on the origin, characteristics, history, or background of the wise men who came to worship Jesus. We don't even know how many traveled from afar to reach the precious and promised Christ Child, though popular convention imagines three wise men because of the three gifts they offered: Gold, frankincense, and myrrh.

By long tradition, the wise men are called *magi*, a word used in the ancient Persian Empire to describe "learned priests" and "holy men." Incidentally, our word *magic* comes from that same word, because those who did not understand the priesthood, or who falsely sought to misuse the power of God, attempted to deceive people through magic.

What we can deduce is that these wise men from the east, whom we call magi, were likely holy men and priests trained in the arts of interpreting ancient scriptures and the signs of the times. They anxiously awaited the Messiah and were prepared in heart, body, and mind when He arrived.

The Master Teacher

Though Jesus was not in an active position of being a teacher in this episode, He was still in a position to receive love and service from others. Even the best teachers know how to graciously receive from others. Jesus did not stop others from serving, from loving, from giving. Jesus allowed others to use their agency to do good. For example, according to Luke 7, when Jesus was eating at a Pharisee's home, a sinful woman washed His feet with her tears, dried His feet with her hair, and anointed Him with expensive oils and perfumes. The Pharisee accused Jesus of not being a prophet, for otherwise He would have known that the woman was a sinner. (Remember that Pharisees were zealous for living righteously on the straight and narrow.) Jesus taught the Pharisee the power of love, forgiveness, and understanding while He graciously received the kind service from the woman.

POSSIBLE APPLICATIONS FOR LEARNERS

How can we serve and help the teachers who bring forth truth to us? How can we seek to share the good news with others about the truths dedicated teachers share with us? Great teachers do not need to always be in the spotlight. They do not need to be the only ones *doing*. In fact, the best teachers empower learners to act for themselves. Great teachers do not get in learners' ways or stop learners from serving, acting, and doing. And great learners do not wait to be commanded in all things. Instead, they do much good of their own free will and volition. Great learners are proactive and self-directed. They find ways to grow and improve and put their efforts into those causes, with or without the direction of a teacher.

HELPS FOR TEACHERS

Outside of His own family, the first people to learn of Jesus are the wise men who model for the rest of us what to do: worship him. The Greek word used for "worship" here and abundantly throughout the New Testament is *proskuneo*. It means to bow down or fall down with the head touching the ground as a sign of extreme reverence. Homage is offered to the one being worshipped with, perhaps, petitionary kissing of the hands or feet.

And wise men seek Him still.

- In all of our teaching, are we encouraging worship of Jesus? No one needs to fall down to the ground as they did in Bible times. But are learners feeling the love of Jesus? Do they feel a sense of awe and worshipfulness about Jesus?
- Do all of your lessons point to Jesus?
- Why did wise men visit Jesus?
- What lessons can this story teach us about the nature and mission of Jesus?

Here are some questions that can help class members become involved in the discussion:

- How does the coming of these wise men from the east provide evidence that God does indeed speak to all His children, as taught in 2 Nephi 29:7–11?
- What does the fact that the wise men came from somewhere in the "east," looking for the Christ Child, show us about God's concern and care for others of His children besides those spoken of in the Bible?
- How do you suppose that these wise men found out about the coming birth of the Savior?
- How many wise men were there? (We don't know.)
- Why does tradition say that there were three wise men? (Because they brought three gifts—gold, frankincense, and myrrh. See Matthew 2:11.)

FINDING JESUS IN THE TEMPLE

LUKE 2:41–52

41 Now his parents went to Jerusalem every year at the feast of the passover.

> The Feast of the Passover is celebrated each year by the Jews in March or April, to commemorate the "passing over" of the angel of death over the Israelite homes in Egypt, when God smote (or killed) the firstborn of the Egyptians. See Bible Dictionary, under "Feasts."

42 And when he was twelve years old, they went up to Jerusalem after the custom of the feast [*as was the custom, to celebrate the Passover feast*].

43 And when they had fulfilled the days [*when they were finished*], as they returned [*to their home*], the child Jesus tarried [*stayed*] behind in Jerusalem; and Joseph and his mother knew not of it.

44 But they, supposing him to have been in the company [*they thought he was with friends or relatives in their traveling group*], went a day's journey; and they sought [*looked for*] him among their kinsfolk [*relatives*] and acquaintance.

45 And when they found him not, they turned back again to Jerusalem, seeking him.

46 And it came to pass, that after three days they found him in the temple, sitting in the midst of the doctors [*teachers, men of high education*], both hearing them, and asking them questions.

> As you will see, as you read the JST for verse 46, above, it makes a significant change. Jesus was teaching them, rather than they teaching Him.
>
> JST Luke 2:46
>
> 46 And it came to pass, that after three days they found him in the temple, sitting in the midst of the doctors, and they were hearing him, and asking him questions.

47 And all that heard him were astonished at his understanding and answers.

48 And when they [*Joseph and Mary*] saw him, they were amazed: and his mother said unto him, Son, why hast thou thus dealt with us [*why did you give us such a scare*]? behold, thy father and I have sought thee sorrowing [*we have been looking for You, very worried!*].

49 And he said unto them, How is it that ye sought me [*why were you looking for me*]? wist ye not [*didn't you know*] that I must be about [*be doing*] my Father's [*Heavenly Father's*] business?

50 And they understood not the saying which he spake unto them. [*Joseph and Mary didn't understand His explanation.*]

51 And he went down [*home*] with them, and came to Nazareth, and was subject [*obedient*] unto them: but [*JST "and"*] his mother kept all these sayings in her heart.

52 And Jesus increased in wisdom and stature, and in favour with God and man.

> When he was born, Jesus had the veil over his memory of the premortal life, just as all do. Elder James E. Talmage taught,
>
> "He came among men to experience all the natural conditions of mortality; He was born as truly a dependent, helpless babe as is any other child; His infancy was in all common features as the infancy of others; His boyhood was actual boyhood, His development was as necessary and as real as that of all children. Over His mind had fallen the veil of forgetfulness common to all who are born to earth, by which the remembrance of primeval existence is shut off. The Child grew, and with growth there came to Him expansion of mind, development of faculties, and progression in power and understanding" (Talmage, *Jesus the Christ*, page 111).
>
> President Joseph F. Smith said that Jesus did not know who He was as He lay in the cradle. See April 1901 general conference. As stated in verse 52, above, He gained wisdom as He grew. No doubt the veil was gone before He reached age twelve, for He knew who He was and felt the urgency of being about His Heavenly Father's business, as expressed to Joseph and Mary in verse 49, above.

Background, Culture, and Setting

Jesus was the adopted son of Joseph the Carpenter. In ancient Jewish times, young boys often learned the trade and followed in the footsteps of their father. Though Jesus knew who His real Father was, declaring to Mary and Joseph, who were seeking after Him after He had stayed behind at the Jerusalem temple for several days, "[Did you] not know that I must be about My Father's business?" (Luke 2:49), Jesus followed in the footsteps of His earthly father, Joseph, to become a carpenter. Significantly, the underlying Greek word to describe Jesus's profession, *tekton*, means more than a simple carpenter. A *tekton* is one who is a craftsman, a planner, an organizer, an author and finisher of a planned project. Jesus is our *tekton*, the author and finisher of our faithful lives.

The Master Teacher

Jesus, the master *tekton* of the universe, came to the temple to teach. Sitting in the Holy House of God that was still under construction by Jewish builders, under the direction of the *tekton* Herod the Great, Jesus chose to "build" the lives of his listeners, which was the business of His Heavenly Father. Jesus understood what His true role was, and He recognized who His real Father was. Though Jesus was raised as a carpenter's son to an adoptive father, Jesus clearly knew what His real business was and Whom He truly served: "Wist ye not that I must be about my Father's business?" And though others did not understand Jesus's mission, including His earthly parents, "And they understood not the saying which he spake unto them," He continued to pursue His mission.

Possible Applications for Learners

Though He hinted at these things, Jesus did not reveal everything to His parents about His identity and mission. As teachers, we are not obligated to teach everything we know, to share everything we have studied. Instead, one of the most important roles of a teacher is to recognize the needs of the learners and to meet those needs. If we, as teachers, instead seek to meet our own needs to "deliver a lesson" or to "get through content," we miss the opportunity to be like the Master Teacher who gave people line upon line and precept upon precept. As exemplified in the case of His mother, Jesus gave people space and time to ponder, reflect, and act upon what had been taught before they received more. Just as we wouldn't continue to feed a child who is already satiated by a satisfying meal, so too we should not overfeed our learners or expect them to gorge on multiple thanksgiving meals of spiritual content. Just as that same child needs time to digest and then use that energy in a variety of pursuits, our learners need time to practice what they have learned. Pacing, pausing, and not sharing all at once everything there is to share will help learners to, like Jesus, steadily increase "in wisdom and stature, and in favour with God and man."

Helps for Teachers

- As you prepare to teach, have you considered the learning needs of those in your care? What do they already know? What do they not know? And what do they need to know and why?
- How will participants in your class be different because of the lessons you have prepared? How will they have new or reinforced knowledge of truth? How will they be empowered to live revealed truths?
- Why was Jesus at the temple?
- What was the business of Jesus?
- How did Jesus treat those who did not recognize or understand His mission?

Questions to foster involvement in class discussion:

- What significant change does the JST provide to this scripture block, as seen in Luke 2:46 footnote c?
- What do these verses tell us about whether or not Jesus knew who He was at this point in His life?
- What does the fact that Joseph and Mary were not initially worried about the whereabouts of Jesus as they began the journey home from Jerusalem tell us about how they traveled? (They apparently traveled with a large group of relatives and friends such that it was common for children to stay with others during the journey.)
- What does verse 52 tell us about whether or not Jesus had the veil over His memory when He was born? (He did. See commentary for verse 52, above.)

The Baptism of Jesus

Matthew 3:13–15

13 Then cometh Jesus from Galilee to Jordan unto John, to be baptized of him.

14 But John forbad him, saying, I have need to be baptized of thee, and comest thou to me?

15 And Jesus answering said unto him, Suffer [*allow*] it to be so now: for thus it becometh us to fulfil all righteousness [*to do the will of the Father*]. Then he suffered him.

> JST Matthew 3:42–44
>
> 42 But John refused him, saying, I have need to be baptized of thee, and why comest thou to me?
>
> 43 And Jesus, answering, said unto him, Suffer me to be baptized of thee, for thus it becometh us to fulfill all righteousness. Then he suffered him.
>
> 44 And John went down into the water and baptized him.

Background, Culture, and Setting

The word *Jordan* is a Hebrew word that means "to descend," "to go down," and "to flow down." All rivers flow downward in elevation, so we may think that this name is not particularly creative as a name for a river. And yet, what beautiful and symbolic lessons we learn about humility and the work of God of "going down" from the word *Jordan*. First, Jesus came down from a higher elevation (the Galilee region) to the area where John was baptizing at the Jordan River, likely near where it flows into the Dead Sea, the lowest spot on the earth. Second, Jesus demonstrated humility by "going down" to John to be baptized, even though John correctly perceived, "I have need to be baptized of thee [Jesus]." Third, Jesus's baptism was a similitude of His "going down" into the grave and coming alive again. Fourth, Jesus came down from heaven. He condescended in full humility to leave His heavenly throne and become mortal. Finally, when we follow Jesus to "go down" into the grave of baptismal water, the blessings of God will "flow down" to us from on high, most specifically through the reception of the Holy Ghost.

As teachers, we should strive to keep all the commandments and to live the principles we are teaching. Let our example be a powerful teacher.

The Master Teacher

Here we see the Master Teacher set the master example. He is the master example of following the Father's commandments perfectly. Jesus is the most humble of all God's children. Having achieved divine status in the premortal world, Jesus was nevertheless willing to come to this earth in the same type of flesh bodies we all inhabit. He had to endure all the vicissitudes of life and to suffer with us. He did not exercise His divine prerogatives to avoid heartache, pain, labor, sacrifice, and ultimate suffering. He came down from on high to be one with us. That is what it means to condescend—"to go down together." As the Master Teacher, He did not lead from the back of the group. Rather, He led from the front, modeling for all of us how to lead lives dedicated to God.

POSSIBLE APPLICATIONS FOR LEARNERS

One of the most important applications for each of us is that we likewise submit ourselves to baptism into the Lord's true Church. The Savior set the example for us. For those who are born in the Church, we follow the example of parents, friends, and other family members. For converts, we set the example for those around us, including our children now or in the future, friends, neighbors, and the list goes on and on. The only possible way to get onto the "straight and narrow path" is through the gate of baptism (2 Nephi 31:17–18).

HELPS FOR TEACHERS

Questions to help students be involved in learning might include

- Did Christ really have to be baptized (since He was perfect) or was He mainly doing it to set a good example? (He had to be baptized to fulfill the commandment of the Father. See 2 Nephi 31:5–7.)
- What does the phrase "to fulfill all righteousness" mean? (To fulfill the will of the Father.)
- How might you use this scriptural passage to show that immersion was the necessary form of baptism, as taught and demonstrated by John the Baptist? (The Jordan River was a long way from population centers and was a lot of extra trouble if sprinkling or some alternate form of baptism was sufficient to fulfill the law of baptism.)
- How do you show humility in teaching?
- How do you show humility in learning?
- What actions must you take to receive the promised blessings that will "flow down" from on high?
- How can you help yourself and others to receive the gift of the Holy Ghost to magnify learning?
- How are we helping learners to fulfill all righteousness?
- How are we seeking to fulfill all righteousness?

The Father Proclaims Jesus to Be His Beloved Son

Matthew 3:16–17

16 And Jesus, when he was baptized, went up straightway out of the water [*evidence that He was baptized by immersion*]: and, lo, the heavens were opened unto him, and he [*John the Baptist*] saw the Spirit of God [*the Holy Ghost*] descending like a dove, and lighting upon him [*the Savior*]:

17 And lo a voice from heaven, saying, This is my beloved Son, in whom I am well pleased.

> The JST gives verses 16–17 as follows (remember, the numbering is sometimes different in the JST):
>
> JST Matthew 3:45–46
>
> 45 And Jesus when he was baptized, went up straightway out of the water; and John saw, and lo, the heavens were opened unto him, and he saw the Spirit of God descending like a dove and lighting upon Jesus.
>
> 46 And lo, he heard a voice from heaven, saying, This is my beloved Son, in whom I am well pleased. Hear ye him.
>
> Because of these and other verses in the scriptures, some people have come to believe that the Holy Ghost occasionally turns into a dove. Such is not the case. The Prophet Joseph Smith taught that the Holy Ghost does not transform himself into a dove. He said,
>
> "The Holy Ghost is a personage, and is in the form of a personage. It does not confine itself to the *form* of the dove, but in *sign* of the dove. The Holy Ghost cannot be transformed into a dove; but the sign of a dove was given to John to signify the truth of the deed, as the dove is an emblem or token of truth and innocence" (*Teachings of the Prophet Joseph Smith*, Deseret Book, 1977, pages 275–76).

Background, Culture, and Setting

The Holy Ghost "descended" upon Jesus after baptism (remember that the word *Jordan* means "to descend"). Again, we see the use of the word *Jordan* and its meaning saturating this portion of the narrative with symbolism and significance. At this point in the narrative, we read of one of the few times the voice of God Himself is recorded in scripture. He says in humility, without any need for focus and attention on Himself: "This is my beloved Son."

This language is significant for several reasons. First, God the Father calls Jesus "beloved." Since we are all children of God and He loves us all, why does God reserve the word "beloved" only for his Son Jesus Christ? In this, and similar words in the English language that start with "be" (beget, below, betray, beyond, betrothed, beguile, begin, become, befriend, behave, believe), the "be" means "completely, thoroughly, fully." "Beloved" means "fully loved," "thoroughly loved," and "completely loved" because He alone is the one who fully, thoroughly and completely pleases God. Second, we should recognize that when God calls Jesus His Beloved Son, this in no way diminishes how God loves us all perfectly. "Beloved Son" is language from the royal Psalms in the Old Testament where God identifies the king as His son: "The Lord hath said unto me [*the Davidic king*], Thou art my Son; this day have I begotten thee" (Psalm 2:7). In other words, Beloved Son = The Chosen King. Because Jesus is the King, He is the Beloved Son.

The Master Teacher

Jesus was chosen and appointed by God. Similarly, teachers are appointed by God through His priesthood-bearing servants. Just as God gave specific blessings, strength, and honor to Jesus to support Him in His divine role, so too, God will give to each duly called Church teacher the power and strength equal to their charge to teach others to come unto Jesus. Just as Jesus is God's Beloved Son, we are God's beloved teachers, fully empowered through the priesthood to teach and testify of the truth and to challenge learners to be more like Jesus.

Possible Applications for Learners

Though only Jesus is *the* Beloved Son of God, we are all beloved children of God. As children of God, we should continuously seek to grow and develop in righteousness. That is, we should vigorously pursue learning and growth. As children of God, we have the capacity to be like Him. The all-encompassing Atonement of the Beloved Son paves the way for us to pursue continuous improvement.

Helps for Teachers

- "This is my beloved Son, in whom I am well pleased. Hear ye him." What is the significance of this phrase as God the Father's recorded direct communication with His children?
- What obvious evidence do you see in this scriptural passage that Jesus was indeed baptized by immersion?
- What symbolism of our confirmation do you see here, with Jesus as the example?
- Does the Holy Ghost sometimes turn Himself into a dove? (No. In *Teachings of the Prophet Joseph Smith*, pages 275–76, the Prophet said that "the Holy Ghost is a personage, and is in the form of a personage. . . . The Holy Ghost cannot be transformed into a dove; but the sign of a dove was given to John [the Baptist] to signify the truth of the deed.")
- Does a person become a member of the Church by baptism alone, or does he or she also have to be confirmed? (He or she also has to be confirmed.)
- What does it take for us to be pleasing to God?

Christ Goes into the Wilderness to Be with God, Is Tempted by the Devil

Matthew 4:1–11

The JST makes many changes to Matthew, chapter 4. You will see a number of them referenced in footnotes in your LDS printing of the Bible. (Remember, several JST changes are not contained in our Bible, simply because they would take up too much space. Therefore, some JST changes that we give in this book are not found in your Bible.) We see a significant difference in verse 1 comparing the King James Version translation (KJV) to the JST.

1 Then was Jesus led up of the Spirit into the wilderness to be tempted of the devil.

> JST Matthew 4:1
>
> 1 Then Jesus was led up of the Spirit, into the wilderness, to be with God.
>
> As you can see, in the JST verse quoted above, the Prophet Joseph Smith teaches us that the Savior went into the wilderness to be with His Father. From this we learn that He did not go specifically to confront the devil nor to be tempted by him. Perhaps one of the things we can learn from this is that we should not deliberately put ourselves in a position to be tempted. In fact, the Savior said, "lead us not into temptation" (Matthew 6:13). And if you look at Matthew 6 footnote 13b, in your Bible, you will see that "do not let us enter into temptation" is given as another translation of this phrase.
>
> Thus, we understand that temptation will come to us simply as a result of being here on earth, but we should not deliberately place ourselves in tempting circumstances.
>
> The JST provides important additions to verse 2, next.

2 And when he had fasted forty days and forty nights, he was afterward an hungred.

> JST Matthew 4:2
>
> 2 And when he had fasted forty days and forty nights, and had communed with God, he was afterwards an hungered, and was left to be tempted of the devil.

3 And when the tempter [*Satan*] came to him, he said, If thou be the Son of God, command that these stones be made bread [*temptation to yield to physical appetite*].

4 But he answered and said, It is written [*in Deuteronomy 8:3*], Man shall not live by bread alone, but by every word that proceedeth out of the mouth of God.

5 Then the devil taketh him up into the holy city [*Jerusalem*], and setteth him on a pinnacle of the temple,

> JST Matthew 4:5
>
> 5 Then Jesus was taken up into the holy city and the Spirit setteth him on the pinnacle of the temple.

6 And saith unto him, If thou be the Son of God, cast thyself down: for it is written [*in Psalm 91:11–12*], He shall give his angels charge concerning thee: and in their hands they shall bear thee up, lest at any time thou dash thy foot against a stone [*temptation to yield to vanity, pride*].

> JST Matthew 4:6
>
> 6 Then the devil came unto him and said, If thou be the Son of God, cast thyself down, for it is written, He shall give his angels charge concerning thee, and in their hands they shall bear thee up, lest at any time thou dash thy foot against a stone.

7 Jesus said unto him, It is written again [*in Deuteronomy 6:16*], Thou shalt not tempt the Lord thy God. [*Note that Jesus answers each temptation with a scriptural quote. This is a reminder of the power of the scriptures to safeguard us against temptation.*]

8 Again, the devil taketh him up into an exceeding high mountain, and sheweth him all the kingdoms of the world, and the glory of them;

> JST Matthew 4:8
>
> 8 And again, Jesus was in the Spirit, and it taketh him up into an exceeding high mountain, and showeth him all the kingdoms of the world and the glory of them.

9 And saith unto him, All these things will I give thee, if thou wilt fall down and worship me [*temptation to yield to materialism and power*].

> JST Matthew 4:9
>
> 9 And the devil came unto him again, and said, All these things will I give unto thee, if thou wilt fall down and worship me.

10 Then saith Jesus unto him, Get thee hence [*leave Me*], Satan: for it is written [*in Deuteronomy 6:13*], Thou shalt worship the Lord thy God, and him only shalt thou serve.

11 Then the devil leaveth him, and, behold, angels came and ministered unto him.

Background, Culture, and Setting

In these scriptures, Jesus is in the wilderness, then at the temple, and then directly confronting Satan.

Matthew 4:1–4 calls upon our memory of the Old Testament. Just as Jesus is now spending 40 days in the wilderness, so too did the Israelites wander for 40 years in the wilderness. Jehovah created a type of bread, called manna, for the Israelites when they wandered in the wilderness. The adversary tempted Jesus to do the same for Himself, to fulfill His bodily needs easily. As Jesus demonstrated with the force of power and will that reverberates across the centuries, the adversary was *not* the master over Jesus. Jesus was the master. He is the master. And if we are to be like Jesus, we must learn to control all our appetites and passions and keep them within the bounds that God has established.

Matthew 4:5–7 takes place at the temple. The temple in Jerusalem at the time of Jesus was the largest religious building anywhere in the vast Roman Empire. Conceived and executed by Herod the Great (yes, the baby killer Herod; he was called "Great" because of his prodigious building spree throughout the land of Israel), the temple was under construction for more than 40 years. In fact, even though the temple was actively used for worship and sacrificial purposes, workmen were toiling away for many years after the time of Jesus to complete this massive public works project. Though the temple took years to build, many of its significant features were complete by the time of Jesus. For example, at the southwestern corner of the temple, there was a staircase that led to the top of the wall overlooking the open public plaza just to the south of the temple and the public marketplace that ran along the west of the temple. From this vantage point, a temple priest would blow the *shofar* (ram's horn) trumpet at regular intervals to announce time for prayers and sacrifice. What is particularly relevant about this location is the public view it had of the city and what a long drop it was from the pinnacle (or place of trumpeting) to the street below. If one were to jump from that pinnacle, thousands of people would see that death-plunge of more than 100 feet. That act would be the talk of the town for years to come. And if you wanted to garner attention, what better way to do so than in the most public and dare-devilish way possible? To top it all off, if angels came sweeping in at the last moment to save you from death, you'd be an instant hero to last the ages.

As we see in Matthew 4:8–11, it is a common tactic for the adversary to tempt the children of God with visions of power, glory, kingdoms, riches, and dominion. "We have learned by sad experience that it is the nature and disposition of almost all men, as soon as they get a little authority, as they suppose, they will immediately begin to exercise unrighteous dominion" (D&C 121:39). We know the story of Moses who, because of his experiences with God, could immediately tell the difference between the lack of glory and the lies of Satan and the power and light of Jesus:

> Blessed be the name of my God, for his Spirit hath not altogether withdrawn from me, or else where is thy glory, for it is darkness unto me? And I can judge between thee and God; for God said unto me: Worship God, for him only shalt thou serve. Get thee hence, Satan; deceive me not; for God said unto me: Thou art after the similitude of mine Only Begotten. And he also gave me commandments when he called unto me out of the burning bush, saying: Call upon God in the name of mine Only Begotten, and worship me. And again Moses said: I will not cease to call upon God, I have other things to inquire of him: for his glory has been upon me, wherefore I can judge between him and thee. Depart hence, Satan. (Moses 1:15–18)

Like Jesus and Moses, we can successfully detect and confront the adversary through immersion in the word of God and by regularly experiencing God's presence in our lives.

THE MASTER TEACHER

The adversary tempted Jesus to fulfill His physical needs easily. Who would have known? Jesus was by Himself in a howling wild place (the word *wilderness* literally means the wild areas). He could have acted, created bread for Himself, and provided nourishment to His famished body. No one would have ever known. Who would it have hurt? In a sea of rocks, would anyone have missed a single, apparently useless rock used to make bread for Jesus? Wouldn't that rock have cried out to save its Creator? And who would criticize Jesus for such an action? Wouldn't our collective humanity cry out, "Yes, save the starving Savior by any means necessary!" Fully divine Jesus is also fully human. He had cravings and hunger every bit as real as any one of us has ever experienced. But He let His spirit master His body, even in the face of persistent cravings and alluring temptations from the adversary.

Now consider this, can Jesus's work be done if no one knows who He is? Can you exercise faith in Jesus Christ if you don't know His name? Can you repent of your sins and feel forgiveness if you have no conception of Jesus Christ? We can all agree that to be saved, every knee must bow and every tongue confess that Jesus is the Christ. (See Romans 14:11 and D&C 76:110.) Today we understand the power of sensationalism to gather an audience and a following. We live in the YouTube sensationalized world, where people gather millions of viewers by the most audacious acts and words. These followers may last a lifetime. Sensationalists have created for themselves the opportunity to influence millions upon millions of people because of some sensationalist act. Why didn't Jesus take up the opportunity to get an immediate following of tens, if not hundreds of thousands, or even millions? Wouldn't that have been much faster instead of walking around the dusty roads of the Galilee, going from poor hamlet to uneducated poor hamlet, meeting with individuals, one-on-one to listen to them, to teach, and to heal? Wow, Jesus took the slow route to gathering a crowd. Satan really seemed to be on to something when he suggested that Jesus jump off the pinnacle.

But Jesus knew better. He knew that His message was about truth. How could He expect people to accept and live truth if He garnered a crowd on false pretenses and sensationalism? Jesus's humility was so thorough that His response was genuine and immediate, "Thou shalt not tempt the Lord thy God." Of course, Jesus was speaking truth to Satan, "I, Jesus Christ, am Lord and God. I will therefore not hand over My crown by acting under your direction."

POSSIBLE APPLICATIONS FOR LEARNERS

The devil used three major categories of temptations, that we likewise face constantly, in his tempting of the Savior: (1) Physical appetites, (2) vanity and pride, and (3) materialism and power. But you will see another form of temptation associated with the above temptations. It is the word "if" in verses 3, 6, and 9. The devil challenged Jesus that *if* He was indeed the Son of God, He could prove it by doing certain things. This "if" challenge can be an effective tool for Satan as he likewise challenges us to "prove it." People often find themselves committing sin or taking foolish chances in order to respond to someone who is suggesting that they are not what they claim to be.

The Savior Himself was subjected to temptation by the devil. Likewise, God does not constantly protect us from the temptations of the devil and his evil followers, because we need opposition to exercise our agency. This principle is taught in the Book of Mormon as follows: "For it must needs be, that there is an opposition in all things" (2 Nephi 2:11). We can be like Jesus, though tempted of the devil, strengthened in the opposition to endure to the end.

Helps for Teachers

- How much effort and sacrifice are you willing to endure to be a learner? Or a teacher?
- How much do you listen to the adversary? Do you pay attention to his false lies about your abilities, your appearance, your testimony, your love, and your standing before God? Or do you strive to cast him away as Jesus did?
- As a teacher or a learner, how often do you use the scriptures to answer questions? How can you increase your ability to do this? (One answer is by increasing your consistency in daily scripture study.)
- As a teacher or a learner, how does the adversary tempt you to show off to others and thus forget the things of the Lord?
- What are your temple pinnacles, your areas of pride that you'd love having the crowd see and acknowledge you for?
- What efforts are you making as a teacher or learner to have angels minister to you?
- What devil's bargains do you grapple with? How have you called down the powers of heaven for strength to overcome?

Rejection of Jesus in His Hometown of Nazareth

Matthew 4:13–17

13 And leaving Nazareth, he came and dwelt in Capernaum, which is upon the sea [*Sea of Galilee*] coast, in the borders of Zabulon and Nephthalim [*the area where Zebulon and Naphtali, two of the Twelve Tribes, settled when Joshua brought the children of Israel into the promised land*]:

> Here, you will see yet another example, beginning with verse 14, of the emphasis by Matthew that Jesus was the fulfillment of Old Testament prophecies concerning the Messiah.

14 That it might be fulfilled which was spoken by Esaias [*Isaiah*] the prophet [*in Isaiah 9:1–2*], saying,

15 The land of Zabulon, and the land of Nephthalim, by the way of the sea, beyond Jordan, Galilee of the Gentiles;

16 The people which sat in darkness [*spiritual darkness*] saw great light [*the Savior and His gospel*]; and to them which sat in the region and shadow of death [*spiritual darkness*] light is sprung up.

17 From that time Jesus began to preach [*Jesus now begins His formal ministry*], and to say, Repent: for the kingdom of heaven is at hand [*salvation is now being made available to you*].

Background, Culture, and Setting

(for Matthew 4:13–17)

The ancient Israelite prophet Isaiah spoke of the time when Jesus would bring light to the world, describing in prophecy the area where Jesus would conduct his ministry. The Israelite tribal territories of Zebulon and Naphtali encompassed the region surrounding Nazareth where Jesus grew up, as well as the town of Capernaum where Jesus lived at times during His ministry. Isaiah specifically identifies "Galilee of the Gentiles" as the area in which Jesus would live. In the times of the Israelite conquest of the Holy Land, under the guidance of Joshua, the eastern portion of the Galilee "beyond Jordan" (that is, on the east side of the Jordan River) remained in the hands of non-Israelites. In the days of Jesus, that land was still primarily occupied by Gentiles; it was the land of the ten gentile cities, otherwise known as the "Decapolis."

Born in Bethlehem, raised in Nazareth, Jesus lived out the remaining years of his adult life primarily in Capernaum, after announcing his Messianic mission in Nazareth.

The name of the town *Capernaum* comes from two ancient Hebrew words meaning "the town of Nahum" which could further be translated as "town of consolation, sorrow, or repentance." The meaning of the name of this town is appropriate, because it underscores Jesus's primary message, "Repent."

Luke 4:16–30

16 And he came to Nazareth, where he had been brought up: and, as his custom was, he went into the synagogue on the sabbath day, and stood up for to read.

> Watch now as the Master reads two verses of scripture from Isaiah in the synagogue of His hometown, and then tells the people gathered there that the verses apply to Him.

17 And there was delivered unto him [*brought to Him at His request*] the book of the prophet Esaias [*Isaiah*]. And when he had opened the book, he found the place where it was written [*Isaiah 61:1–2*],

18 The Spirit of the Lord is upon me [*Christ*], because he hath anointed [*called*] me to preach the gospel to the poor; he hath sent me to heal the brokenhearted, to preach deliverance [*remission of sins*] to the captives [*those under the bondage of sin*], and recovering of sight to the blind [*spiritually as well as physically*], to set at liberty [*redeem*] them that are bruised [*by sins*],

19 To preach the acceptable year of the Lord [*the time designated by the Father for Jesus to perform His mission as a mortal on earth; see McConkie,* Doctrinal New Testament Commentary, *vol. 1, page 161*].

20 And he closed the book, and he gave it again to the minister, and sat down. And the eyes of all them that were in the synagogue were fastened on him.

21 And he began to say unto them, This day is this scripture fulfilled in your ears. [*In other words, I am the fulfillment of this prophecy of Isaiah.*]

22 And all bare him witness [*spoke well of him (for a few minutes)*], and wondered at the gracious words which proceeded out of his mouth. And they said [*to each other*], Is not this Joseph's son?

> The men of the synagogue, who heard Jesus claim to be the Messiah, after reading the passage from Isaiah, now begin to have doubts. They have heard of the many miracles and things a man named Jesus has been doing throughout the country. Now, when they see that He is the Jesus who grew up in their town, they say, in effect, "Now wait a minute. Isn't this Jesus who is Joseph the carpenter's son? We know His family. He grew up here. He is just a common man, one of us. How can He possibly think He is the Messiah?"

23 And he said unto them, Ye will surely say unto me this proverb, Physician, heal thyself: whatsoever we have heard done in Capernaum, do also here in thy country. [*Prove that You are something special by doing the same miracles You have done elsewhere.*]

> You have probably heard the last phrase of verse 24 many times. It is often quoted to mean that a person who is famous among people elsewhere is criticized and put down among people he or she grew up with.

24 And he said, Verily I say unto you, No prophet is accepted in his own country.

25 But I tell you of a truth, many widows were in Israel in the days of Elias [*Elijah*], when the heaven was shut up three years and six months, when great famine was throughout all the land;

26 But unto none of them was Elias [*Elijah*] sent, save [*except*] unto Sarepta, a city of Sidon, unto a woman that was a widow.

27 And many lepers [*people with leprosy*] were in Israel in the time of Eliseus [*Elisha*] the prophet; and none of them was cleansed, saving [*except*] Naaman the Syrian [*2 Kings 5:14*].

> The point Jesus is making to these men of His hometown seems to be that it wasn't necessary for prophets such as Elijah and Elisha to heal every person in the land or perform the same miracles for everyone to be accepted as a prophet sent from God. So why should it be different with Jesus? Why should He be required to perform the same miracles for the people of Nazareth, as for others, to be accepted by them? Couldn't they exercise faith in what had been done elsewhere?

28 And all they in the synagogue, when they heard these things, were filled with wrath [*were very angry*],

29 And rose up, and thrust him out of the city, and led him unto the brow [*cliff*] of the hill whereon their city was built, that they might cast him down headlong [*headfirst*].

30 But he passing through the midst of them went his way,

> It will be interesting to get the rest of the details as to what happened here. This was a great miracle, if these wicked and hardhearted men would pay attention to it.

Background, Culture, and Setting

(for Luke 4:16–30)

Nazareth, set up in the limestone hills north of the Jezereel valley, was a poor, out-of-the-way spot of the Galilee region. Accessing this small village was not necessarily easy, especially since sheer cliffs created a natural barrier to the southeast.

Not on any major roads and bereft of educational or other advancement opportunities, the synagogue would have been the community of Nazareth's lifeline to learning, opportunity, and socialization. The Jews gathered at synagogues to read scriptures and share interpretations. Synagogues were typically built to have their front door oriented to Jerusalem. Benches lined the walls so that everyone could see each other. They took turns reading and interpreting scripture. The custom was that for whoever's turn it was to read, they would stand and read the assigned scriptural passages out loud. Standing identified who was teaching that day and made it easier for everyone to see that person. After the designated individual read the scriptures out loud, they would sit down, signaling that they would now explain the scriptural passages. Though we don't have exact certainty, evidence suggests that underneath a Crusader chapel tucked away in the market area of modern-day Nazareth is the original synagogue where Jesus taught.

The Master Teacher

Looking at the above verses in Matthew, we see that Jesus, basing His ministry in "the town of repentance," kept His message simple and relevant, in other words, "repent." That is a word we seldom hear today outside of religious contexts. Even then, the word "repent" is not one most people like to hear, evoking a sense of dread, guilt, and the potential for significant punishment. If we peel back the meaning of this word, as it is expressed in the Greek of the New Testament, the word *repent* does not convey the fire-breathing wrath of an offended God. Instead, invitingly, the word literally means "to change your mind." Can any repentance happen without change? And doesn't that change initially happen in our mind or heart? We have to decide to change. That is the first step. (Incidentally, ancient people believed that the heart was the origin of thinking, which is why we have the phrase "a change of heart" when what we really mean is "a change of mind.")

With this understanding, we do not have to feel to avoid the call to repent. We can embrace the opportunities and possibilities inherent in change. Isn't learning all about change? Isn't it having our minds changed by new experiences, new information, new perspectives, new stories, and new ideas?

Looking at the Savior's example, we see that master teachers share principles and then illustrate them with case studies, examples, metaphors, analogies, expansions, and other relevant information to make the principle memorable, useful, and applicable. Though, as teachers, we will likely never declare ourselves as fulfillers of specific prophecies of Isaiah, Jesus used scripture to illustrate to His listeners how He was like other past Israelite prophets who had also been rejected by the people. Jesus even challenged His Jewish listeners' sense of order and justice when He reminded them that the only person cleansed during the famine of Elijah's day was the gentile Syrian Naaman.

Master teachers challenge learners to expand their understanding and perspective but must do so without offense, anger, or pride.

Possible Applications for Learners

As learners or teachers, we need not be eloquent to be instruments in the hands of God. We need not be so-called gospel scholars or gospel intellectuals to share with simple love and humility the saving truths so powerfully revealed in Jesus, the son of God. Should we pursue gospel learning? Absolutely, with all diligence. Should we seek to expand our scriptural understanding and capacity? Without a doubt. But our scripture mastery is not meant to be a tool with which we impress others as though there is a competition with our fellow brothers and sisters in the Lord for our interpretative supremacy of scripture.

Helps for Teachers

As teachers, we should follow the example of Jesus to not overly complicate the message of the gospel. There is so much sophistry and wordsmithing in the world. Our words should never be used to cloud, diminish, dilute, or distract from the plainness of the gospel, and especially not to call attention to ourselves as being intellectually amazing. The message of Jesus is simple: "Repent and come unto me." Two Book of Mormon prophets said it well. Nephi declared that we should speak "in plainness, even as plain as word can be . . . because I glory in plainness; I glory in truth; I glory in my Jesus, for he hath redeemed my soul from hell" (2 Nephi 32:7; 2 Nephi 33:6). And Alma the Elder reminded us that we "should preach nothing save it were repentance and faith on the Lord, who had redeemed his people" (Mosiah 18:20).

When scriptures are read, can everyone hear? The ancient synagogues were laid out in such a manner that everyone could see and hear everyone else. Our modern-day Sunday School classrooms are typically not so laid out, privileging the teacher over joint participation. Though we want everyone to participate, many problems abound when there are rows of people, such as difficulties in seeing and hearing everyone. That being the case, the teacher should carefully consider how to ensure that everyone can hear and see, and, when possible, arrange the classroom accordingly.

Let's take the example of reading scriptures in Sunday School. Is it really necessary to change readers with every verse? Often such an activity, meant to involve more people in the Sunday School lesson, actually distracts from learning from scripture: Those in the front row may not be able to hear those who are in the back row. People might lose track of what verse they should read, and then there is a pause and fumbling around with scriptures until the right scripture is located. So, if you feel tempted to have everyone take turns reading one verse at a time out loud in class, consider other ways to help everyone hear the scriptures without disruption.

Helpful questions to start good class discussion might include

- What factors might have caused the Jews who rejected Jesus here in His hometown to fail to acknowledge Him as the Savior?
- Are you aware of some issues where some members reject the words of our living prophets?
- How can we avoid treating some of the messages of our living prophets like the Jews did the Savior's words?
- What role does a strong personal testimony of the gospel play in our following the prophet?

Miraculous Catch of Fish

Luke 5:4–9

4 Now when he had left speaking, he said unto Simon [*Peter*], Launch out into the deep, and let down your nets for a draught [*a catch of fish*].

5 And Simon answering [*in response*] said unto him, Master, we have toiled [*worked hard fishing*] all the night, and have taken nothing: nevertheless at thy word I will let down the net.

> By way of information, it was the practice at this time for those who fished for a living on the Sea of Galilee to fish during the night.

6 And when they had this done, they inclosed a great multitude of fishes: and their net brake [*started to break; see Luke 5 footnote 6a*].

7 And they beckoned [*waved*] unto their partners, which were in the other ship, that they should come and help them. And they came, and filled both the ships, so that they began to sink.

> There is beautiful symbolism here. As Peter and others follow the Savior's instructions in faith, they have great success in catching fish. Symbolically, as Peter and the others follow Christ, He will make them "fishers of men," and they will have a large "catch" of converts. See end of verse 10 below.

8 When Simon Peter saw it, he fell down at Jesus' knees [*very humble*], saying, Depart from me; for I am a sinful man, O Lord. [*I am not worthy to be in Thy presence.*]

9 For he was astonished, and all that were with him, at the draught [*catch*] of the fishes which they had taken:

10 And so was also James, and John, the sons of Zebedee, which were partners with Simon. And Jesus said unto Simon, Fear not; from henceforth thou shalt catch men.

Background, Culture, and Setting

The Sea of Galilee, a massive freshwater lake in the north of Israel, is a significant source of life to the Holy Land. The Jordan River flows out of its southern shores, watering the rich farmland of the Jordan River Valley. The Sea of Galilee lies in a deep depression at some 600+ feet below sea level. There is some farmland surrounding the Sea of Galilee, but not much. Mountains surround the sea and create inclines that make farming on the slopes impractical. Volcanic rocks also mar sections of the mountains, discouraging any capable farmer from risking his plow in such unforgiving territory. In ancient times, the primary moneymakers near the Sea of Galilee were fishing, trade, tax collecting, and some limited farming (where arable land was available). Compared to today's living standards in the modern West, the majority of those ancient Jews living near the Sea of Galilee struggled to have sufficient resources for their needs, and seldom, if ever, sufficient for any wants. Theirs was a hardscrabble life that required ongoing toil, effort, sacrifice, failure, undergirded with faith in God and hope for success.

The Master Teacher

Simon Peter was a fisherman living on the north side of the Sea of Galilee in the town of Capernaum. Though poverty was the common lot for most Galilean Judeans during the time of Jesus, Peter had a fishing business with several boats and partners. Peter seems to have experienced some success and prosperity as a fisherman. What does this suggest about Peter? He knew what he was doing as a fisherman. After a fruitless night of toil on the unpredictable waters of the Galilee, why did Peter listen to Jesus command "Launch out into the deep, and let down your nets for a draught"? Wasn't Jesus a lowly carpenter from Nazareth, the out-of-the-way town that future disciple Nathaniel wonderingly questioned, "Can there any good thing come out of Nazareth?" (John 1:46). What would a carpenter know about fishing? Where to take the boat? Where or when to let down the net? Peter could have responded with pride, "Jesus, I appreciate the suggestions, but leave it to me, the expert fisherman in this region, to know how to do my job. I have nothing to learn from you." Jesus challenged Peter, within Peter's own domain of experience and expertise. Similarly, good teachers do likewise for their learners. Heeding Jesus's call to action, Peter experienced unexpected success. Good teachers do not shy away from inviting their learners to try again, to work harder, to exercise faith, to experience unexpected success, even within their own areas of expertise. And good learners willingly learn from others, even if they may be (or think they are) an "expert" on a topic the teacher is not.

Possible Applications for Learners

As teachers, we cannot be experts in all things. Often we will be treading on the expertise of others when we invite them to answer questions, share insights, or to act. Everyone can learn. Everyone can be challenged to grow and progress, even if they are already an "expert" and have lots of experience. Teachers should not shy away from challenging learners to exercise their faith. Learners should be willing to act on invitations. When humility encompasses these interactions, both teacher and learner are edified.

We authors have friends who teach in the CES system who faithfully attend Sunday School each week as learners, even though they teach the scriptures full time as their day job. Some in the class, and sometimes even the teachers in these Sunday School classes, want to call upon these CES teachers to answer all the questions, thinking along these lines, "We might as well have the expert sitting in the room tell us the answers." We have observed how these CES teachers respond with simple humility in such settings: "I am a learner. I am here to learn from others. If I do all the talking, what will I ever learn?"

None of us are beyond learning. Without learning, we may miss significant opportunities to experience the Atonement. Without the Atonement, learning is not possible. Let us be like Peter, ever willing to act on faith to learn, to try, to experiment, and to experience. We are liable to be surprised by the draught of miracles we catch as we exert our efforts to lower our nets.

Helps for Teachers

- Why did Jesus ask Peter to continue fishing after such a grueling, unsuccessful night?
- When has Jesus challenged you to act for yourself?
- How has God taught you humility?
- When has God showered His unexpected miracles upon you?
- When have you learned a profound truth from a nonexpert or an unexpected source?

The Lamp under the Bushel

Matthew 5:14–16

14 Ye are the light of the world. A city that is set on an hill cannot be hid.

JST Matthew 5:16

16 Verily, verily, I say unto you, I give unto you to be the light of the world; a city that is set on a hill cannot be hid.

It is helpful to know that in the Holy Land, cities were built upon the hills, saving valuable land in the valleys for agricultural and pasture use.

The wording in JST Matthew 5:16, above, reminds us of the responsibility of those who are given the blessings of Abraham, Isaac, and Jacob (as often stated in patriarchal blessings) to take the gospel and accompanying blessings of the priesthood to all the world. (See Abraham 2:9–11.)

15 Neither do men light a candle, and put it under a bushel [*a bushel basket*], but on a candlestick; and it giveth light unto all that are in the house.

JST Matthew 5:17

17 Behold, do men light a candle and put it under a bushel? Nay, but on a candlestick; and it giveth light to all that are in the house.

16 Let your light so shine before men, that they may see your good works, and glorify your Father which is in heaven.

JST Matthew 5:18

18 Therefore, let your light so shine before this world, that they may see your good works, and glorify your Father who is in heaven.

The topic now changes, starting with verse 17, to the Savior's role with respect to the Law of Moses. Misunderstanding of this issue, or deliberate refusal to accept Jesus as the fulfillment of Old Testament prophesies about the Messiah, led the Jewish religious leaders to demand that the Master be crucified.

Background, Culture, and Setting

Some New Testament passages are so familiar it seems as though they need no introduction and no explanation. We may feel tempted to read Matthew 5:14–16 and Jesus's call to not hide our light and move on to the next passage since we immediately know what He is teaching. Yet pausing will allow us to experience afresh the incredible insights, object lessons, and visual aids that Jesus used to make His message unforgettable.

The Sea of Galilee sits in a natural depression ringed by steep mountains on all sides that at their summits spread away and level off into plains. At the time of Jesus, numerous villages populated the upper reaches overlooking the Sea of Galilee. At night, the towns at the top of the mountains were impossible to miss, their firelights twinkling in the gathering darkness, spreading light that would be discernible for many dozens of miles. The scene is magical and encompassing. Anyone living near the Sea of Galilee would have experienced these lights around the Sea of Galilee each night, as surely as they would see the stars peeking through the enveloping darkness of the night sky, unless there was bad weather obscuring the vista.

The Master Teacher

Jesus's audience was mostly poor, illiterate farmers eking out an existence in a physically and politically oppressive land. Jesus did not need long discourses, academic dissertations, or sophisticated analogies drenched in philosophical subtleties and sesquipedalian vocabulary. (We use the word *sesquipedalian* tongue-in-cheek because it means "of really long words" that are typically incomprehensible to normal readers.) Instead, Jesus knew His audience. He understood them, He loved them, and He showed that love by teaching them in ways that helped them learn. He found examples in their surrounding environment that would be unmistakable in conveying the principles He wanted His listeners to understand and apply.

Possible Applications for Learners

The lesson is obvious: why would you remove the light you have to plunge the world into darkness? Our light does not have to be overbearing or overpowering. Our light does not need to overshadow other light. We simply need to let our light shine in its place. As we let our light shine, it provides illumination and context for those who see it. We may never know who needs to see more burning light in their lives. Perhaps they are discouraged by the darkness of life's experiences recently endured, and they find themselves lost on a storm-tossed sea. But then they spy your light shining simple and unobscured, making the shore known and accessible. What hope might you bring to others when your light so shines?

Helps for Teachers

- How do we use object lessons to reinforce principles?
- How do we call upon learners' experience with everyday life to help them make sense of the gospel?
- How do we create experiences for learners so that their learning is not simply listening to words but something they do, see, feel, or try?

The Parable of the Good Samaritan

Luke 10:29–37

29 But he, willing to justify himself [*wanting to make himself look good in front of the people who were standing around; see Luke 10 footnote 29a, which sends you to Luke 16:15 for a similar situation*], said unto Jesus, And who is my neighbour?

30 And Jesus answering said, A certain man went down from Jerusalem to Jericho, and fell among thieves [*was attacked by robbers*], which stripped him of his raiment [*clothing*], and wounded him, and departed, leaving him half dead.

31 And by chance there came down a certain priest [*Jewish priest*] that way: and when he saw him, he passed by on the other side.

32 And likewise a Levite [*another Jewish priest*], when he was at the place, came and looked on him, and passed by on the other side.

> JST Luke 10:33
>
> 33 And likewise a Levite, when he was at the place, came and looked upon him, and passed by on the other side of the way; for they desired in their hearts that it might not be known that they had seen him.

33 But a certain Samaritan [*a man from Samaria*], as he journeyed, came where he was: and when he saw him, he had compassion on him,

34 And went to him, and bound up his wounds, pouring in oil and wine [*gave him first aid*], and set him on his own beast, and brought him to an inn, and took care of him.

35 And on the morrow when he departed, he took out two pence [*money representing two days' wages*], and gave them to the host [*the innkeeper*], and said unto him, Take care of him; and whatsoever thou spendest more [*beyond what I have paid you*], when I come again, I will repay thee.

> Did you notice that it costs to be a good Samaritan? Certainly, that is one of the important messages for us in this parable.

36 Which now of these three, thinkest thou, was neighbour unto him that fell among the thieves?

37 And he [*the lawyer*] said, He that shewed mercy on him. Then said Jesus unto him, Go, and do thou likewise.

Background, Culture, and Setting

So beloved and well-known is the Good Samaritan parable that we can simply name the parable and remember the major take away: treat your neighbors *and* your enemies as they wish to be treated.

Most of us know that the Samaritans and the Jews were long-time, bitter enemies. And most of us know that the Jews thought the Samaritans were less than the dust of the earth. Why?

Seven hundred years before the time of Jesus, during the time of King Hezekiah and the Prophet Isaiah, Israel was separated into two kingdoms. The northern kingdom of Israel consisted of the ten tribes. The southern kingdom of Judah consisted of the tribes of Judah and Benjamin. When the formidable Assyrian empire conquered the ten northern tribes and led them into captivity in about 722 B.C., the Assyrians let many of the poor and dispossessed of the northern tribes remain in the land. The Assyrians then seeded the land with Gentiles from other conquered peoples from elsewhere in the Assyrian empire. Over time, this situation created a mixed people in the northern areas of Israel—part Israelite and part gentile. These individuals and their descendants lived in the area of Samaria and were thereafter called Samaritans.

For Jews who prized ancestral and blood purity, they saw the Samaritans as both degenerate and as a warning to any Jew of what will happen to the pure descendants of Israel if they are not zealous for maintaining every requirement of the Law of Moses. This attitude led the Jews to treat Samaritans in inhumane ways. About 150 years before the time of Jesus, the inhumanity Jews practiced against Samaritans culminated in the Jews waging war against them, destroying the Samaritan temple, and forcibly converting Samaritans to Judaism. One wonders about possible evidence of divine justice when 200 years later Romans destroyed the Jewish temple and forced many Jews to convert, or rather, to no longer practice their ancient faith.

The Master Teacher

Learning is hard to achieve when the learning experience does not evoke deep feelings, emotional and intense. Our bodies and brains are designed in such a way that we only remember what we have spent a lot of time thinking about or what we've had a deeply emotional experience with.

As the Master Teacher, Jesus shared spectacularly unexpected stories for the truths He wished to sink deep into the hearts and minds of His listeners.

Nothing would have been more shocking to a Jewish listener than that a Levite and a priest left a fellow Jew to die. The very people we expect to provide a helping hand become prime examples of selfishness. On the other hand, the lowest person in the social order, someone that no self-respecting Jew would ever dare associate with—in this case a Samaritan—was set up as a pinnacle of righteousness and neighborly love. This story has all the ingredients for being unforgettable.

Possible Applications for Learners

Think about the most important things you have learned in your life. Where did you learn those things and with whom? Many of us would answer that the most important things we have learned in life came through experiences together with people that we love. That being the case, what can you do as a learner to find loving environments where you can have transformative learning experiences? And what can you as a good neighbor do to create loving relationships or a loving environment that help those around you to learn?

HELPS FOR TEACHERS

As you study the Master's teaching approach here, it is obvious that He tips His listeners off-balance in a good way, such that they end up with a strong motivation to resolve the situation in their own minds. If you use such teaching techniques in your class, it will create an ideal environment for students to express their ideas and feelings in class discussion. Thus, they will "teach one another the doctrines of the kingdom" (D&C 88:77). In other words, the students will teach each other, and the teacher will guide them as needed.

For example, questions you might ask could be

- In what situations might you find yourself being a "priest or Levite" if you are not careful?
- Can you think of a time when you were a good Samaritan toward people who have mistreated you?
- What did it cost the Samaritan to be a good Samaritan?
- Have you noticed that it often costs to be a good Samaritan?
- Can you think of a time when it cost you either time or money to go out of your way to help someone who had not treated you well?
- Can you think of a time when you loaned an acquaintance one of your things and it came back in worse shape than when you loaned it? What did you do about the feelings it brought up in you?

Teachers need to find ways to repeat key principles in multiple ways. Otherwise, the human brain and heart won't remember the message. Or, teachers must find a deeply emotional or spiritual connection between the learners and the principles being taught. When truth is taught in boring, non-compelling ways, our unstirred souls deflect the penetration. Finally, love is the most important ingredient in long-term, transformative learning experiences. Teachers have the power to create loving environments where the wounds and brokenness of misconceptions and false ideas melt away with the healing oil of love and truth.

Jesus Teaches Us How to Pray Effectively (The Lord's Prayer)

Matthew 6:5–13

5 And when thou prayest, thou shalt not be as the hypocrites are: for they love to pray
standing in the synagogues [*church buildings where the Jews worshiped*] and in the cor-
ners of the streets, that they may be seen of men. Verily I say unto you, They have their
reward.

6 But thou, when thou prayest, enter into thy closet, and when thou hast shut thy door,
pray to thy Father which is in secret; and thy Father which seeth in secret shall reward
thee openly.

7 But when ye pray, use not vain [*useless, meaningless, ineffective*] repetitions, as the hea-
then [*non-Jews, non-Christians*] do: for they think that they shall be heard for their much
speaking.

8 Be not ye therefore like unto them: for your Father knoweth what things ye have need
of, before ye ask him.

> The Savior now gives us what is commonly known as "The Lord's Prayer." It is a beautiful example of prayer and may be considered one example of appropriate prayer, rather than a rigid form to be followed without deviation.

9 After this manner therefore pray ye: Our Father which art in heaven, Hallowed [*sacred,
holy*] be thy name.

10 Thy kingdom come. Thy will be done in earth, as it is in heaven.

11 Give us this day our daily bread.

12 And forgive us our debts [*sins, faults, offenses; see Matt. 6 footnote 12a*], as we forgive
our debtors. [*This is an important formula for our obtaining forgiveness for our own sins.*]

13 And lead us not into temptation [*we should avoid purposely putting ourselves into temp-
tation*], but deliver us from evil: For thine is the kingdom, and the power, and the glory,
for ever. Amen.

Background, Culture, and Setting

Prayer has been a standard form of communication between God and his people from time immemorial. However, by the time of the Savior's earthly ministry, customs had developed that often stood in the way. Because priests were specifically set apart and commissioned to commune with God on behalf of the people in sacred locations (such as the tabernacle or the temple) on sacred and holy days (incidentally, our word *holiday* comes from a combination of the two words "holy" and "day"), Jewish commoners may have felt, over time, that they were barred from encountering God through prayer in their personal, private lives. Delegating or giving over personal spiritual matters to a priestly class disempowered normal individuals from the realm of God. Jesus upended that culture by modeling personal and fervent communion with God and inviting His followers to do as He did.

The Master Teacher

Jesus empowered the agency of His listeners. Instead of being bound by the set and rote prayers that were common among some of the Jewish groups, Jesus invited the people to let their voices and their inner needs be heard by God. Jesus provided a simple template, a simple example that anyone can follow to engage in more fervent, heart-felt, sincere prayer. First, address God. Second, recognize that God's plan is at work in the world, and you'll experience His kingdom come as you see His hand in your life. Third, give unto others as you yourself need. That is, forgive. All of us stand in ever present need of forgiveness. We can engage in no more divine act of love and godliness than to forgive others. As we do, we feel the power of God's love enliven our hearts. We experience a bit of what it is to be like God. Fourth, ask God's assistance in avoiding and overcoming temptation, weakness, and difficulty. End with the acknowledgement that God is in charge and His kingdom is one of power, justice, glory, and goodness.

The Master Teacher opened a door for His listeners to be set free from having someone in officialdom do their praying for them and invited them to be effective in communicating with God themselves.

Possible Applications for Learners

We should want to take full advantage of the power of personal prayer for many reasons. We can petition God in all sincerity to expand our learning, open our hearts and minds, and help us see where we have been wrong or in error and where we have misconceptions or blind spots. We should pray to find learning in all our experiences. We should pray for our teachers to be inspired to help us learn. We should pray for those around us that they might assist us on our quest to become more like God through learning. We can ask for divine help in daily living. We can pray over everything, as counseled by Alma (Alma 37:36–37).

Helps for Teachers

The Church has been making a strong emphasis for teaching to more actively involve learners, including having the learners do more teaching. If students simply show up to a classroom, passively waiting for the teacher to act upon them by teaching, then they will miss much of the vibrant opportunities to grow and develop, and the class may be boring to them. Teachers can model and demonstrate applicable patterns for learning and then provide opportunities in class for participants to try those learning approaches and conclude with an invitation to learners to practice those learning patterns in their personal study.

Perhaps you have noticed that the questions you ask can make or break the learning experience. Effective questions can immediately set class members on the front of their chairs, anxious to get their turn to respond. Other questions can lead to dead silence in the class, squelching any desire for participation.

For this scriptural event, examples of effective questions might be

- The Savior taught to avoid using vain repetitions (Matt. 6:7.) Is it possible that some of the things you pray for every time in your daily prayers might be vain repetitions? What, for example?
- What are some things you might pray for every day that would definitely not be vain repetitions?
- What are some possible meanings of "Give us this day our daily bread"?
- What does it do to us if we don't forgive our debtors?
- What if we can't bring ourselves to forgive our debtors? For example, someone who has really hurt us physically or emotionally. (One answer might be to turn their judgment over to the Savior (D&C 64:11).)

The Parable of the Rich Fool

Luke 12:16–21

16 And he spake a parable unto them, saying, The ground of a certain rich man brought forth plentifully:

17 And he thought within himself, saying, What shall I do, because I have no room where to bestow [*store*] my fruits [*crops*]?

18 And he said, This will I do: I will pull down [*tear down*] my barns, and build greater [*bigger ones*]; and there will I bestow [*store*] all my fruits and my goods.

19 And I will say to my soul [*I will say to myself*], Soul [*self*], thou hast much goods laid up for many years [*you have enough to last for several years*]; take thine ease [*relax, take it easy*], eat, drink, and be merry.

20 But God said unto him, Thou fool, this night thy soul shall be required of thee [*tonight you will die*]: then whose shall those things be, which thou hast provided [*then who will all your stuff belong to*]?

21 So is he that layeth up treasure for himself, and is not rich toward God. [*So it is with people who allow their possessions to take the place of God in their lives.*]

Background, Culture, and Setting

There are dozens of parables in the New Testament. We can profitably divide them using the following categories: Three-point (or three character) parables, two-point (or two character) parables, and one-point (or one character) parables. Three-point parables have three main characters: a master or God, and two subordinates who usually are in stark contrast to teach other.

Three-point parables typically have three obvious lessons (and an untold number of other lessons to tease out). A majority of parables in the New Testament follow the three-point pattern. The two-point parable typically sets up two obviously contrasting characters. Listeners are invited to consider each character, imagine themselves in each role, consider the consequences of the characters and their choices, and, for the listeners, choose accordingly. One-point parables usually have only one central character who illustrates a specific principle.

Again, all parables can provide an endless supply of lessons, though we should recognize that the major lessons from the parables are meant to be obvious. We are more likely to derive the best benefit from seeking out and applying the obvious lessons rather than opaque or tortured interpretations.

The Parable of the Rich Fool, as Luke 12:16–21 is popularly known, follows the one-point parable format with the obvious lesson being to avoid the greed of wealth that distracts from God and His kingdom. Instead with all the wealth you acquire, do so with an eye single to the glory of God.

If, for our purposes here, we were to interpret wealth to mean learning, we could have a profitable conversation about the advantages and disadvantages of so much learning. If someone believes that because they have learned so much in their lives that there is nothing left to learn, they may become complacent, turning to eating, drinking, and merry-making (instead of continual life-long learning), like the rich man of this parable who said, "Soul, thou hast much goods laid up for many years; take thine ease, eat, drink, and be merry." We should never become complacent in our pursuit of becoming like God. Life-long learning is the path to become like God.

THE MASTER TEACHER

Jesus was derided by the educated of His day. Perhaps they had built up so many treasures of the learning of men that they were unaware of when the Master of Learning came to them. This parable, so straightforward in its immediate interpretation, conveys the idea that those who do not put God first will discover it matters not what they have accomplished in this life. Jesus had an eye single to the glory of God. In all of His obtaining, which was little in terms of the material goods of this world, but rich in the learning available to Him and all of us, He did so with the express intent to grow closer to God and to help others do the same. The best teachers are first the best learners—learners who have God as the reason for all they do.

POSSIBLE APPLICATIONS FOR LEARNERS

We are at cross currents in our culture. There is a culture of defying authority, of denying rigorous science and learning, trusting instead on uninformed opinions, often from the Internet. On the other side, there is also much of trusting in the arm of flesh, building up learning simply for the sake of learning and not for any utility that could benefit human society. We must be careful to guard against both temptations. We should be humble and willing to learn from those who have far more experience than we do. For example, I am not trained in electric work. Given my current level of learning, which includes almost no experience in this area, I struggle to imagine a scenario where my current range of learning would give me enough ability to tell electricians how to do their job correctly. Similarly, I've had years of experience studying the Middle East, including studying their cultures, regions, languages, religions, and customs. I'm surprised by those who have no direct experience with the Middle East who have all sorts of opinions about it and tell me how I am wrong. It's important that we thoughtfully listen to experts. We are not required to slavishly follow whatever they say. However, we are fools to think that in the audacity of our ignorance we can do better than the experienced. On the other hand, those who have more experience are under responsibility to be humble, to not strut around as though they are something special. And experts should not act as though they are owed deference or any special treatment. We need to guard against both extremes: fanatical ignorance on one side, and arrogant expertise on the other. Good learners known how to hew a middle path.

The point here is that like the rich man who had no room for God before it was too late, we should have care in all the accumulation of our riches (in other words, learning) that we are learning for God, to build His kingdom, to spread His truth, and to help others become more like Him. If we are learning to gratify our pride, to put ourselves into positions of power and authority that we might fulfill our lusts for personal praise and influence, we will discover that we have perverted the very reasons God has granted us these abundant riches of learning.

HELPS FOR TEACHERS

Perhaps, in your experience, you have known teachers or individuals in a position in the Church to teach others, and they preach their own wisdom. They set themselves up as a light unto the children of men, and they seem to only believe and live the first half of Jacob's declaration, "But to be learned is good if they hearken unto the counsels of God" (2 Nephi 9:29). Just as in this parable where a man had great success but took no thought for the kingdom of God, so too is the temptation to let our learning get in the way of what matters most to the progress of God's children. As teachers, we should ask ourselves: Are we teaching truth? Are we teaching the most important truths? Are we teaching principles that are useful? Understandable? Informative? Relatable? If what we have to teach does not immediately help learners grow closer to God, then it shouldn't be shared. In the Church, teachers are empowered to accomplish God's work, to build His kingdom, not to promote their own agenda or to build their own kingdom.

Nicodemus, and the Samaritan Woman at the Well

John 3:1–8, 17–21

Many members of the Church are extra familiar with this chapter because of verse 3, which is much quoted in teaching the necessity of baptism.

1 THERE was a man of the Pharisees [*who was a Pharisee*], named Nicodemus, a ruler [*leader*] of the Jews:

> The Pharisees were prominent religious leaders among the Jews. Jesus's popularity has begun to threaten their position of power and control over the Jews. They will play a prominent role in getting Him crucified. However, Nicodemus is a good man and will oppose the majority of the Pharisees. He now sincerely seeks Jesus out to ask Him questions. He is probably many years older than Jesus. After the crucifixion, he will help Joseph of Arimathea take Christ's crucified body, prepare it for burial, and gently place it in the tomb. See John 19:38–42.

2 The same [*Nicodemus*] came to Jesus by night, and said unto him, Rabbi [*"my master," a humble, respectful term for "my teacher"*], we know that thou art a teacher come from God: for no man can do these miracles that thou doest, except God be with him.

3 Jesus answered and said unto him, Verily, verily, I say unto thee, Except a man be born again, he cannot see the kingdom of God.

> Simply put, being "born again" means to be baptized and then to be directed by the Holy Ghost to become a new person, cleansed from sin and worthy to comfortably enter into the celestial kingdom.
>
> In effect, Jesus is saying to Nicodemus, "I want you to be My child, spiritually, to be born again spiritually, and then let the Holy Ghost teach you in the ways of righteousness so that you can live with Me in celestial glory." (Compare with Mosiah 5:7.)
>
> Obviously, Nicodemus does not understand the symbolism at first, and so asks a good question, seeking clarification.

4 Nicodemus saith unto him, How can a man be born when he is old? can he enter the second time into his mother's womb, and be born?

5 Jesus answered, Verily, verily [*this is the main point; listen carefully*], I say unto thee, Except a man be born of water [*baptized*] and of the Spirit [*receive the gift of the Holy Ghost*], he cannot enter into the kingdom of God [*he cannot be taught the things he must do to become celestial*].

6 That which is born of the flesh is flesh; and that which is born of the Spirit is spirit [*there is a difference between being a common person and being a spiritual person*].

7 Marvel not that I said unto thee, Ye must be born again.

8 The wind bloweth where it listeth [*where it will*], and thou hearest the sound thereof, but canst not tell whence it cometh [*where it comes from*], and whither it goeth [*where it is going*]: so is every one that is born of the Spirit. [*Perhaps meaning that that's how it is with one who has the gift of the Holy Ghost. Promptings come and inspiration is given. We don't demand it or control it any more than we can control the wind, but it does come, and it comes according to the will of the Lord.*]

17 For God sent not his Son into the world to condemn the world; but that the world through him might be saved.

18 He that believeth on him is not condemned [*stopped in progress*]: but he that believeth not is condemned already, because he hath not believed in the name of the only begotten Son of God.

> JST John 3:18
>
> 18 He who believeth on him is not condemned; but he who believeth not is condemned already, because he hath not believed on the name of the Only Begotten Son of God, which before was preached by the mouth of the holy prophets; for they testified of me.
>
> The JST addition, "testified of me," is a most significant addition, because it tells us that Jesus was telling Nicodemus clearly that he, Jesus, is the Son of God.

19 And this is the condemnation [*this is the reason people get condemned, in other words, stopped in their spiritual progress*], that light is come into the world [*because the gospel is presented to them*], and men loved darkness rather than light [*and people choose wickedness rather than the gospel*], because their deeds were evil.

20 For every one that doeth evil hateth the light [*wickedness, by its very nature, makes you hate light and truth*], neither cometh to the light, lest his deeds should be reproved. [*People involved in wickedness won't come to the light, because they don't want to face the consequences of their sins.*]

21 But he that doeth truth [*lives righteously*] cometh to the light, that his deeds may be made manifest [*made known*], that they are wrought in God [*accomplished through God's help*].

> JST John 3:21–22
>
> 21 But he who loveth truth, cometh to the light, that his deeds may be made manifest.
>
> 22 And he who obeyeth the truth, the works which he doeth they are of God.
>
> The Savior's personal teaching session with Nicodemus ends with verse 21 (JST 21–22), above. We are left not knowing the outcome, but we do know that he defended Jesus to the Pharisees (John 7:50) and assisted with the Savior's burial (John 19:39).

John 4:5–10

5 Then cometh he to a city of Samaria, which is called Sychar, near to the parcel of ground that Jacob gave to his son Joseph [*who was sold into Egypt*].

The fact that the Master is weary as they arrive at Jacob's well is a reminder that He suffered "hunger, thirst, and fatigue" (Mosiah 3:7) during His mortal sojourn and thus understands our physical trials through His own personal experience. As He sits down on the side of the well, the stage is set for each of us to drink deeply from the well of "living water" offered us by the Savior.

6 Now Jacob's well was there. Jesus therefore, being wearied with his journey, sat thus on the well: and it was about the sixth hour [*about noon*].

7 There cometh a woman of Samaria to draw water [*to get water from the well*]: Jesus saith unto her, Give me to drink [*please give Me a drink*].

8 (For his disciples were [*had*] gone away unto the city to buy meat [*food, provisions*].)

The following account of the Savior and the Samaritan woman is both delightful and profoundly moving. For our purposes, we will imagine her to be somewhat feisty and a bit sharp-tongued. We might imagine also a bit of a twinkle in the eyes of the Savior as He begins this conversation.

9 Then saith the woman of Samaria unto him, How is it that thou, being a Jew, askest drink of me, which am a woman of Samaria? for the Jews have no dealings with the Samaritans. [*In other words, why would a Jew like You ask a Samaritan woman like me for a drink? Don't You know that Jews don't have anything to do with us?*]

JST John 4:11

11 Wherefore he being alone, the woman of Samaria said unto him, How is it that thou being a Jew, askest drink of me, who am a woman of Samaria? The Jews have no dealings with the Samaritans.

Watch, now, as the Savior gets her curiosity up.

10 Jesus answered and said unto her, If thou knewest the gift of God, and who it is that saith to thee, Give me to drink; thou wouldest have asked of him, and he would have given thee living water. [*In effect, if you knew about the gift Father in Heaven has for you, and who I am, you would have asked Me for a drink, and I would have given you "living water."*]

The phrase "living water" was a familiar Old Testament phrase, having been used by Old Testament prophets to describe the blessings that flow from Jehovah to His faithful people. We will quote Jeremiah as an example:

Jeremiah 2:13

13 For my people have committed two evils; they have forsaken me the fountain of living waters, *and* hewed them out cisterns, broken cisterns, that can hold no water.

We will quote from the Institute of Religion's *New Testament Student Manual* regarding the term "living water."

"Israel's prophets had repeatedly declared that the Lord was as a fountain of living water that Israel had rejected. (See Jeremiah 2:13; Isaiah 8:6.)

"Jesus himself, as Jehovah, had pled with ancient Israel to repent and return to him so that he could nourish and sustain them. And in his pleading, Jehovah had used the word water as a figure of speech. (See Isaiah 58:11.)" (*Life and Teachings of Jesus and His Apostles*, page 38.)

Bruce R. McConkie taught about "living water." He said,

"His solemn invitation, 'If any man thirst, let him come unto me, and drink,' was a plain and open claim of Messiahship. In making it he identified himself as the very Jehovah who had promised drink to the thirsty through an outpouring of the Spirit. After such a pronouncement, his hearers were faced with two choices: Either he was a blasphemer worthy of death, or he was in fact the God of Israel." (McConkie, *Doctrinal New Testament Commentary*, vol. 1, pages 445–46.)

You can find other references in the Topical Guide under "Living Water." As you know, we use the phrase often today in referring to the gospel of Jesus Christ, which brings blessings that flow from heaven into our lives, providing refreshment, cleansing, and eternal life to the faithful.

Background, Culture, and Setting

In the ancient world, teachers would often use polar opposites to capture interest, to highlight, to instruct, and to make lessons more obvious. Jesus, as the Master Teacher, uses contrast to that effect in this example. Two stories are placed side-by-side: Jesus talking with Nicodemus and Jesus talking with the woman at the well. The pattern of comparing and contrasting is a powerful teaching and learning tool. Other scriptures make use of this tool. In the Book of Mormon, whining and disobedient Laman and Lemuel contrast with obedient and diligent Nephi. Would Nephi's example be as brilliant and shining without the dark backdrop of his brothers? In the Old Testament, comparison and contrast is profitably employed by sharing the story of Joseph of Egypt being tempted by Potiphar's wife (Genesis 39), which immediately follows the story of Judah and his daughter-in-law Tamar (Genesis 38). Why? The prophetic writers wanted readers to compare and contrast similar situations involving sexual morality and the consequences of different choices.

The Master Teacher

Instead of us giving away all the answers in this chapter, we'll encourage teachers and learners to ask the questions below and discover for themselves how Jesus sought to increase learning by using comparisons and contrasts.

John 3:1–21 Story of Nicodemus	**Questions to Consider**	**John 4:1–42 Story of Samaritan Woman**
	Who is the main character that interacts with Jesus?	
	Is the main character named or unnamed?	
	Is the main character male or female?	
	Is the main character educated or uneducated?	
	Is the main character a Jew or not?	
	Is the main character a leader or powerless?	
	Where does this chapter take place?	
	What time of day is it in this chapter?	
	Does the main character seek out Jesus or not?	
	Does the main character believe Jesus or not?	
	Who initiates the conversation?	
	How does the main character make use of questions?	
	How perceptive is the main character?	
	Which character has doubts and further questions?	
	What is the main character doing before interacting with Jesus?	

	What is the role of light and dark in this chapter?	
	How does the main character address Jesus?	
	Does the character recognize who the Messiah is?	
	How much speaking does Jesus do?	
	How much speaking does the main character do?	
	What is the nature of the questions that Jesus asks?	
	How many questions does Jesus ask?	
	How many questions does the main character ask?	
	How many questions does Jesus answer?	
	How many questions does the main character answer?	
	What does the main character do after talking with Jesus?	
	Which character would you expect to be talking with Jesus?	
	Which character do you believe would most likely follow Jesus?	
	What is the role of water in this chapter?	
	What is the role of the theme "life" in this chapter?	
	Which character would you expect to be saved in the light and which one condemned to the darkness?	

Possible Applications for Learners

As a learner, after completing this exercise consider answering these additional questions:

- Which character are you?
- How are you like Nicodemus? And how are you like the woman at the well?
- Based on your answers, what would Jesus ask you to do?

Helps for Teachers

- How can you show or demonstrate opposites to make gospel principles shine more clearly?
- Invite learners to think of a gospel principle and its opposite. Invite them to think of stories that represent a gospel principle and its opposite. What new insights do they gain when they compare and contrast the stories they thought of?

The Cleansing of a Leper

Matthew 8:1–4

1 When he was come down from the mountain [*after giving the Sermon on the Mount*], great multitudes followed him.

2 And, behold, there came a leper and worshipped him, saying, Lord, if thou wilt, thou canst make me clean [*heal me*].

> Leprosy is described in *Webster's New World College Dictionary*, 2nd ed., 1980, as follows: "a chronic infectious disease . . . that attacks the skin, flesh, nerves, etc.; it is characterized by nodules, ulcers, white scaly scabs, deformities, and wasting of body parts."

3 And Jesus put forth his hand, and touched him, saying, I will; be thou clean. And immediately his leprosy was cleansed.

> Every time you read of a physical healing of the sick performed by the Savior, you can consider it symbolic of His ability to heal us spiritually through His Atonement. Thus, every healing will remind you of the Master's power to heal you spiritually, through your repentance and His forgiving you. In this case of the healing of a leper, leprosy could be symbolic of very serious sin that can gradually destroy us spiritually.

4 And Jesus saith unto him [*the leper who had been healed*], See thou tell no man [*keep this spiritual experience very private*]; but go thy way, shew thyself to the priest, and offer the gift that Moses commanded, for a testimony unto them [*keep the requirements of the Law of Moses with respect to the cleansing of lepers*].

Background, Culture, and Setting

According to the Mosaic law, if lepers touched anyone, they made that person unclean. In Leviticus 13, God gives instructions to priests to "shut up him that hath the plague," essentially imprisoning or quarantining anyone suspected of leprosy until the priest can determine if the leprosy is real or not. During the time of quarantine, no one touches the leper. Eventually the priest will again "see" the potential leper (not touch him), and if the priest sees an improvement, he is to pronounce the individual clean. If there is no improvement, the priest declares leprosy: "And the leper in whom the plague is, his clothes shall be rent, and his head bare, and he shall put a covering upon his upper lip, and shall cry, Unclean, unclean" (Leviticus 13:45).

Humiliatingly, lepers were supposed to stay away from all other people. How devastatingly lonely. If they did come upon anyone, they were supposed to cry out with full conviction and warning "unclean!" How could they have friends? Family? Loved ones?

These unfortunate souls would be wholly cut off from society because of something they did not do and could not control. Imagine having to shout in all public places for the rest of your life, "Don't come near me. I could ruin your life!" No one would touch you. No one would talk to you. You would be cut off from all that is good about human relationships, society, and sociality.

THE MASTER TEACHER

Wait, what did Jesus do? Jesus did not turn away from those unclean, socially shunned lepers. Unexpectedly, shockingly, Jesus put forth His hand to touch the leper! Why didn't Jesus simply say, "Be healed"? In other New Testament stories, supplicants petitioned Jesus to, "Speak the word only, and my servant shall be healed" (Matthew 8:8). Jesus could have simply spoken the words of healing and physical salvation. Instead, He truly ministered to the leper's needs by doing the unexpected. Jesus was willing to make Himself ritually unclean to make someone ritually pure. There was healing power in Jesus's touch.

The leper must have been humbled that his cursed disease was finally lifted. But perhaps what "healed" him more than the socially ostracizing leprosy disappearing from his life is that Jesus touched him. How many years had this child of God been deprived of touch? One of the most important things we need as humans is kind and loving touches from other humans.

POSSIBLE APPLICATIONS FOR LEARNERS

Are we held back by society's expectations of us? Do we think less of ourselves than our divine nature would suggest? Do we go about thinking to ourselves, or telling others that we are "unclean," that is, incapable to change, to learn, to achieve? Learners should remember that the Lord's touch can be with us.

HELPS FOR TEACHERS

Here are some possible questions to stimulate class discussion:

- What ways can you think of in which we, today, might treat some people as if they were "lepers"?
- In what ways might bullying in our culture be like the treatment of lepers in the days of the Savior's ministry?
- What evidence do you see in the scriptural passage (Matthew 8:1–4) that the leper had heard of the Savior previously?
- What evidence do you see that the leper had faith in the Savior?
- Under what circumstances might we need faith like that of the lepers?
- What does it take to have faith like that of the lepers?
- Why do you think the Savior told the leper who was miraculously healed not to tell anyone? (We don't know for sure, but one possible answer might be that large crowds were already following the Master, and word of such a healing might cause impossible crowds to throng Him. Another possible answer might be that such personal miracles are often best kept private in order to avoid,

among other things, showing off to others and getting puffed up in pride over one's importance.)

- Why do you think that Christ instructed the healed leper to follow the rules given in the law of Moses for the cleansing of lepers? (One possible answer is that He had not yet completed His Atonement, thus fulfilling and replacing the law of Moses. Another reason might be for the benefit of the leper, himself, so that people around him might see that he was in compliance with the law of Moses and could now be allowed back into society without being shunned.)

Jesus Heals the Centurion's Servant

Matthew 8:5–13

5 And when Jesus was entered into Capernaum, there came unto him a centurion [*a Roman soldier in charge of 100 soldiers*], beseeching him,

> The Romans were Gentiles, and thus were considered by the Jews to be inferior in the eyes of God, compared to the Jews, who considered themselves to be God's only chosen people. All others, despite their best efforts, were considered second class citizens in the kingdom of God.

6 And saying, Lord, my servant lieth at home sick of the palsy, grievously tormented.

7 And Jesus saith unto him, I will come and heal him.

8 The centurion answered and said, Lord, I am not worthy that thou shouldest come under my roof: but speak the word only, and my servant shall be healed.

9 For I am a man under authority, having soldiers under me: and I say to this man, Go, and he goeth; and to another, Come, and he cometh; and to my servant, Do this, and he doeth it.

10 When Jesus heard it, he marvelled, and said to them that followed, Verily I say unto you, I have not found so great faith, no, not in Israel.

> JST Matthew 8:9
>
> 9 And when they that followed him, heard this, they marveled. And when Jesus heard this, he said unto them that followed,

11 And I say unto you, That many shall come from the east and west [*many foreigners, including Gentiles*], and shall sit down with Abraham, and Isaac, and Jacob, in the kingdom of heaven [*will be saved along with Abraham, Isaac, and Jacob in celestial glory*].

12 But the children of the kingdom [*those Jews who considered themselves to be elite, above all other people*] shall be cast out into outer darkness [*probably not meaning into perdition, with Satan, rather, in the spirit world prison, as explained in Alma 40:11–13*]: there shall be weeping and gnashing of teeth.

13 And Jesus said unto the centurion, Go thy way; and as thou hast believed, so be it done unto thee. And his servant was healed in the selfsame hour.

Background, Culture, and Setting

The story of Jesus healing the centurion's servant immediately follows the story of Jesus cleansing a leper and immediately precedes the story of Jesus healing Peter's mother-in-law. This series of healing stories is shared rapid-fire to convey some significant insights about Jesus, His mission, and His power.

In the modern west, we are blessed with an abundance of trained medical personnel, and we typically have access to medical facilities to meet our health needs. So familiar are we with the modern marvels and blessings of medical advancements that we have to exercise significant creative imagination to picture the ancient world where medical understanding and facilities were essentially nonexistent. What medical knowledge they had was typically only available to royalty, the very rich, and to those in power. Even then, ancient medical understanding was generally not much better than quackery. Anciently, you were more likely to experience greater suffering at the hands of a well-meaning but incompetent doctor than if you had stayed at home to quietly endure whatever ailment afflicted you. There is a reason the word "patient" is used to identify the sufferer under medical care and that doctors call their activities medical "practice." (Coincidentally Taylor Halverson wrote this section in a hospital while the doctors and nurses prepped his wife for surgery. He marveled at the modern miracles of medicine, medical training, and medical technology.)

The Master Teacher

We learn that Jesus, as Son of God (a term referring to His kingship), has come to demonstrate what the kingdom of God is like. That kingdom is full of soundness, healing, and wholeness. Each healing that Jesus does demonstrates, or gives a taste of, what the kingdom of God is like. We also learn from these various healing stories that Jesus is no respecter of persons. He will heal an Israelite man (the leper) who shouldn't be touched, a gentile servant (who, according to Jewish tradition, shouldn't be bothered with), and a woman (women represented the lowest, forgotten class in that culture).

Jesus pays attention to the individual. He recognizes their humanity, their individuality, and their personal needs. He ministers one-on-one. Though He made use of opportunities to address the masses and the crowds who thronged Him, Jesus often demonstrated the importance of ministering to the one.

Possible Applications for Learners

As learners, are we willing to trust Jesus, as did the centurion? Are we willing to ask Jesus for salvation even when we recognize our human failings, weaknesses, and sins? Or are we afraid that we are not worthy of God's love, forgiveness, and salvation? The centurion recognized that he was sinful and that he was not of the house of Israel and therefore didn't outwardly "qualify" for the mercy of Jesus. Still, he petitioned Jesus, recognizing His power to heal. Finally, though Jesus can physically heal us if we have faith, even more important in the eternal perspective is His ability to heal our ignorance, fears, misconceptions, and errors.

HELPS FOR TEACHERS

As teachers, how are we reaching and touching the lives of individuals? Are we making time to know and understand the learners in our care? Are we listening to their needs and seeking to find ways to teach them that meet them where they are in their lives right now?

Here are some possible involvement questions leading to discussion wherein students basically teach the class:

- How were the Jews at the time likely to view both the centurion and his servant compared to fellow Jews?
- In the Lord's eyes, what is the worth of Gentiles compared to members of the House of Israel? (Hint: D&C 18:10.)
- How can we correct our own thinking if we tend to think of fellow Church members as being above nonmembers? Or is that a problem?
- What role do you suspect the humility of the centurion played in the healing of his servant by Jesus?
- What do you think Jesus meant when He said, "That many shall come from the east and west, and shall sit down with Abraham, and Isaac, and Jacob, in the kingdom of heaven"? (Most likely, He is responding to the belief among the Jews that they were above all other people in the eyes of God, and thus, all others, Gentiles included, were below them. They are shocked that He has just said that many from all over, from the east and west, will end up with Abraham, Isaac, and Jacob in heaven. He is teaching them that the worth of all souls "is great in the sight of God" [see D&C 18:10], and all who qualify can be in heaven.)
- What damage can personal prejudice on our part play in our relationships with others? (For example, nonmembers, less active members, people who are different than us, etc.)
- What do you see as the main point of the healing of the centurion's servant?

PETER'S MOTHER-IN-LAW HEALED

MATTHEW 8:14–15

14 And when Jesus was come into Peter's house, he saw his wife's mother laid, and sick of a fever.

15 And he touched her hand, and the fever left her: and she arose, and ministered unto them [*attended to their needs*].

BACKGROUND, CULTURE, AND SETTING

When Jesus moved from Nazareth to Capernaum (on the northwest coast of the Sea of Galilee), He settled in the home of Peter. Also living in that home was Peter's mother-in-law. In the ancient world, multiple generations of family lived together in homes that would be considered small by the standards of American homes today. Having three or four generations living under one roof was the norm. When we hear the Old Testament phrase, "to the third and fourth generation" (see for example Deuteronomy 5:9), this phrase doesn't simply refer to a time period of approximately 75–100 years as though each generation equaled 25 years. Instead, this phrase specifically refers to the family unit living within one Israelite household. That household would be led by a grandfather/patriarch (first generation). Living in his home or his domain would be his sons and their wives (second generation), and the children of those sons (the third generation), and in some instances, the families of the male grandchildren (constituting the fourth generation). The head of the household, as the leader of the family, set the standard for faithfulness. If the grandfather was faithful, the blessings of God would be available to everyone in his home to the third and fourth generations, that is to his sons, grandsons, and great-grandchildren and their families all living in the home. On the other hand, if the grandfather/patriarch was unfaithful, the curses of God would be on that household.

In the instance of Matthew 8:14–15, we may conjecture that Peter's father-in-law had passed on and that Peter, as the head of his own household, had invited his mother-in-law to join his family unit. As a righteous father-leader, literally a *patriarch* (from the word *patri* = father, and *arch* = leader), Peter faithfully followed and listened to Jesus and thereby reaped blessings for himself and those in his household.

THE MASTER TEACHER

One of a teacher's major resources for affecting his or her students positively is showing love for them. Here, the Master Teacher shows His blessings to Peter as patriarch by blessing his mother-in-law. And, in effect, Jesus blesses the household of Peter to the third and fourth generation. That is, everyone under Peter's roof is blessed by Peter's faithfulness to have Jesus in his home. And that faithfulness leads to Jesus healing Peter's mother-in-law.

POSSIBLE APPLICATIONS FOR LEARNERS

How do we model faithfulness to those in our home? Do we model the teachings of the Savior, inviting His gospel teachings to attend our families to bring healing, light, life, and learning? Do we avoid needing the counsel of Jacob in the Book of Mormon, who cautioned parents (specifically fathers) to "remember your children, how that ye have grieved their hearts because of the example that ye have set before them; and also, remember that ye may, because of your filthiness [*or lack of faithfulness*], bring your children unto destruction, and their sins be heaped upon your heads at the last day" (Jacob 3:10). Those living within the household to the third and fourth generation will be blessed according to the faithfulness of the father-leader in the home. We can all strive to be more sensitive to the needs of others in our households and respond in appropriate ways to provide comfort and healing.

HELPS FOR TEACHERS

Teachers are like parents or patriarchs. They are under responsibility to teach the truth to those in their care. Jacob, brother of Nephi, understood this principle well when he taught, "And we did magnify our office unto the Lord, taking upon us the responsibility, answering the sins of the people upon our own heads if we did not teach them the word of God with all diligence; wherefore, by laboring with our might their blood might not come upon our garments; otherwise their blood would come upon our garments, and we would not be found spotless at the last day" (Jacob 1:19). And further he cried out, "O, my beloved brethren, remember my words. Behold, I take off my garments, and I shake them before you; I pray the God of my salvation that he view me with his all-searching eye; wherefore, ye shall know at the last day, when all men shall be judged of their works, that the God of Israel did witness that I shook your iniquities from my soul, and that I stand with brightness before him, and am rid of your blood" (2 Nephi 9:44).

The imagery in these scriptures may seem a little strange at first glance. However, with some insight we'll understand how significant these words of Jacob are. In the ancient world, blood was a symbol of responsibility. When covenants were made between two parties, they typically would sacrifice an animal. The blood of the animal would represent the blood of the covenant makers and their responsibility to keep the covenant. The blood also symbolized that the covenant was in force and ratified. Remember that Jesus is the Lamb of God that has been slain, meaning that He ratifies and enforces the covenant of God.

Returning to the story of Jacob—because of his priesthood covenants, he was under covenant responsibility to teach the truth. If he did not teach the truth to those in his care (as a spiritual father/patriarch, the Nephite nation constituting his household), then he would be responsible for their sins. Their "blood" (in other words, the responsibility for their sins) would be upon his garments (or, upon his soul). Because he taught the truth to his people (as though they were children in his household), that is why Jacob declared he could "stand with brightness before" God at the last day, having rid his garments (his soul) of their blood (of the responsibility of their sins).

Helpful questions that might lead students in the class into a discussion include

- What frustration might have been on Peter's mother-in-law's mind as she lay sick? (Possible answer: She was accustomed to serving guests and was too sick to do so.)
- In addition to healing her physically, what other important blessing did Jesus give her?
- As a teacher, how is your role similar to that of an ancient patriarch or leader?

The Calling of the Twelve Apostles

Luke 6:12–16

12 And it came to pass in those days, that he went out into a mountain to pray, and
continued all night in prayer to God.
13 And when it was day, he called unto him his disciples [*some of His close followers*]: and
of them he chose twelve, whom also he named apostles;
14 Simon, (whom he also named Peter,) and Andrew his brother, James and John, Philip
and Bartholomew,
15 Matthew and Thomas, James the son of Alphæus, and Simon called Zelotes,
16 And Judas the brother of James, and Judas Iscariot, which also was the traitor [*who
would betray Jesus*].

Background, Culture, and Setting

Jesus had many disciples but called only twelve to serve as Apostles. He empowered them to do His works on His behalf. Symbolically, these twelve men represented the twelve tribes of Israel. In biblical numerical symbolism, "twelve" was also a symbol of completion, signifying that all God's children can be invited into the covenant family of Israel. It also symbolized divine organization, including God's government.

The Master Teacher

Since Jesus is the Son of God, why would He need to delegate any power or authority to anyone? Isn't it His role to save God's children (Moses 1:39)? Isn't Jesus powerful enough to touch every heart, speak every word of truth, heal all that is broken, and bring all the willing back to God? If so, then why would He need any help?

That is obviously not the point. We have all been given agency. The only way we can be brought back into the presence of God and enter exaltation is by good choices. And the whole purpose of the Father's plan of salvation is to teach us and involve us such that we grow in understanding and spiritual strength to the point that we think as Christ thinks, see as He sees, and love as He loves.

If Jesus never invited us, challenged us, empowered us, or allowed us to participate in His work, we could never become like Him. We could never exercise our agency. We could never fail and then learn to apply faith unto repentance. God needs us, and we need God. God needs us to love His children as He does, to serve, to listen, and to teach.

When we act like God, we become more like Him. These principles of teaching certainly apply to His newly called Apostles.

As the Master Teacher, after calling His Apostles, Jesus spent significant time teaching and training them so they would be prepared to lead the Church after His crucifixion and resurrection.

Possible Applications for Learners

Jesus prepared Himself to invite others to be involved in the gospel. When we re-read the passage above, we notice that Jesus spent all night alone, praying on a mountain. Why alone? Likely because He didn't want distraction. Why on a mountain? Mountains are symbolic of temples, which bring us spiritually and physically closer to God.

As teachers, we should prepare through private prayer, and perhaps in prayer at the modern spiritual mountains we call temples. We should use prayer to receive inspiration about whom to actively invite to participate in the class. We should create meaningful learning experiences where participants are empowered to be more than simple passive receivers of the word of God.

Helps for Teachers

Some possible questions you might pose to your students are as follows:

- How do you suppose these original Twelve felt about their call?
- How do you suppose their role changed at this point as they went from disciples (followers of Christ) to Apostles?
- How are new Apostles called in our day? (Answer: only the Prophet calls new Apostles. Then they are presented to the members of the Church for sustaining.)
- Have you ever seen an Apostle in real life? If so, how did you feel?

Take My Yoke upon You

Matthew 11:28–30

28 Come unto me, all ye that labour and are heavy laden, and I will give you rest.

29 Take my yoke [*make covenants through which you, in effect, put yourselves in the harness with the Savior*] upon you, and learn of me; for I am meek and lowly in heart [*I am humble and love to help you*]: and ye shall find rest unto your souls.

30 For my yoke is easy, and my burden is light.

> Above, the Savior teaches us that the path to exaltation is actually the easiest way as well as the happiest. The "burdens" one carries as a devout follower of the Master are nothing compared to the burdens of guilt and shame carried by those who choose wickedness as a lifestyle.

Background, Culture, and Setting

Jesus's primary audience for much of His ministry was the poor, the outcast, the illiterate, the unschooled, the forgotten, the overworked, the overburdened, the ceaseless toilers. How stunning would it have been, perplexing and confusing even, to hear Jesus pronounce "my yoke is easy, and my burden is light"? For a class of people who likely never knew a day of easy or light burdens, Jesus was a miraculous and unexpected marvel. Undoubtedly, some of His listeners saw the connection between the yokes Jesus would break from off their backs just as God had saved their ancestors from the yoke of Egyptian bondage, "I am the LORD your God, which brought you forth out of the land of Egypt, that ye should not be their bondmen; and I have broken the bands of your yoke, and made you go upright" (Leviticus 26:13). What was the yoke Jesus offered them and all of us? That he would carry the yoke, or the burden of our sins, as represented by the heavy cross He carried on the way to His Crucifixion.

The Master Teacher

Notice that Jesus did not say, "You'll find rest unto your *bodies*." He instead promised, "You'll find rest unto your *souls*." Jesus made appropriate promises. And Jesus came to fulfill the promises of Isaiah, "And it shall come to pass in that day, that his burden shall be taken away from off thy shoulder, and his yoke from off thy neck, and the yoke shall be destroyed because of the anointing" (Isaiah 10:27).

Possible Applications for Learners

What do we learn from this episode of Jesus the Master Teacher? Making appropriate promises. We obviously are not Jesus and must exercise caution with the promises that we make to learners in our midst. Still, we know from modern day revelation that "There is a law, irrevocably decreed in heaven before the foundations of this world, upon which all blessings are predicated—And when we obtain any blessing from God, it is by obedience to that law upon which it is predicated" (D&C 130:20–21). Well-prepared teachers understand the connection between gospel principles they teach and blessings that flow from living those gospel principles. When appropriate, teachers invite learners to live principles taught and then describe the attendant promises related to the principles.

Helps for Teachers

- What promises have you received as a learner?
- What are you doing to live faithful to your blessings, promises, and opportunities?
- What learning burdens do you have? Have you shared those with the Lord?
- Have you joined with him, equally yoked, in your learning journey to grow and develop and become more like God?

Healing a Crippled Man on the Sabbath

John 5:1–9

1 AFTER this there was a feast [*Passover; see John 5 footnote 1a in your LDS scriptures*] of the Jews; and Jesus went up to Jerusalem.

2 Now there is at Jerusalem by the sheep market a pool, which is called in the Hebrew tongue Bethesda, having five porches.

3 In these [*porches*] lay a great multitude of impotent [*crippled*] folk, of blind, halt [*lame*], withered, waiting for the moving of the water.

4 For an angel went down at a certain season into the pool, and troubled the water: whosoever then first after the troubling of the water stepped in was made whole [*healed*] of whatsoever disease he had.

> Apparently, there was a belief that gave sick and crippled people hope that they would be healed if they were the first to get into the water after the water was moved by an unseen force. This is superstition and not the way God works.

5 And a certain man was there, which had an infirmity thirty and eight years.

6 When Jesus saw him lie [*laying there*], and knew that he had been now a long time in that case, he saith unto him, Wilt thou be made whole [*would you like to be healed*]?

7 The impotent [*crippled*] man answered him, Sir, I have no man, when the water is troubled, to put me into the pool: but while I am coming, another steppeth down before me [*when I try to get into the water first, someone else always beats me to it*].

8 Jesus saith unto him, Rise, take up thy bed, and walk.

9 And immediately the man was made whole, and took up his bed, and walked: and on the same day was the sabbath [*this all happened on the Sabbath*].

Background, Culture, and Setting

In John 5, Jesus is yet again in Jerusalem for a feast, that is, for a holy day. Footnote 1a for John 5:1 informs us that this was Passover. These passages remind us that Jesus was an observant Jew. He followed the commands of God to gather with His people in Jerusalem three times a year to celebrate these holy days: "Three times in a year shall all thy males appear before the Lord thy God in the place which he shall choose; in the feast of unleavened bread, and in the feast of weeks, and in the feast of tabernacles: and they shall not appear before the Lord empty: Every man shall give as he is able, according to the blessing of the Lord thy God which he hath given thee" (Deuteronomy 16:16–17). Jesus was in Jerusalem to worship God as commanded by God through Moses.

North of Jerusalem's walls was a set of two pools called collectively The Pool of Bethesda. These pools were used for a variety of purposes. First, the pools provided water storage for the city. Second, pilgrims would come to these pools to ritually purify themselves before entering into the city and the holy temple. Third, over the years stories of miraculous healings at these pools circulated. Those in need gathered, waiting to be healed.

Jesus found the paralytic despondent, who after 38 years of immobility was incapable of getting into the water before anyone else after it stirred. Why did the paralytic believe he could be healed by these waters? According to tradition, an angel would stir the water, imbuing it with some unexplained healing properties that were available only to the first person to get into the water.

There are several interesting things to note about this tradition. First, the best ancient biblical manuscripts don't contain this portion of John 5:3–4: "waiting for the moving of the water. For an angel went down at a certain season into the pool, and troubled the water: whosoever then first after the troubling of the water stepped in was made whole of whatsoever disease he had."

What does that mean? A later scribe or editor, seeking to make sense for readers of the paralytic's words about needing help to reach the water when it stirred added the traditional or folkloric story that an angel stirred the water. Second, Jesus did not correct the fact that the paralytic believed that the moving water would heal him, for the paralytic had said to Jesus, "I have no man, when the water is troubled, to put me into the pool: but while I am coming, another steppeth down before me." Jesus likely would have known the true mechanism that perturbed the water. Did He stop and give a scientific and rationalistic explanation of how the pool keeper would open a sluice gate connecting the upper pool to the lower pool so that water would then flow from the upper pool into the lower pool, thus churning up sediment in the lower pool, creating a movement in the water as though it had been disturbed by some unseen force? Did Jesus take time to point out to this immobile man that his worldview about the water was unscientific and wrong? Did Jesus "heal" this man's misunderstanding? Is that what the man needed, even if he was in error? No. Jesus focused first on what was most important: the physical healing of this man who had been lame for nearly four decades.

The Master Teacher

Jesus chooses the better part. Jesus did not come to immediately correct every error in thinking, every misconception, every false piece of culture or folklore that impedes our understanding and progress. Yes, all these things must eventually be shed if we wish to be like Jesus, *full* of light and truth. But Jesus focuses first on what matters most. Good teachers do the same. Teach the most empowering and liberating truths first. Do not be distracted by the minor or inconsequential false ideas floating in the minds of your learners. There is only so much time in the teaching and learning context to make a transformative difference. Good teachers plan accordingly.

POSSIBLE APPLICATIONS FOR LEARNERS

Learners should practice self-reflection and self-correction. There are many false ideas and perspectives floating around, and we should diligently test what we think we know. How many of us, metaphorically, lay around for decades waiting for some magical solution because the world told us a story that may not be true? Instead, we should be up and walking, looking for Jesus, to bring Him into our lives. Good learners never rest on their laurels (that is, on their past accomplishments) *or* on their infirmities. Good learners trust that when they rise up and act, God will make them whole, or He will help them grow closer to being whole.

HELPS FOR TEACHERS

Teachers should stay focused on "healing," that is, teaching what matters most. All of us as humans walk around with false ideas and ill-conceived worldviews. If we had and acted on all truth, well, this entire world and all its inhabitants would likely have been translated back into God's presence already. Our role as teachers is to not correct every misconception, every falsehood, and every ill-conceived worldview. There is not enough time in life to do so. Instead, we should focus on teaching and healing the most important things—those misunderstandings or infirmities that are the biggest obstacles to growth—that comprise our ability to use agency or to build thriving lives centered on God.

This principle is clearly taught in the allegory of Zenos (Jacob 5:65–66):

> 65 And as they begin to grow ye shall clear away the branches which bring forth bitter fruit [*symbolic of false ideas, traditions, worldviews, etc.*], according to the strength of the good and the size thereof; and ye shall not clear away the bad thereof all at once, lest the roots thereof should be too strong for the graft [*symbolic of people who are young in the gospel, new converts, and so forth*], and the graft thereof shall perish, and I lose the trees of my vineyard.
>
> 66 For it grieveth me that I should lose the trees of my vineyard; wherefore ye shall clear away the bad [*false notions, ideas, and so forth*] according as the good [*gospel truths, teaching, etc.*] shall grow, that the root and the top may be equal in strength, until the good shall overcome the bad, and the bad be hewn down and cast into the fire, that they cumber not the ground of my vineyard; and thus will I sweep away the bad out of my vineyard.

These sample questions might help stimulate student involvement in the class:

- What false traditions or legends can you think of that, over time, have attained the status of truth in the eyes of the general public? (Possible responses might include that everyone has a guardian angel assigned full time to them; if you think an unclean thought, the Holy Ghost will immediately leave you; the Holy Ghost will leave you if you stay out on a date past midnight.)
- Why wouldn't God make it so that our being healed depends on our beating someone else in some kind of physical competition?

- How do you think the Savior feels when He heals us, either physically or spiritually? (Possible responses might include that He loves to bless and heal us; it brings Him joy whenever He helps us, no matter what our situation is; specific situations, such as the crippled man's, allow Him to extend His perfect love to us.)
- How can we maintain our faith and commitment to God if we desire such a miracle for ourselves or a loved one but it does not come?
- Why do you suppose the Savior did not first take time to correct the false belief that an angel, from time to time, stirred the water so that the first one to step in was healed? (Answers might include that it was not an appropriate priority at that point. It could come later.)

(Just a final note: this chapter was written while Taylor's wife was lame for days and not able to walk because of foot surgery. It's hard to imagine nearly four decades of lacking ambulatory capabilities.)

Christ Heals a Crippled Woman on the Sabbath

Luke 13:10–17

10 And he was teaching in one of the synagogues on the sabbath.

11 And, behold, there was a woman which had a spirit of infirmity [*had been weak and sickly*] eighteen years, and was bowed together [*was bent over*], and could in no wise lift up herself [*could not straighten herself out at all*].

12 And when Jesus saw her, he called her to him, and said unto her, Woman, thou art loosed from thine infirmity [*you are set free from being crippled*].

13 And he laid his hands on her: and immediately she was made straight, and glorified God.

14 And the ruler of the synagogue answered with indignation, because that Jesus had healed on the sabbath day, and said unto the people, There are six days in which men ought to work: in them therefore come and be healed, and not on the sabbath day. [*In other words, if you want to be healed in my synagogue, come on any of the six days of the week when work is permitted. But don't come to be healed on the Sabbath.*]

15 The Lord then answered him, and said, Thou hypocrite, doth not each one of you on the sabbath loose [*untie*] his ox or his ass from the stall, and lead him away to watering?

16 And ought not this woman, being a daughter of Abraham, whom Satan hath bound, lo, these eighteen years, be loosed [*freed*] from this bond [*the bondage of being crippled*] on the sabbath day? [*You treat your beasts of burden better that you treat this woman.*]

17 And when he had said these things, all his adversaries [*opponents*] were ashamed: and all the people rejoiced for all the glorious things that were done by him.

Background, Culture, and Setting

Jesus often did acts of healing in synagogues. If synagogues were places of spiritual learning and experience, why is it that so many who needed physical healing were found there? Because synagogues were more than simple places of worship. They were, to use an inexact description, like community centers, hospitals (Jesus often healed people at synagogues, because people went there seeking physical help, even though the synagogue leader told them to come back to the synagogue on a day *other than* Sunday to be healed), hostels, social gathering places, and the center of worship for the community. People came to synagogues not only for spiritual and social sustenance, but also for food and water and to have other physical needs filled. We caution to not take these ideas too far, because synagogues were primarily focal points of worship. But ancient evidence seems to suggest that the infirm would come to synagogues with the hope that if they couldn't find physical relief, the spiritual strength they received from worship might encourage them to endure a little longer.

The Master Teacher

Jesus attended to both the spiritual and physical needs of those He taught. We love the use of the word *loosed* in these passages, when Jesus declared, "thou art loosed from thine infirmity." In modern vocabulary, the word *loose* is seldom used. Typically, we hear expressions of "be healed" or "be whole," which sound more immediate and descriptive. If we peel back the language translation, our minds may be expanded to learn that the word *loose* comes from the Greek word referring to breaking the chains of bondage. Isn't that what infirmity is, the bondage of not being whole? Whether we are healed from physical or spiritual debilitations, they are chains that keep us from growing, developing, learning, and experiencing. God's power is sufficient to loosen those shackles from our lives so that we are put at liberty to act. Isn't that what Jesus came to do as He declared in soberness in the small-town synagogue of Nazareth? "The Spirit of the Lord is upon me, because he hath anointed me to preach the gospel to the poor; he hath sent me to heal the brokenhearted, to preach deliverance to the captives, and recovering of sight to the blind, to *set at liberty* [*loosen*] them that are bruised" (Luke 4:18, emphasis added).

Possible Applications for Learners

Learners should seek to be whole physically and spiritually. Our bodies are temples. If we abuse them, our spirit suffers, and we create unnecessary obstacles to our growth and learning. If we are suffering physically, we should do all in our power to exercise faith in God's healing power and then act to incorporate the best that medical care has to offer. We can hardly be on the path of being whole if we care for our spirit but neglect the body.

A major application suggested by this scripture is the proper use of the Sabbath. Obviously, the leader of the synagogue was so steeped in the laws and traditions of the Jews that he completely failed to see that the healing of the crippled woman by the Savior was a marvelous use of the Sabbath. If we properly understand the divine purposes of Sunday, the Lord's Day, we will be hard-pressed to even begin to do a small part of all the appropriate activities for keeping the Sabbath holy.

Helps for Teachers

What keeps our learners from progressing? What shackles or fetters hold them back? Is it lack of understanding of pure doctrine? Is it festering anger or pride? Is it cultural traditions that are enticing and satisfying yet ultimately inferior to the truth? Is it a lack of strong learning habits? It is a lack of persistence or interest in learning?

Whatever may hold a learner back, teachers have a commission to loosen these infirmities through love, purity of doctrine, and engaging teaching.

Questions that might help your class members become engaged in helping teach the class are

- What might cause some of us to miss the purposes of the Sabbath, and thus make it something we might dread, or at least something we don't really look forward to?
- What activities are appropriate for our Sabbath in addition to going to Church?
- Why do you suppose that Church leaders have not provided us with a fairly long list of dos and don'ts for the Sabbath?
- What are some particularly pleasant and appropriate activities in which you have participated that have made your Sabbath observance satisfying?
- What do you think Jesus meant when He said "The sabbath was made for man, and not man for the sabbath" (Mark 2:27)?
- What did the leader of the synagogue not understand about the true purposes of the Sabbath?
- Why do you think the adversaries of Jesus were ashamed?
- What messages can you see in these verses that would caution us not to be judgmental of how other members of the Church choose to keep the Sabbath? (One possible answer is that the ruler of the synagogue was applying his own interpretation of Sabbath Day observance by telling the people not to come to the synagogue on the Sabbath in order to be healed.)

Comparing the Kingdom of Heaven to a Mustard Seed

Matthew 13:31–32

31 Another parable put he forth unto them, saying, The kingdom of heaven is like to a grain of mustard seed, which a man took, and sowed in his field:

32 Which indeed is the least [*smallest*] of all seeds: but when it is grown, it is the greatest among herbs, and becometh a tree, so that the birds of the air [*symbolic of angels, see* Teachings of the Prophet Joseph Smith, *page 159*] come and lodge in the branches thereof.

Joseph Smith explained this parable:

> "And again, another parable put He forth unto them, having an allusion to the Kingdom that should be set up, just previous to or at the time of the harvest, which reads as follows—'The Kingdom of Heaven is like a grain of mustard seed, which a man took and sowed in his field: which indeed is the least of all seeds: but, when it is grown, it is the greatest among herbs, and becometh a tree, so that the birds of the air come and lodge in the branches thereof.' Now we can discover plainly that this figure is given to represent the Church as it shall come forth in the last days." (For more of the Prophet's explanation, see *Teachings of the Prophet Joseph Smith*, pages 98–99 and page 159.)

Background, Culture, and Setting

The word *parable* means "to throw together side by side" (*para* = side, alongside; and *bole*, shortened to *ble* = throw). That is, place two ideas side by side in order to compare and contrast them to enhance learning. The word parable is related to another word we all know: *problem*, which is something you "throw in front of" someone (*pro* = before, or in front of). Our word *ball* (an object that we "throw") derives from the ancient root word *bole* that shows up in the words "para*ble*" and "pro*ble*m." And because so much of the gospel is conveyed through sym*bol*ism, it's useful for us to know that it means "to throw together" or "to be brought together" (*sym* = together, *bol* = throw). Symbols bring together in our mind two things that are connected that, if separated, may not initially appear to be connected.

Jesus regularly used parables (and symbols) to help His people better understand the truths He communicated. Jesus did not simply list truths in bullet point fashion, tack them up on a wall for all to read and commit to heart, and then hope for the best that everyone would both understand and apply the truths. No. He taught using story, metaphor, and examples. Sometimes He used multiple yet diverse examples to teach one core idea, as is the case in Matthew 13 where Jesus used a variety of parables to describe the kingdom of heaven. The scriptures are full of stories, metaphors, analogies, and parables that help prepare the soil of our souls to receive the seeds of truth.

Incidentally, the phrase "kingdom of heaven" is unique to Matthew. Gospel writers Mark and Luke say "kingdom of God." Both phrases "kingdom of heaven" and "kingdom of God" refer to the same thing in these books of the New Testament. Whereas, in some other scripture references, such as Doctrine and Covenants 65:6, "kingdom of God" means the Church here on earth, and "kingdom of heaven" means the celestial kingdom, Christ's kingdom, which will come with Him from heaven when He comes to rule during the Millennium. (See Bible Dictionary, "Kingdom of Heaven or kingdom of God.")

The Master Teacher

Many of us know that mustard seeds are very small, some as small as a grain of sand, such as those God referred to when he told Abraham that if he could count them all, he would know the number of his posterity. Many of us recognize Jesus's teaching technique of using surprise or the unexpected to catch a learner's attention and focus them on a core idea. Something as small as a little grain of sand growing into a large tree is amazing and unexpected. So, too, is God's kingdom. What is more stunning is the miracle that Jesus may be hinting at in this parable. That miniscule mustard seed *transforms* to become something entirely new and different than what it was. Think of it. All of us can be transformed by the love of God to become something entirely new and different, lustrous and productive, far beyond comprehension, just as a mustard seed transforms into a mighty tree. Looking at a cache of various seeds, could any one of us, without prior experience with those seeds, ever predict what those seeds would become? Impossible. So too is it with our lives and Jesus's invitation for us to become part of the kingdom of heaven. If we follow Christ, we will be transformed in ways beyond our imagination. We will become greater, mightier, and wholly different than what we started out as. God, the Master Gardner, is only just starting to cultivate us!

Possible Applications for Learners

As learners, we should be patient with ourselves and take the long view of our growth and development. Learning takes time. Learning things that matter takes even more time. Mastering that which matters most may take the most time, but it is where we should spend our most devoted, patient, and faithful efforts. We should trust God that He can transform us into something unexpectedly different that who we currently are. We should embrace change for good, even when change can be uncomfortable. With persistence, the change will become as natural as a seed becoming a tree.

Helps for Teachers

Teachers should see learners as God sees them. Teachers should pray to God to understand the eternal nature and destines of their learners. Teachers should be patient with learners as they grow, develop, and transform. Learning is a process not a destination. Teaching moments are like feeding moments, one act of nourishment at a time to fill the wells of faith.

Examples of questions that can foster good class discussion:

- What are some ways that this parable can be encouraging to us? (One possible answer is that some of our good attributes at present might look insignificant, even weak, but with the help of the Holy Ghost and the gospel, including repentance, they can grow to be strong and powerful.)
- How might understanding this parable help us to be less judgmental of others? (An answer might be that if we compare others to a mustard seed and its potential growth into a mighty tree, we can see them more as God sees them.)
- What prophecy from this parable do you see being fulfilled with the Church today? (From tiny beginnings at its organization with six members on April 6, 1830, it is now growing toward filling the whole earth. See Daniel 2:35.)
- How might this parable apply to our testimonies? (One possible answer is that they may start out small but can continue to grow as we nourish them under the direction of the Holy Ghost until they become strong and unshakable.)

The Pearl of Great Price

Matthew 13:45–46

45 Again, the kingdom of heaven is like unto a merchant man, seeking goodly pearls:

46 Who, when he had found one pearl of great price, went and sold all that he had, and bought it.

Background, Culture, and Setting

Anciently, as today, pearls were prized possessions. But unlike today, pearls were much harder to acquire anciently, before the modern-day inventions of underwater breathing equipment and rapid modes of transportation and trade.

What was the constitution of an intrepid pearl diver? These treasure seekers endured unparalleled challenge and difficulty. Pearl divers would climb into a boat, cast off from shore into the sea, and then position the boat to hover above a pearl bed. Before diving in, they would tie a rope around their ankle. This would allow them to not lose the boat. Their pearl diving companions could also help haul them back up to the surface in case of an emergency. The divers would then take a deep breath that could sustain them for 30 seconds or more, dive into the sea, and swim to the depths in search of pearls. This was an exhausting ordeal full of peril. Pearl divers suffered from the pain of salt stings to the eyes (remember there were no swim goggles to use); their lungs burned with fire, screaming for a new breath; and sea creatures lurking in the depths could unexpectedly attack.

Once the pearls were acquired from the forbidding depths, how would one on land eventually access such a rare and treasured possession? Only through extensive trade networks, unless you wanted to personally find your own. In that case, one of the most productive and sought-after sources of pearls in ancient times was off the coasts of Bahrain in the Persian Gulf. So, if you were an ancient Israelite in search of a pearl, what were your options if you were unwilling to trade but would rather obtain your pearl through sweat equity? You'd have to go to Bahrain yourself. Would you seek to save time by taking a shortcut from Israel to travel through the howling wilderness of the Arabian Desert's Empty Quarter to visit Bahrain? Or would you travel the more secure trade paths north through Syria; south along the Euphrates River to the Persian Gulf; and then further south, following the coast until you reached Bahrain? This would require passing through a babble of languages and cultures. You'd hope no one robbed or beat you along the way. The entire one-way trip might require more than two months of travel time and cover a distance of roughly 1500 miles, passing varied terrain and climates. This is not a trip for the faint of heart, because you'd have to do much of it, if not all of it, by foot. Once you arrived in Bahrain, you'd have to find a sea-going vessel captained by those willing to divulge the secrets of the locations of the pearl-bearing oyster beds. You'd then need someone to teach you how to dive; how to not lose your composure at 30, or 50, or in extreme cases, more than 100 feet under water; how to force yourself to keep your eyes open from the burning salt water; how to appropriately handle water pressure changes; how to pry an oyster from its cemented base; and how to persist in searching until a pearl of great price and worth was ultimately found. Of course, once you've made the spectacular discovery, how will you protect your prize possession, especially as you have to retrace 1500 miles of footsteps through foreign and likely unfriendly territory?

Personally finding your own pearl of great price was nigh impossible, so you'd have to turn to trade to obtain the prize. But what would one have to trade to secure such a prize? All that you had. No one who had gone through the effort described above to acquire a pearl would easily and quickly depart from their treasure unless they received in exchange something of significant and hard-to-obtain value. All that you could offer is all that you had. That is what we see in this short analogy Jesus shares of the merchant selling *everything* he has to obtain the pearl of great price.

Pearls were prized for more than their unparalleled beauty, rarity, and difficulty of acquisition. Pearls represented something far more significant. Pearls represented eternal life. Ancient peoples believed that these rare and prized possessions restored youth to the owner. Whoever possessed a pearl of great price would have ever-restored youth. They would live forever.

This folklore, that a pearl is the source of eternal life, is old—even ancient. One of the most ancient stories in the world tells of the travels and deeds of warrior king Gilgamesh who, having conquered all, feels that he needs to conquer life by achieving eternal life. In his long and winding story, he eventually hunts for pearls (represented by a special plant at the bottom of the sea). The ordeal of diving to the bottom of the sea to wrest the symbol of eternal life from the sea floor exhausts him. He returns to shore and falls into a prolonged state of sleep. When he awakes, he discovers that a snake has stolen his prized and long-sought possession, his plant of eternal life (or the pearl of great price). Gilgamesh later learns that he cannot obtain eternal life on his own. He needs help from God.

The Master Teacher

Notice how Jesus shared a two-verse analogy that was packed full of significant insights and instructive value. Jesus, as the Master Teacher, did not need to launch into lengthy and descriptive discourses to enliven the minds of His people and to empower their hearts to act. So, often less is more. Good teachers find ways to use analogies that are simple yet deep and comprehensible yet expansive in the lessons they convey. Good teachers use such analogies and then provide time for learners to ponder, reflect, share, and act.

Possible Applications for Learners

Learners should be willing to devote the time and energy necessary to develop their God-Given abilities to learn. To be human is to learn. To be a child of God is to learn. Our natural disposition to grow and transform is what eventually will help us become like God. Sadly, many compromise or put on hold their agency. They believe that learning happens only based on what others do to them. For example, some learners blame their lack of learning on a teacher who didn't teach them well, failing to realize that their agency to learn is the most powerful tool they have to be transformed. Diligent learners don't wait for others to teach them. They do not wait for others' agency to move before they are willing to act for themselves. Like ancient pearl divers, good learners understand the efforts and risks required to learn, and they willingly and persistently embrace these opportunities.

HELPS FOR TEACHERS

Teaching is a complex skill that requires sustained effort and practice. Teaching is more than simply talking. Teaching involves loving the people you teach, loving the message you have to share, thoughtfully considering the needs of the learners, and designing appropriate learning experiences to help learners become more than what they were when they entered your class. Sometimes being a teacher feels as long, arduous, and unglamorous as traveling 1500 miles of ancient roads in search of treasure. But just like the wise merchant, we must give all we have to obtain the prize of being a teacher like Jesus.

Possible questions to involve students in class discussion:

- How might the pearl of great price be compared to the Church?
- How might the pearl of great price be compared to Jesus?
- What lessons in living the gospel might be seen in selling all to obtain the "pearl of great price"?
- What does "of great price" mean in the parable?
- Why do we need to "sell all that we have" in order to live the gospel?
- How do we "sell all that we have" in order to live the gospel?
- What part of the plan of salvation would the "pearl of great price" represent? (Ultimately, it would represent exaltation.)
- What kinds of things in our lives would we need to "sell," so to speak, in order to obtain the "pearl of great price"? (Answers could include our sins, priorities and activities that keep us from giving complete loyalty to the gospel, involvement in social media that prevents us from spending adequate time studying the scriptures and serving others, and so forth.)

Feeding of the 5000

John 6:5–13

5 When Jesus then lifted up his eyes, and saw a great company [*huge crowd*] come unto him, he saith unto Philip, Whence [*where*] shall we buy bread, that these may eat [*to feed all these people*]?

> In verse 6, next, John points out to us the Master Teacher's technique as He provides learning opportunities for His Apostles. They are, in effect, involved in their own personalized "MTC" training.

6 And this he said to prove [*test*] him: for he himself knew what he would do.

7 Philip answered him, Two hundred pennyworth of bread is not sufficient for them, that every one of them may take a little. [*Two hundred days' wages would not buy enough for everyone to have more than a little; see Mark 6 footnote 37a.*]

8 One of his disciples, Andrew, Simon Peter's brother, saith unto him,

9 There is a lad here, which hath five barley loaves, and two small fishes: but what are they among so many?

10 And Jesus said, Make the men sit down. Now there was much grass in the place. So the men sat down, in number about five thousand [*plus women and children; see Matthew 14:21*].

11 And Jesus took the loaves; and when he had given thanks, he distributed to the disciples, and the disciples to them that were set down; and likewise of the fishes as much as they would [*everyone ate as much as they wanted*].

12 When they were filled [*when the people in the crowd were full*], he said unto his disciples, Gather up the fragments that remain, that nothing be lost [*wasted*].

13 Therefore they gathered them together, and filled twelve baskets with the fragments [*leftovers*] of the five barley loaves, which remained over and above unto them that had eaten.

Background, Culture, and Setting

One of the great miracles of Jesus's ministry is the feeding of the five thousand. The crowd was so hungry for the word of God that they completely failed to provide for their own physical needs. Imagine the spiritual thirst that would drive individuals to forget about their own physical needs, and multiply that by five thousand. Jesus, who was filled with compassion, knew that without physical sustenance, the people would struggle to experience the spiritual feeding He had to offer.

But what was the source of the miracle? Bless the soul of the little lad who appears to be the only one who had packed a lunch that day: five loaves of barley bread and two little fishes. Doubly bless the soul of that faithful Jewish mother who packed a lunch for her young son, likely unaware that her act of service that day, an act she had repeated daily across her years, which has been repeated by mothers across the ages and across the lands, was the source of physical nourishment to thousands and spiritual sustenance to millions in the millennia that have followed.

Though we aren't sure which type of "little fish" the young lad brought, even if it was the famous St. Peter's fish (a delicious tilapia white meat fish), we, the authors, can tell you from experience visiting the Sea of Galilee and consuming St. Peter's fish that one of these fish is not enough for even a single person. Today, St. Peter's fish is consumed alongside a healthy portion of Israeli salad, French fries, hummus, and pita bread. But eating the fish alone? Tasty, yes. Filling? No.

THE MASTER TEACHER

The people, apparently, were both spiritually and physically famished. Note that Jesus did not scold the people for coming to the learning experience unprepared. He met the people in the condition in which they arrived at the learning moment, and He provided for them what they needed when they needed it, regardless of any prior teaching plan He may have devised.

Jesus also acted in a way to call up the memory of former prophets in the minds of the people. Just as they honored and listened to the word of God through ancient past prophets, they should listen to Him now. Effective teachers build upon the shoulders of those who have gone before.

How did Jesus connect His lessons to those of the prophets past? Let's consider some surprising connections. Remember that in the 40 years of wilderness wandering, God provided physical sustenance for His people as He sought to teach them covenantal truths. He gave them bread and flesh. He daily sent them a honey-flavored, bread-like substance called manna. And on several occasions, He sent them quail to eat. The miracle of feeding the five thousand allowed Jesus to show that He is the new Moses and the Mediator before God who provides for His people. We should also remember that the Jews of Christ's day held Moses to be the highest and most important of all the ancient prophets. So Jesus serving as the new Moses should have been a clear sign to the Jews that God had called Him to bring truth.

Many years after the time of Moses, another prophet like Moses also miraculously provided food for those in need. That prophet was Elijah. In 1 Kings 17, in the midst of a raging famine, Elijah found the widow of Zarephath gathering sticks to make one last meal and then die with her son. Elijah challenged her faith, asking her to bring him some bread to eat. Using the last of her flour, she gave him all that she had. Elijah then blessed her that she would not want during the famine. Subsequently, she miraculously had enough flour to make bread for herself and her son until the famine abated. Though we don't know if the mother of the lad at the feeding of the five thousand gave away all that she had, we do know that the lad gave away all his food that day, and, like in the story of Elijah, it was miraculously multiplied.

Possible Applications for Learners

Good learners come prepared. This young lad was, apparently, the only one among five thousand people to have brought sustenance. Perhaps this physical sustenance was provided by his mother. Perhaps the fishes and loaves were symbolic of the drop-by-drop spiritual nourishment she provided to him in daily interactions. Perhaps she was like the mothers of the stripling warriors (Alma 56:47–48), having taught her son the truths of the gospel so that they sunk deep into his heart.

Helps for Teachers

Teachers need not deliver everything they have prepared. Good teachers recognize, use, and multiply the contributions of others. Good teachers, like good parents, have the long view. They recognize that no simple word, no individual truth, no one lesson, no single day will create lasting and transformative learning. Every day, drop by drop, persistently and consistently over time, over the years, over a lifetime, the regular engagement with the word of God, the regular interaction with the Spirit, will build a spiritual life that endures to the end. As teachers, our role is to be there, day-by-day (or week by week) assisting learners as they persistently endure to the end.

Possible learning involvement questions might include

- What lessons might we learn from the fact that the Savior did not scold the five thousand for following Him to a "desert place" (Matthew 14:13) without bringing food with them? (Possible answers could include that He is mercifully willing to help us in our lives, even when we do foolish things. Another answer could be that we should be forgiving and willing to help others even when they get themselves in trouble by doing foolish things. Yet another response might be that God does not expect us to be perfect in order for him to be willing to help us.)
- What lessons might we learn from the fact that the five thousand followed the Savior into a wilderness in order to hear Him? (Answers could include that living the gospel often requires us to leave our comfort zones.)
- What character traits of the Savior are demonstrated by these verses?
- What might you surmise about the lad who brought five barley loaves and two small fishes along as he followed Jesus into the wilderness? What possible things might you guess regarding his mother? How can you be like that lad when you come to church or any other gospel-oriented learning experience?
- What do you think might have been going on in Andrew's and the other Apostles' minds as Jesus instructed them to have the people sit down? What principle of faith is demonstrated?
- What lessons could you teach from the fact that after everyone had eaten, there was more bread left over than what the boy had originally brought? (One possible response is that the Savior can make far more of our lives when we strive to follow Him than we could possibly do without His help.)

Healing the Canaanite Woman's Daughter

Matthew 15:21–28

21 Then Jesus went thence, and departed into the coasts [*borders*] of Tyre and Sidon [*a bit north and then west of the Sea of Galilee*].

22 And, behold, a woman of Canaan [*a Gentile, non-Israelite*] came out of the same coasts [*from the same area*], and cried unto him, saying, Have mercy on me, O Lord, thou Son of David [*thou Messiah, who was prophesied to be a descendent of King David*]; my daughter is grievously vexed [*is very sick*] with a devil.

23 But he answered her not a word. And his disciples came and besought him, saying, Send her away; for she crieth after us.

24 But he answered and said, I am not sent but unto the lost sheep of the house of Israel.

> As he states here, Jesus's mortal mission was limited to the house of Israel, specifically, the Jews. This limitation will be done away with later, as exemplified by Mark 16:15 and Peter's dream in Acts 10:9–48.

25 Then came she and worshipped him, saying, Lord, help me.

26 But he answered and said, It is not meet [*appropriate, necessary*] to take the children's bread [*the gospel nourishment designated at this time for the Jews; see note above*], and to cast it to dogs.

27 And she said, Truth, Lord: yet the dogs eat of the crumbs which fall from their masters' table.

> The word "dogs" in this context means "little dogs" or household pets (a term of endearment). A Bible scholar named Dummelow explains as follows:
>
> "The rabbis often spoke of the Gentiles as dogs . . . (Jesus) says not 'dogs,' but 'little dogs,' i.e. household, favourite dogs, and the woman cleverly catches at the expression, arguing that if the Gentiles are household dogs, then it is only right that they should be fed with the crumbs that fall from their master's table." (Dummelow, *Commentary*, pages 678–79.)

28 Then Jesus answered and said unto her, O woman, great is thy faith: be it unto thee even as thou wilt. And her daughter was made whole from that very hour.

Background, Culture, and Setting

Jesus's primary message was to the house of Israel. The gospel writers do not provide background details as to why Jesus traveled out of the lands of Israel into the western neighboring lands of Sidon and Tyre. In other gospel narrative episodes, Jesus travels east into the gentile Decapolis. Though His primary declared mission was to the house of Israel, these stories suggest that Jesus was anxious to spread the message a bit further, into the lands of the Gentiles.

This story might surprise us since we might superficially think of Jesus as *always* being loving and kind. We might wonder, why would Jesus not have immediately responded to the real and desperate need from this gentile woman? She cried out to Him, and He passed on by without responding to her as though He didn't hear her. When she continued to press Him, even Jesus's disciples sought to reinforce Jesus's initial reactions (or inactions) to the woman. The fact that in the ancient world women and children were highly vulnerable only raises our level of surprise.

THE MASTER TEACHER

Upon further reflection, we recognize Jesus was doing several things. First, He was seeking to be true to His mission to first preach to the covenant people of God. The Gentiles would soon have their dispensation, but their time was not yet. Second, though the overall timing for sharing His ministry with the Gentiles had not yet arrived, Jesus ministered to the individual. Jesus saw her righteous desires and honored her noble petition. He was specifically moved by her faith and her ability to reason and communicate cogently and persuasively about her needs while acknowledging Jesus's mission to the Israelites. We should remember that Jesus's full love and mercy is available to *all* people. Though Jesus did not grow up in every nation of the earth, the gospel is for everyone. Everyone will have the chance to receive or reject the gospel of Jesus Christ.

POSSIBLE APPLICATIONS FOR LEARNERS

Good learners are persistent, even in the face of disappointment, frustration, injustice, or in facing overwhelming odds. All that is worthwhile takes significant effort and time. Too often as learners we can be lulled into carnal security, thinking that we can have all of our learning needs met by simply having a teacher (or the internet) deliver all the answers. But we can never know the joy of learning, we can never know the reality of owning our own learning without effort and sacrifice and persistence, just as the woman of Canaan who was unyielding in her desire to receive from Jesus.

HELPS FOR TEACHERS

Teachers appropriately challenge learners to demonstrate their thirst and desire to learn. If learning was easily and readily accessible at the snap of the fingers, if learning required no effort and no sacrifice, then learning would be useless. It would be as dross to be cast out. Good teachers are also open to the needs of learners. Sometimes as teachers, we have a plan, lesson preparations for what we want to accomplish, and that may induce us to ignore the pleas of learners in class to address a different topic. Like Jesus, we can listen thoughtfully and weigh the opportunities. Who knows, there may be an opportunity to "heal" that we had not previously recognized, and the learner's request can be the spark that lights a teaching moment that blesses the individual learner and potentially everyone else in the teaching environment.

Possible involvement questions are

- Since the gospel and plan of salvation is ultimately for all of God's children, why do you suppose that the Master only focused on teaching the Jews during His mortal ministry? (Answers might include that He only had a limited time in His mortal ministry to establish His Church in the Holy Land, thus it was necessary to focus only on them.)
- What possible lessons might we learn from the fact that Jesus ultimately yielded to the Canaanite woman's pleading? (One answer is that prayers often need to be fervent and very heart-felt to be effective. Another is that Jesus, as well as our Father in Heaven, have deep feelings for us, and our sincere prayers move Them emotionally.)

Peter Bears Witness That Jesus Is the Christ

Matthew 16:13–20

13 When Jesus came into the coasts of [*area around*] Caesarea Philippi [*about 25 miles north of the Sea of Galilee*], he asked his disciples, saying, Whom do men say that I the Son of man am?

14 And they said, Some say that thou art John the Baptist: some, Elias [*Elijah*]; and others, Jeremias [*Jeremiah*], or one of the prophets.

15 He saith unto them, But whom say ye that I am?

16 And Simon Peter answered and said, Thou art the Christ, the Son of the living God.

17 And Jesus answered and said unto him, Blessed art thou, Simon Bar-jona [*son of a man named Jona*]: for flesh and blood [*man*] hath not revealed it unto thee, but my Father which is in heaven [*you have received your testimony of Me through revelation*].

18 And I say also unto thee, That thou art Peter, and upon this rock [*the "rock" of revelation, see TPJS, page 274; also, Christ is the "rock" upon which the Church is based, see Matt. 16 footnote 18a*] I will build my church; and the gates of hell shall not prevail against it. [*Satan's kingdom absolutely will not ultimately win against Christ's kingdom, a very comforting fact!*]

19 And I will give unto thee the keys [*including the sealing power*] of the kingdom of heaven [*Peter is authorized to serve as the president of the Church after the Savior leaves*]: and whatsoever thou shalt bind [*seal*] on earth shall be bound in heaven: and whatsoever thou shalt loose [*unseal*] on earth shall be loosed in heaven.

20 Then charged he his disciples that they should tell no man that he was Jesus the Christ. [*Apostle Bruce R. McConkie explained verse 20, above, as follows: "For the time being, to avoid persecution and because the available hearers were not prepared to heed their witness, the apostles were restrained from bearing witness of the divine Sonship of their Master" (McConkie,* Doctrinal New Testament Commentary, *vol. 1, page 390).*]

Background, Culture, and Setting

One of the greatest truths ever taught in scripture is Peter's statement to Jesus, "Thou art the Christ, the Son of the living God." That statement is true no matter the season of the year, the time of day, or the location where uttered, indoors or out of doors, domestically or foreign. It is truth, plain and simple.

The context of this scriptural story occurs at "the coasts [*or borders*] of Caesarea Philippi," about 25 miles north of the Sea of Galilee, at the foot of Mount Hermon.

This city was near the border of several other ancient provinces and sat on the major international road connecting Syria and Lebanon to Israel. Caesarea Philippi was a cosmopolitan city made up mostly of non-Jews: Greeks, Romans, and native inhabitants of the region. The various peoples worshipped their favorite gods at pagan temples in Caesarea Philippi.

There are a host of teaching and learning reasons why Jesus created this learning experience. This story, whose truths are so beloved, needed to occur at this specific place.

When Jesus posed the question to his disciples "Whom do men say that I am?" He was likely standing in front of the temple in Caesarea Philippi, dedicated to Caesar Augustus. That pagan temple was built directly in front of a massive cave that was a source of the Jordan River, which emanated from out of the deep, blue, spring pool at the base of Mount Hermon.

In ancient times, pagans believed that the cave and spring of water were a gateway to the underworld. Worshippers would come to the pagan temple to make a sacrifice and to ask a question of the gods they worshipped. The questions were typically "yes or no," something like, "Should I marry so and so?" or "should I go on a long journey?" or "should I join a particular business venture?" The pagan temple priests would conduct the sacrificial ritual. The worshipper would take the remains of the sacrificial animal and throw it into the pool of spring water. The worshippers believed that the gods of the underworld would provide an answer to their petition. If the animal carcass sank, as though consumed by the underworld gods, then that was the sign that the gods accepted of the sacrifice and said "yes" to the petition. If the gods of the underworld rejected the sacrifice, the answer was "no," and the sacrificial remains would bubble back up to the surface.

Let's review this passage and see the significance of the context. First, listen to Peter's sincere declaration, "Thou art the Christ, the Son of the living God." Peter didn't say, "Thou art Jesus." Peter didn't use Jesus's given and proper name, a name revealed by an angel to Joseph's adoptive father, "and thou shalt call His name Jesus, for He shall save His people from their sins" (Matthew 1:21). The name *Jesus* in Hebrew means "to save," which is mentioned in revelation as "He shall save." (Variants of the name include Joshua, Josh, Hosea, Hoshea, and Isaiah.) Peter instead calls Jesus "the Christ," identifying not Jesus's name, but His role in salvation. *Christ* is a Greek word that means "anointed." The same word in Hebrew is "messiah." Priests, prophets, and kings were anointed. Using the phrase *Christ*, Peter signals that Jesus is the promised anointed king, priest, and prophet who will save God's chosen people.

But Peter doesn't simply stop at naming Jesus's role as the one who saves. He continues. He elaborates on Jesus's identity. He says that Jesus is "the Son of the living God." Does that addendum really matter? Whether we declare Jesus is the Son of the living God or not doesn't change His role and purpose in saving us, it seems. Still, Peter must have had a reason for making this specific statement.

For Romans living in this area of Israel, they wanted to honor the first Roman emperor Caesar Augustus, so they built a temple in his name. Caesar Augustus brought peace to the war-torn Roman Empire. For his deeds in bringing peace to the world, Augustus was known throughout the Roman world as the prince of peace. His success at bringing civility once again to a civilization ripped by civil war was heralded as "the good news" (or rather, the gospel) of the day. Augustus was the nephew and adopted son of another formidable and famous Roman, Julius Caesar. Julius Caesar was one of the most capable Roman generals and administrators of all time. But he had grand ambitions that deeply worried many in the free Roman republic, including some of his senator friends. These friends conspired to murder Julius Caesar before he became a permanent king over the Roman Republic. Unfortunately, that murder set off out-of-control events that led to massive violence and Roman civil war that was only put to peace years later by Caesar Augustus.

Though Julius Caesar had been feared by some to become a tyrant, he was beloved by many Romans, including many in positions of power and leadership. Those in power, seeking to honor Julius Caesar, voted divine honors to him, installing him in the pantheon of Roman gods. And what did that make Caesar Augustus? The son of god.

Think of it. Jesus was standing in front of a Roman temple only a two-day's journey from His missionary base at Capernaum. And this temple was dedicated to Augustus, the same man that the Roman world proclaimed as the son of god and the prince of peace.

Bold Peter had the audacity to declare in such a setting, "Thou art the Christ, the Son of the living God." Again, it wasn't sufficient for Peter to call him Jesus, or even Jesus the Christ. Peter made a bold declaration that Jesus was the Christ, the Son of the living God.

But why didn't Peter say more simply, "Thou art the Christ, the Son of God"? In the Old and New Testament, "Son of God" was a title of kingship. The name Caesar eventually became a title of kingship and rulership, and we see the descendants of that name in titles such as Kaiser or Czar. Peter wanted to highlight that Jesus was not simply the real and true king. He was the Son of the *living* God in stark contrast to Caesar Augustus who was the son of a *dead* god. Furthermore, even Caesar Augustus, who also received divine honors at his death, was himself a *dead god*. Augustus was nothing more than a dead god who was the son of a dead god.

Those with ears to hear certainly could not have missed the momentous and stunning contrast voiced by Peter that day.

Jesus responded to Peter, saying, "Blessed art thou, Simon Barjona: for flesh and blood hath not revealed it unto thee, but my Father which is in heaven." What we learn from Jesus's statement is that Peter was moved by revelatory utterance to testify of Jesus's divine role in salvation as the living Son of God. We also see Jesus setting up an unmistakable contrast between the false and empty pagan attempts to receive revelation. Standing in front of the Roman temple, where animal flesh and blood sacrifices were thrown into the depths of the underworld in hopes of hearing from the gods, Jesus plainly declared that it is the Father who grants revelation. Peter did not receive that revelation through the flesh and blood petitionary sacrifice at a Roman temple. Peter did not enter a Roman temple with the question on his mind "Is Jesus the Christ, the Son of the living God?," slaughter an animal, throw its flesh and blood into the water, and wait for a yes or no response. Peter received direct revelation—simple, clean, pure, and beautiful, just like the water of the Jordan River, gushing forth from the base of Mount Hermon, before it was tainted by pagan sacrifices. The Jordan River itself symbolized ongoing and everlasting access to revelation.

Jesus continued speaking to Peter. Just as Peter identified Jesus by means of revelation, Jesus now returned the favor. Speaking through revelation, He said, "That thou art Peter, and upon this rock I will build my church; and the gates of hell shall not prevail against it." For generations, Biblical scholars have delighted in the fact that the name *Peter* (both in Greek and Aramaic) is a variant on the word for "rock." Scholars have used this wordplay to demonstrate that Peter was the chief apostle, the one to whom the keys were entrusted, the one who was to be the head of the Church once Jesus was gone (even though Jesus didn't call Peter the head, but rather the rock, or the foundation). The literary beauty and message of this passage is delightful to see and consider. Yet, because we only have words to read, we may only detect these literary symbols and miss the visual contextual backdrop for a larger message Jesus wanted to teach.

Stunningly, Jesus and His disciples were standing at the foot of the largest rock in any direction for approximately five hundred miles—Mount Hermon! This object lesson was unmistakable. This mountain looms in the distance over the Sea of Galilee. The disciples would have grown up in the gaze of this spectacular mountain that inescapably dominated the landscape. And hiking to Caesarea Philippi for two days from the Sea of Galilee, there would be only one major object to look at during the entire hike: the largest, most unmovable rock any of these men would ever see. So when Jesus said, "And I say also unto thee, That thou art Peter, and upon this rock I will build my church; and the gates of hell shall not prevail against it," he was simultaneously playing on the literary meaning of Peter's name, while demonstrating with the most massive object lesson conceivable, how stable and solid the kingdom of God was. Furthermore, the very cave and spring where pagans practiced their attempts at revelatory sacrifice were considered by these same pagans to be the gateway to the underworld, or in other words, the gates of hell. As Jesus said, "the gates of hell shall not prevail against" the Church, just like the spring of water at the base of Mount Hermon was inconsequential to any attempts to move the mountain.

Why did Jesus make His disciples hike for two days to answer a seemingly simple question "Who am I?" Because He wanted them to experience unmistakable revelatory learning firsthand in the context of unforgettable object lessons.

THE MASTER TEACHER

Did you notice how Jesus created the need for His disciples to learn and find answers? He used comparison and contrast (especially using the contextual clues of their setting) to encourage them to ask and answer questions about His identity. And when Peter answered, did you notice how the Master Teacher reinforced Peter's answer, complimenting him on his response ("Blessed art thou, Simon Bar-jona") and following up with additional instruction, including that his testimony came not from intellectual study and observation but rather from on high? Did you notice how the Lord "strikes while the iron is hot," so to speak? While He had Peter's undivided attention, He gave additional instruction that tied in beautifully to the contextual setting. He taught that revelation from God will guide the Church, and if we heed that revelation, Satan cannot succeed against the Church. We also learn that the keys of the priesthood, as part of the true Church, can make things done on earth by proper authority also valid in heaven.

Did you also notice that while Christ was aiming the discussion directly at Peter (one class member), He skillfully taught the other disciples (class members) as they paid rapt attention?

POSSIBLE APPLICATIONS FOR LEARNERS

With the help of the Holy Ghost, applications to your personal life are virtually infinite. That is the marvelous thing about learning "even by study, and also by faith" (D&C 88:118). The Holy Ghost becomes the teacher, in effect, your personal tutor, and thus your scripture study becomes progressively richer and deeper throughout your life. Here are a few possible applications:

- If we listen to the many voices in the world around us concerning Christ, we can be pulled in all different directions as to who He really was and is. We can even conclude that there is no way to come to a satisfactory answer. However, with the sure witness that comes only from the Spirit, we can join Peter in knowing that Jesus is indeed "the Christ, the Son of the living God" (Matthew 16:16).
- We can focus on the teaching in verse 18 and learn that we can have much stability and satisfaction in our lives if we build upon the "rock" of revelation, upon which the Church is built. And, we can be reminded of the incredible opportunity we have as members of the Church to listen to ongoing revelation through the apostles and prophets who lead the Church today.
- By applying verse 18 to ourselves, we can draw strength from the promise that, for those who strive to live the gospel and follow the promptings of the Spirit, "the gates of hell shall not prevail against" them. This is an iron-clad promise!
- Yet another application might be found in verse 19 regarding "keys" of the priesthood and the authority to "bind on earth" such that it "shall be bound in heaven." Because of the restoration of the sealing power (D&C 110:13–16), we can be married in the temple and look forward to having our marriages and families last throughout the eternities.
- Have you noticed that it was a lot of work for the Savior's disciples to keep up with Him during his travels? How might this apply to you in terms of keeping your covenants and commitments regarding the gospel and the Church? How might the fact that it took considerable effort for them to "stay close to Him" physically apply to your efforts to "stay close to Him" spiritually?

HELPS FOR TEACHERS

Good questions provide the foundation for good class discussions, such that class members fulfill the instruction to "teach one another the doctrine of the kingdom" as given in Doctrine and Covenants 88:77. Here are a few sample questions that might help encourage the productive participation of your students:

- Why is it that the witness of the Holy Ghost is the only way to gain a sure testimony of Jesus Christ?

- Peter was told that he would have power to bind on earth such that it would be bound in heaven. How do we qualify to have our temple sealings in force in eternity?
- What effect can temple marriage have on the day-to-day lives and relationships of married couples and families?
- What hope is there for a faithful member of the Church who has not yet had the blessing of temple marriage and sealing?
- How does one obtain a testimony like Peter exemplified in verse 16?
- Can a person who has, so far, not had any spectacular spiritual manifestations have as strong a testimony as Peter expressed in verse 16?
- How can we keep the "gates of hell" from winning against us (verse 18)?
- What possible applications might we find in our lives for Brother McConkie's explanation of verse 20? (There might be times when it would not be wise to bring up the gospel because of the nature and attitudes of those around us.)
- How do people, who are not acquainted with the gospel and thus are not able to have the ordinances of salvation "bound on earth," gain access to these blessings?
- Referring to verse 17, how does Heavenly Father generally give a testimony to His children that Jesus is the Christ? (Revelation through the Holy Ghost. John 15:26; 1 Corinthians 12:3.)

Counting the Cost

Luke 14:25–35

25 And there went great multitudes with him: and he turned, and said unto them,

26 If any man come to me, and hate not his father, and mother, and wife, and children,
and brethren, and sisters, yea, and his own life also, he cannot be my disciple.

> JST Luke 14:26
>
> 26 If any man come to me, and hate not his father, and mother, and wife, and children, and brethren, and sisters, or husband, yea and his own life also; or in other words, is afraid to lay down his life for my sake, he cannot be my disciple.

27 And whosoever doth not bear his cross, and come after me [*whoever is not willing to
sacrifice whatever is necessary to follow Me*], cannot be my disciple.

> The JST adds a verse here, as follows:
>
> JST Luke 14:28
>
> 28 Wherefore, settle this in your hearts, that ye will do the things which I shall teach, and command you.
>
> The whole point here is that if you are half-hearted about following the Savior, you will be unsuccessful.
>
> Next, beginning with verse 28, the Master emphasizes again that one must plan and accept the cost in order to successfully follow Him.

28 For which of you, intending to build a tower, sitteth not down first, and counteth the
cost, whether he have sufficient to finish it?

29 Lest haply [*JST "unhappily"*], after he hath laid the foundation, and is not able to
finish it, all that behold it begin to mock him,

30 Saying, This man began to build, and was not able to finish.

> JST Luke 14:31
>
> 31 Saying, This man began to build, and was not able to finish. And this he said, signifying there should not any man follow him, unless he was able to continue; saying,

31 Or what king, going to make war against another king, sitteth not down first, and
consulteth whether he be able with ten thousand to meet him [*the enemy*] that cometh
against him with twenty thousand?

32 Or else, while the other is yet a great way off, he sendeth an ambassage [*ambassador, negotiator*], and desireth conditions of peace.

33 So likewise, whosoever he be of you that forsaketh not all that he hath [*is not willing to sacrifice everything for the gospel*], he cannot be my disciple.

The JST adds the following after verse 33 and overlapping verse 34:

JST Luke 14:35–37

35 Then certain of them came to him, saying, Good Master, we have Moses and the prophets, and whosoever shall live by them, shall he not have life?

36 And Jesus answered, saying, Ye know not Moses, neither the prophets; for if ye had known them, ye would have believed on me; for to this intent they were written. For I am sent that ye might have life. Therefore I will liken it unto salt which is good;

37 But if the salt has lost its savor, wherewith shall it be seasoned?

34 Salt is good: but if the salt have lost his savour, wherewith shall it be seasoned?

35 It is neither fit for the land, nor yet for the dunghill; but men cast it out. He that hath ears to hear, let him hear.

BACKGROUND, CULTURE, AND SETTING

Salt is a fabulously simple yet deeply meaningful symbol. First, salt was essential in the ancient world, because it provided flavor to otherwise bland food. Consider this. Our modern word *salsa* (a word used to discuss flavoring that we add to our foods) comes from the ancient word for salt, *sal*. Second, the only way to preserve food without refrigeration or freezing is by drying and salting the food. Salt is therefore a preservative. Third, salt is hard to come by, at least it was anciently. Today, salt is in such super abundance that we throw it onto snow-covered roads without a second thought. Anciently, you'd have to find a salt mine, a salt lick, or a salt sea (like the ocean or the Dead Sea) where you could extract salt through evaporation. All of these required intensive time and labor. Once the salt was made, you still faced difficulty in obtaining it if you weren't the one mining it or extracting it through evaporation. That required extensive and expensive trade networks. Clearly, salt was highly valuable and expensive. So valuable was salt that at times the Roman Empire paid their soldiers their salary in salt. Ever hear the phrase, "Worth his salt?" That phrase originated when salt was highly prized and highly valuable. And where does our modern word *salary* come from, the regular monetary payment a career worker receives? You guessed it—salt! As we said a moment ago that the Roman soldiers received salt as payment, that tradition became known as their *salary* and has continued to be used in our language today.

For all these reasons and others we haven't discussed, Jesus used in His ministry the symbol of salt to describe His true disciples. They were valuable and hard to find. They brought flavor to everything they did, and they preserved what mattered for the future.

One more thought we should add here on the topic of salt, and perhaps this is the most significant.

Salt is also a symbol of blood. And blood in turn is a symbol of life.

Because salt can substitute symbolically for blood, and blood for life, when we read passages in scripture discussing salt, such as those we've reviewed above, we can also connect our minds to the idea of life. So when Jesus says "Ye are the salt of the earth," we can understand another level of meaning to be "Ye are the life of the earth. If you have lost or given away your life to things other than God's work, what value are you to your friends, your neighbors, the earth, and to God and His kingdom? When you gain the world at the expense of your soul, you lose your life and are worth nothing more than to be trodden under foot of men." Isn't that what Korihor in the Book of Mormon achieved? He gained fame and fortune at the expense of truth and his soul. In the end, he was trodden under foot, because he had no real salary, no real value, no real life to give that mattered to anyone.

Truly, when we live disciplined in the doctrine of the real Doctor, we have our salary, our life. And our lives become blessings that can spread around the world to bring life, flavor, and preservation to all we encounter.

THE MASTER TEACHER

These four words are interrelated: Doctor, doctrine, disciple, discipline. Doctors teach doctrine to disciples. Disciples show discipline (or faithfulness) in living the doctrine. Initially, Jesus had many disciples who followed His doctrine. But as He continued to reveal doctrine, some disciples felt that the discipline was too much and left the cause. For example, one day in the synagogue at Capernaum Jesus declared, "Verily, verily, I say unto you, Except ye eat the flesh of the Son of man, and drink his blood, ye have no life in you. Whoso eateth my flesh, and drinketh my blood, hath eternal life; and I will raise him up at the last day. For my flesh is meat indeed, and my blood is drink indeed" (John 6:53–55). A superficial interpretation of these statements may lead one to think that Jesus is advocating heinous cannibalism.

In fact, this is exactly what some of his disciplines determined: "Many therefore of his disciples, when they had heard this, said, This is an hard saying; who can hear it? . . . From that time many of his disciples went back, and walked no more with him" (John 6:61, 66). They missed the symbolism. Such leaving still happens today when disciples misunderstand doctrine or think the gospel is too hard to live.

For this and other reasons, Jesus reminds His listeners in Luke 14 to have eyes wide open about what they are getting into. They have to plan in advance. They have to count the costs. They have to be as prepared as possible. Real disciples of Jesus should not simply think that because He is with them that there will be no rigor or difficulty expected or encountered. Similarly, those who follow the doctrine of Jesus should not expect life to be a bed of roses. Quite the opposite. President Hinckley taught this principle, quoting Jenkins Lloyd Jones: "Life is like an old-time rail journey—delays, sidetracks, smoke, dust, cinders and jolts, interspersed only occasionally by beautiful vistas and thrilling bursts of speed. The trick is to thank the Lord for letting you have the ride" ("Big Rock Candy Mountains," *Deseret News*, June 12, 1973, A4).

Jesus recognized that those who are willing to throw their lot in with Him will suffer. He even repeated His use of the symbol of salt, "Blessed are they which are persecuted for righteousness' sake: for theirs is the kingdom of heaven. Blessed are ye, when men shall revile you, and persecute you, and shall say all manner of evil against you falsely, for my sake. Rejoice, and be exceeding glad: for great is your reward in heaven: for so persecuted they the prophets which were before you. Ye are the salt of the earth: but if the salt have lost his savour, wherewith shall it be salted? it is thenceforth good for nothing, but to be cast out, and to be trodden under foot of men" (Matthew 5:10–13).

As the Master Teacher, Jesus set high, challenging, yet attainable standards for His disciples. He does the same for us today. Jesus loves us enough to not make life simple or easy. Jesus loves us enough to show us how to live true doctrine in a disciplined way, including counting the costs of discipleship in advance.

Possible Applications for Learners

Learning is crucial. But how many of us adequately prepare and plan? Do we put in enough time? Do we give ourselves the best opportunity to learn in an environment devoid of or with minimized distractions? Have we set appropriate learning goals, or have we failed because we tried to "eat too much at one time"? We can't expect one single gorging Thanksgiving dinner-like learning experience to meet our needs throughout a lifetime. Just as we need regular meals and nourishment, we need regular experiences with learning. Do we lose focus? Are we scattered? Do we endure and persist even when it is difficult? What stories do we tell ourselves about being learners (that we are losers or winners)? Do we create small wins that lead to larger learning victories?

How do we maintain discipline in the face of challenge? How do we, in a disciplined way, seek after and find doctrine from the Living Doctor?

Helps for Teachers

Teachers should be windows to the true Doctor and His doctrine. Teachers should not seek to win disciples for themselves but rather for God. Teachers should be more loyal to the discipline taught by the real Doctor than they are to any other discipline or doctor. Yes, we must seek after and embrace all truth if we are to ever become like God. But truths are built first on the firm foundation of the doctrines given us by Jesus. Teachers are commissioned to model discipleship for others as they teach the doctrines of the Doctor we all hope to follow.

Here are some questions that can help spur involvement in class discussion:

- How does Luke 14:26 apply to us as we strive to live the gospel?
- What does "bear his cross" mean in Luke 14:27? (Answers might include the difficult sacrifices required for us to truly follow Christ.)
- What do verses 27 and 33 imply about claiming to want to follow Christ but remaining lukewarm or half-hearted in obeying some of the commandments? (We need to strive to be fully committed to living the gospel to be a true disciple of Christ.)
- What are some of the costs of living the gospel?

- What are some of the wonderful rewards of "paying" these costs?
- What verses do the JST add to Luke 14:33–34? (Hint: see footnote 34a for Luke 14:34.)
- How could we, as the "salt" spoken of by the Savior here, in effect, lose our "savour"?
- How are you being the "salt" or "life" of the world?

THE UNFORGIVING SERVANT (THE PARABLE OF THE UNMERCIFUL SERVANT)

MATTHEW 18:23–35

23 Therefore is the kingdom of heaven likened unto a certain king, which would take account of his servants [*see who is in debt to him, etc.*].

24 And when he had begun to reckon [*check the accounting records*], one was brought unto him, which owed him ten thousand talents.

> One calculation of this amount, based on an average day's wage, yields a debt which would require sixty million work days to pay off, which, of course, is an impossible debt to repay. A person who starts full-time work at age 15, and works six days a week for 55 years, would have 17,160 days of work in his or her lifetime.

25 But forasmuch as he had not to pay, his lord commanded him to be sold, and his wife, and children, and all that he had, and payment to be made. [*This can be symbolic of the fact that we would lose family and all that counts (see 2 Nephi 9:8–9) without the Atonement and its power to free and cleanse us so we can enter exaltation and dwell in family units forever.*]

26 The servant therefore fell down, and worshipped him, saying, Lord, have patience with me, and I will pay thee all.

27 Then the lord of that servant was moved with compassion, and loosed him, and forgave him the debt [*symbolic of the Atonement*].

28 But the same servant went out, and found one of his fellowservants, which owed him an hundred pence [*an amount equivalent to about 100 days' wages; see Matthew 20:2*]: and he laid hands on him, and took him by the throat, saying, Pay me that thou owest.

29 And his fellowservant fell down at his feet, and besought him, saying, Have patience with me, and I will pay thee all [*the exact words he had used as he begged for mercy in verse 26, above*].

30 And he would not [*he refused to be merciful to the person who owed him and couldn't pay*]: but went and cast him into prison, till he should pay the debt.

31 So when his fellowservants saw what was done, they were very sorry, and came and told unto their lord [*the king, verse 23*] all that was done.

32 Then his lord, after that he had called him [*the man who refused to forgive the relatively small debt of 100 days' wages*], said unto him, O thou wicked servant, I forgave thee all that debt, because thou desiredst me:

33 Shouldest not thou also have had compassion on thy fellowservant, even as I had pity on thee?

34 And his lord was wroth [*angry; righteous indignation*], and delivered him to the tormentors, till he should pay all that was due unto him [*symbolic of the law of justice*].

> Symbolically, "tormentors" would represent the punishment of the wicked who are eventually turned over to the buffetings of Satan (D&C 82:21) to pay for their own sins. Even after they have paid the penalty for their own sins, the highest degree of glory they can enter is the telestial (D&C 76:84–85). Also, this parable teaches the interplay between the law of justice and the law of mercy. The law of mercy allows us to be forgiven of unfathomable debt to God, through obedience to the gospel, including forgiving others. However, if we, through our actions, refuse the law of mercy, then the law of justice takes over and we bear the burden of our sins as explained in D&C 19:15–18.

35 So likewise shall my heavenly Father do also unto you, if ye from your hearts forgive not every one his brother their trespasses. [*This is fair warning to us about forgiving others and quite an answer to Peter's question in verse 21, wherein he asked how often he should forgive others.*]

Background, Culture, and Setting

During the days of Jesus, a hundred pence, or a hundred denarii, would be the equivalent of a hundred days of wages for a Roman solider or day laborer, which is a significant sum, especially in the minds of poor Galilean fishermen and farmers. But this amount was dwarfed by the eye-popping amount of ten thousand talents! Keep in mind that, according to some scholarly estimates, six thousand denarii would equal one talent. The unjust and indebted servant would need to work for more than 164,000 years before the debt had been retired (assuming that no interest had been collecting along the way).

For comparison, the unmerciful servant's debt was six hundred thousand times greater than that of his fellow servant.

The Master Teacher

Jesus used exaggerated stories to make truths and principles unmistakably clear. Here, again, we watch the Master Teacher capture His students' full attention as He presents a case study, so to speak, that quickly elicits strong positive feelings toward the king for his kindness, and equally strong negative feelings toward the unmerciful servant for his hypocrisy and unbelievable lack of mercy.

Possible Applications for Learners

Applications for this parable in our own lives are numerous. The principle of forgiving others if we expect forgiveness from the Lord is the major idea here. We are to not only forgive the small hurts, pains, and offensives we receive from others, but we should also forgive others *fully*. We are to let go the debt others may "owe us" because of how they pained us, no matter the cost, whether a small sum of pain or an enormous sum of pain. If we are petty with others and hold grudges, if we are mean and punishing toward others, if we reject the requests of people who ask our forgiveness, we can hardly expect forgiveness from the Lord for our countless sins and offenses. In short, it is our obligation to forgive others in order to be forgiven ourselves, as commanded in Matthew 6:12: "And forgive us our debts, as we forgive our debtors." The exaggerations of this parable wonderfully illustrate the principle and requirement to forgive. In some cases, those who have hurt us may never ask for forgiveness. We are still required to forgive them whether they "know not what they do," or even if they know what they do.

HELPS FOR TEACHERS

Teachers can help learners find clarity in their learning by placing opposites side by side, or by putting next to each other two extreme examples. A note of caution should be expressed here. We are not advocating for extreme examples simply for the sake of shock and awe. Rather, once the teacher has determined which principle of truth needs to be highlighted, the teacher should consider whether using paired opposites or exaggerated examples would help learners to see the truth. If the exaggerations or extreme examples become distracting, then do not use this approach.

Here are some questions to help encourage participation:

- What are some obvious benefits to each of us if we follow the commandment to forgive others?
- What principles of the law of justice are illustrated in this parable?
- What principles of the law of mercy are illustrated in this parable?
- What principles of the Atonement of Christ are illustrated in the parable? (Answers might include that without the mercy extended to us by the Savior's Atonement, we could never even begin to make payment for our sins. We would be in the bondage of sin forever.)
- Why is hypocrisy, as illustrated by the unmerciful servant, so damaging? To one's self? To others?
- What is illustrated in the parable about daily living and our personal actions by the fact that the man's wife and children were to be sold along with him? (One answer might be that our unkind and unmerciful actions unavoidably affect our families. This is in contrast to the claim by some that what they do is their "own business.")

Parables of the Lost Sheep, the Lost Coin, and the Prodigal Son

Luke 15

1 THEN drew near unto him all the publicans [*tax collectors*] and sinners for to hear him.

2 And the Pharisees and scribes murmured, saying, This man receiveth sinners, and eateth with them.

> The Pharisees and scribes were very strict about not associating with sinners, as a matter of religion. The following parable that the Savior gives is generally known as the Parable of the Lost Sheep. Joseph Smith tells us that it is directed at the Pharisees and scribes in verse 2 who are complaining that Jesus is associating with sinners. (See *Teachings of the Prophet Joseph Smith*, page 277.)

The Parable of the Lost Sheep

3 And he spake this parable unto them [*the grumbling Pharisees and scribes in verse 2*], saying,

4 What man of you, having an hundred sheep, if he lose one of them, doth not leave the ninety and nine in the wilderness, and go after that which is lost, until he find it?

> JST Luke 15:4
>
> 4 What man of you having a hundred sheep, if he lose one of them, doth not leave the ninety and nine, and go into the wilderness after that which is lost, until he find it?

5 And when he hath found it, he layeth it on his shoulders, rejoicing.

6 And when he cometh home, he calleth together his friends and neighbours, saying unto them, Rejoice with me; for I have found my sheep which was lost.

7 I say unto you, that likewise joy shall be in heaven over one sinner that repenteth, more than over ninety and nine just persons, which need no repentance.

> This parable can remind us of the quote from the Doctrine and Covenants dealing with the worth of souls:
>
> D&C 18:10 and 15
>
> 10 Remember the worth of souls is great in the sight of God;

> 15 And if it so be that you should labor all your days in crying repentance unto this people, and bring, save it be one soul unto me, how great shall be your joy with him in the kingdom of my Father!

> Reading verse 7 of Luke 15, above, could make a person feel bad that a repentant sinner makes heaven happier than a righteous person. One could almost be tempted to commit an occasional sin to bring more joy to heaven when he or she repents. But wait! That is not what verse 7 is saying. Using the Prophet Joseph Smith's explanation that the ninety-nine "just persons" represent the Sadducees and Pharisees "that are so righteous; they will be damned anyhow" (*Teachings of the Prophet Joseph Smith*, pages 277–78), we can then understand verse 7 as follows: "There is more joy in heaven over one humble sinner who repents, than over ninety-nine self-righteous hypocrites like you Pharisees and scribes, who claim to be just men who need no repentance!" This verse, then, is actually a scathing rebuke of these evil religious leaders of the Jews, whom the Savior called "whited sepulchres" (Matthew 23:27). In other words, they were like whitewashed coffins that look clean on the outside but are full of rot and filth inside.

This next parable is usually referred to as the Parable of the Lost Coin. Again, it is in response to the criticism of the Pharisees and scribes in verse 2 and reminds us that it is worth whatever effort is necessary to save one lost soul.

The Parable of the Lost Coin

8 Either [*here is another example*] what woman having ten pieces of silver [*equal to ten days' wages for a workman; see Luke 15 footnote 8a*] if she lose one piece, doth not light a candle, and sweep the house, and seek diligently till she find it?

9 And when she hath found it, she calleth her friends and her neighbours together, saying, Rejoice with me; for I have found the piece which I had lost.

10 Likewise, I say unto you, there is joy in the presence of the angels of God over one sinner that repenteth.

The Parable of the Prodigal Son

11 And he said, A certain man [*symbolic of God*] had two sons [*symbolic of different types of people*]:

12 And the younger of them said to his father, Father, give me the portion of goods that falleth to me [*give me my inheritance now, instead of waiting until you die; symbolism: I am not interested in future exaltation, but rather want to enjoy the ways of the world now*]. And he [*the father*] divided unto them his living [*divided up his property between his two sons; symbolism: our Father in Heaven respects our agency*].

13 And not many days after the younger son gathered all together [*put all his financial resources together*], and took his journey into a far country [*symbolism: he fell away from the Church and participated in the ways of the world*], and there wasted his substance [*financial resources; symbolism: his gospel heritage*] with riotous living [*symbolism: he wasted his potential for joy and happiness in the gospel for temporary worldly, sinful pleasures*].

14 And when he had spent all [*symbolism: when he was wasted away by his wicked lifestyle*], there arose a mighty famine in that land [*symbolism: Satan left him with no support, as taught in Alma 30:60*]; and he began to be in want [*in need, poverty, desperation*].

15 And he went and joined himself to [*got a job with*] a citizen of that country [*symbolism: he didn't yet turn to God for help*]; and he sent him into his fields to feed swine. [*Feeding pigs was about the lowest, most humiliating job a person from Jewish culture could have; symbolism: he was totally humbled.*]

16 And he would fain have filled his belly with the husks that the swine did eat [*he got so hungry that even the refuse he was feeding the pigs started to look good to him*]: and no man gave unto him [*no one gave him anything to help him in his poverty; symbolism: there was no worldly source of effective help for him*].

17 And when he came to himself [*came to his senses; symbolism: he started repenting*], he said, How many hired servants of my father's have bread enough and to spare, and I perish with hunger!

18 I will arise and go to my father, and will say unto him, Father, I have sinned against heaven, and before thee [*I have been wicked; symbolic of sincere confession*],

19 And am no more worthy to be called thy son [*symbolism: I am not worthy of exaltation*]: make me as [*let me be*] one of thy hired servants [*symbolism: let me go into one of the other degrees of glory*].

20 And he arose, and came to his father. But when he was yet a great way off, his father saw him [*had been watching for him*], and had compassion, and ran, and fell on his neck [*hugged him*], and kissed him [*symbolism: the Father is merciful and kind and is anxious to "run" to us to help us return to Him*].

21 And the son said unto him, Father, I have sinned against heaven, and in thy sight, and am no more worthy to be called thy son [*symbolism: the son, thoroughly humbled by his wickedness, acknowledges his unworthiness to live with the Father in celestial exaltation*].

22 But the father said to his servants, Bring forth the best robe, and put it on him; and put a ring on his hand, and shoes on his feet:

23 And bring hither the fatted calf, and kill it; and let us eat, and be merry [*symbolic of joy and rejoicing on earth and in heaven when a sinner repents and returns*]:

24 For this my son was dead [*symbolic of being spiritually dead*], and is alive again [*symbolic of rebirth, through the Atonement*]; he was lost, and is found. And they began to be merry.

A question sometimes arises among members of the Church as to whether or not the returning prodigal son could ever repent sufficiently to gain exaltation, especially in view of his intentional wickedness. There is much symbolism in verse 22, above, which can help answer that question:

The "robe" is symbolic of royalty and status. It is also symbolic of acceptance by God, as in 2 Nephi 4:33 where Nephi says "O Lord, wilt thou encircle me around in the robe of thy righteousness! O Lord, wilt thou make a way for mine escape before mine enemies!" See also Isaiah 61:10. In Revelation 7:9, white robes are given to those who live in the presence of God (celestial glory). The "best robe" would be symbolic of potential for highest status, in other words, exaltation.

The "ring" is symbolic of authority to rule. Example: a signet ring which a king would use to stamp official documents and make them legal and binding.

"Shoes on his feet": Shoes were very expensive in the days of the Savior's ministry and were only worn by the wealthy and the rulers. Thus, shoes would be symbolic of wealth, power, and authority to rule.

Summary: The cultural symbolism in this verse would lead us to believe that the father was not only welcoming his wayward son back with open arms, but he was also inviting him to repent and reestablish himself as a ruler in his household, symbolic of potential for exaltation. President David O. McKay, in April Conference 1956, speaking of the prodigal son, said, "The Spirit of forgiveness will be operative" when the prodigal son comes to himself and repents. Elder Richard G. Scott, in October Conference 2002, speaking of Alma the Younger and the four sons of Mosiah, who he said "were tragically wicked," said that there are no "second-class" citizens after true repentance. Said he, "If you have repented from serious transgression and mistakenly believe that you will always be a second-class citizen in the kingdom of God, learn that is not true."

Thus, the prodigal son does not have to remain a "second-class citizen" in the Father's kingdom. However, the older brother may have to change his attitude if he plans to retain his status in the Father's kingdom.

25 Now his elder son [*symbolic of a member who has been active all his life*] was in the field: and as he came and drew nigh to the house, he heard musick and dancing.

26 And he called one of the servants, and asked what these things meant.

27 And he said unto him, Thy brother is come; and thy father hath killed the fatted calf, because he hath received him safe and sound.

28 And he was angry, and would not go in [*this is hardly appropriate behavior for one who is supposed to be a faithful son*]: therefore came his father out, and intreated [*pleaded with*] him.

29 And he answering said to his father, Lo [*now see here!*], these many years do I serve thee, neither transgressed I at any time thy commandment: and yet thou never gavest me a kid, that I might make merry with my friends [*you never killed even so much as a young goat for me to have a party with my friends!*]:

30 But as soon as this thy son [*implies "thy son," not my brother anymore*] was come [*came home*], which hath devoured thy living with harlots [*wasted his inheritance with prostitutes*], thou hast killed for him the fatted calf.

31 And he said unto him, Son, thou art ever with me, and all that I have is thine. [*This presupposes that the older son rethinks his attitude about his returning younger brother, repents, and helps him get reestablished in his father's household.*]

32 It was meet [*needful, good*] that we should make merry [*celebrate*], and be glad: for this thy brother [*emphasizing that he is "your brother," not just "my son"*] was dead [*spiritually*], and is alive again [*has repented, is a new person*]; and was lost, and is found.

Background, Culture, and Setting

Chapter 15 of the Gospel of Luke is a carefully crafted single literary unit. Though we may feel familiar with the three parables shared in the chapter, we often discuss these parables out of context and separated from each other. What is the result? We miss how and why they work together to make one key point.

Luke 15 opens with this scene: Jesus is hanging out with sinners, and the Pharisees and scribes deride Him for it. To answer their concerns, to teach that He was sent to gather the lost, the destitute, the poor, the outcast, the unfit, the broken, and the unhealthy, Jesus shares three thematically interrelated parables.

The first parable speaks of a hundred sheep, but one is lost. The shepherd, leaving the ninety-nine, searches and finds the one that is lost, whereupon he rejoices with his friends.

The second parable speaks of a woman's ten coins, but one is lost. She searches diligently until she finds it, whereupon she rejoices with her friends.

The final parable speaks of a man with two sons, but one is lost. The father rushes out to embrace the lost son when he returns, whereupon the father rejoices with his friends. Yet the father's "faithful" son is angry.

Why does Jesus share these three parables back to back? And did you notice that He begins with large numbers and with each additional parable He reduces by a multiple of ten? One hundred, to ten, to one.

Do we see how Jesus paints an unmistakable picture for the "faithful," accusing him of wrongdoing? God is like the shepherd, or the woman, or the father missing one precious among the many (or the few), who have found what was lost and consequently invite their friends to rejoice at the restoration. Only in the final parable do we see a new character introduced: the "faithful" son. But this "faithful" son angrily complains against the father's merciful treatment of that which had been lost. Who is the so-called "faithful" son in Luke 15? Answer: the Pharisees and the scribes. The message would have been unmistakable for Jesus's listeners. The Pharisees and scribes are the angry "faithful" son who should instead be rejoicing at finding what had been lost. Undoubtedly, many of the Pharisees and scribes left offended.

The Master Teacher

In Luke 15, Jesus told three distinct stories that taught the same principle. What would a shepherd, a woman in a home, and a man with two sons have in common? On the face of it, probably nothing. But Jesus skillfully used three different story settings to teach the same story so that the lesson would be clear and obvious. Furthermore, He structured the stories in such a way that the listeners could feel the increasing value of the "one." First, you have one lamb among a hundred. Would it really be that bad if one was lost? It's only the loss of 1%. The shepherd probably could endure the loss. The next story is of the woman, likely poor, who has lost one coin among ten. We feel more deeply her need to recover the 10% loss of her wealth. Then the last parable discusses humans, beloved sons of a father. Here the loss is of eternal magnitude. The father is set to lose 50% of his posterity. Or, from another perspective, he will lose 100% of a beloved son! The increasing significance of the losses are felt with each new parable. When Jesus concludes His teaching, no commentary is provided. Luke 15 simply ends at the conclusion of the third parable. Why is that? Because the teaching was so thoughtfully constructed that listeners hearing all three of these parables back to back could only conclude that God the

Father is deeply anxious to save all His children, no matter where or how far they have wandered. When they return to Him, rejoicing and joy are the only activities. There is no place for anger, jealousy, or complaining from God, from His friends, or from His other sons and daughters. That is the *summum bonum* (or, in other words, the greatest good) of the plan of happiness.

POSSIBLE APPLICATIONS FOR LEARNERS

Good learners look for repeated patterns. The gospel of Jesus Christ and the scriptures are full of patterns that reinforce principles of truth. Furthermore, good learners read scripture in context. They avoid the temptation to "proof text," that is, to take a specific verse out of context and make it say something that might not have been the original intent of the inspired author. Good learners are willing to put in the time and effort to read scriptures more carefully and diligently, seeking for and reading through the lenses of the patterns established by the prophetic writers to convey meaning and truth.

Good learners rejoice when others succeed in learning, growing, and repenting.

HELPS FOR TEACHERS

The word *teacher* derives from the ancient word "token," which is something that we show or demonstrate to represent a larger reality or truth. Good teachers show and demonstrate. Good teachers show patterns that appear in scripture and in the gospel. Then these teachers demonstrate these patterns, or, that is, they demonstrate to learners how to find and apply these patterns. Finally, good teachers give learners opportunities to practice finding and using the patterns, and the teachers provide relevant feedback to learners as they practice. Carefully formulated questions can help learners get better and better at this. Some examples follow:

- Who was the target audience for these three parables? (The scribes and Pharisees.)
- Why do you think the Savior gave these three parables together?
- What is a common thread that runs through all three of these parables?
- What similar pattern do you see in the attitudes of the scribes and Pharisees and the older son in the above parables? (One possible answer is that they all considered themselves to be "faithful," but, in reality, they were badly missing the point of being truly righteous regarding how they see the value of "lost" souls. And if they were truly faithful, they would think like God does regarding all His children and rejoice in the fact that the lost were back!)
- What pattern do you see in the fact that in all three parables, the shepherd, the woman, and the father invited others to join in rejoicing when the lost were found? (Answers might include that truly righteous people love to share joy and rejoicing with others. Also, truly righteous people forgive freely and want others to share in the joy of a sinner's return to the fold.)
- If you were to write "the rest of the story" for the Parable of the Prodigal Son, how would you want it to end? (Example: "The older son did some serious thinking about his own attitude and decided to forgive his younger brother, gave him part of his herds and flocks so he could start over, and apologized

to his father for criticizing him for throwing a party for his brother upon his return." Or, "The older brother remained bitter and, over time, shriveled up emotionally and ultimately lost his soul.")

- What are some of the emotions you feel likely went through the mind of the prodigal son as he debated whether or not to return to his father's home?

THE WOMAN TAKEN IN ADULTERY

JOHN 8:1–11

It is the day after the Feast of Tabernacles, and large crowds of people gather to listen to Jesus as He teaches in the courtyard of the temple in Jerusalem. The scribes and Pharisees are frustrated, because, despite repeated attempts to discredit Jesus and get Him arrested, they continue to fail to reach their goal. John now reports yet another attempt to trap Jesus in His words as these Jewish leaders drag a woman taken in adultery to Jesus, in front of the crowd, and ask what He recommends be done to her. Their hope is that they can get Him to say something in opposition to the Law of Moses concerning punishment for adultery so they can have Him arrested. See what happens.

1 Jesus went unto the mount of Olives [*about a 10–15 minute walk east of Jerusalem*].

2 And early in the morning he came again into the temple [*the courtyard of the temple*], and all the people came unto him; and he sat down, and taught them.

3 And the scribes and Pharisees brought unto him a woman taken in adultery; and when they had set her in the midst,

> JST John 8:3
>
> 3 And the scribes and Pharisees brought unto him a woman taken in adultery; and when they had set her in the midst of the people,

4 They say unto him, Master, this woman was taken in adultery, in the very act.

> One has to wonder why these Jewish leaders didn't also bring the man who was involved with this woman to the Savior. Perhaps he was one of their own. In JST Luke 16:21, Jesus called these leaders "adulterers." We don't know if the man was a fellow Pharisee, but it is pure hypocrisy to single out the woman for embarrassment and humiliation and let the man escape.
>
> Next, they remind Him of what the Law of Moses said regarding the matter, and then ask a question.

5 Now Moses in the law commanded us, that such should be stoned: but what sayest thou?

> These evil men are still trying to trap Jesus by getting Him to say something against Moses and his laws. Imagine how quiet it was as the crowd hushed in an attempt to watch and hear the Master's response. Imagine also how frightened the woman was.

6 This they said, tempting him [*trying to lure Him into a trap*], that they might have to accuse him [*to build a legal case against Him*]. But Jesus stooped down, and with his finger wrote on the ground, as though he heard them not.

7 So when they continued asking him, he lifted up himself, and said unto them, He that is without sin among you [*perhaps implying whoever has not committed the same sin; see McConkie, Doctrinal New Testament Commentary, vol. 1, page 451*], let him first cast a stone at her.

8 And again he stooped down, and wrote on the ground.

9 And they which heard it, being convicted by their own conscience, went out one by one, beginning at the eldest, even unto the last: and Jesus was left alone, and the woman standing in the midst.

> JST John 8:9
>
> 9 And they which heard it, being convicted by their own conscience, went out one by one, beginning at the eldest, even unto the last; and Jesus was left alone, and the woman standing in the midst of the temple.

10 When Jesus had lifted up himself, and saw none but the woman, he said unto her, Woman, where are those thine accusers? hath no man condemned thee? [*Where did the men go who wanted to stone you? Didn't any of them condemn you to death?*]

11 She said, No man, Lord. And Jesus said unto her, Neither do I condemn thee: go, and sin no more.

> JST John 8:11
>
> 11 She said, No man, Lord. And Jesus said unto her, Neither do I condemn thee; go, and sin no more. And the woman glorified God from that hour, and believed on his name.
>
> Jesus did not forgive the woman at this point. Obviously, she has some serious repenting to do. But He did not condemn her, meaning that she still had time and opportunity to repent. The JST, cited above at the end of verse 11, confirms that she began repenting.

Background, Culture, and Setting

This scriptural account takes place at the temple in Jerusalem. To understand the significance of the temple, we'll spend some time discussing its size and layout. (For a free visual of the ancient Jerusalem temple, visit virtualscriptures.org/virtual-new-testament.) When in Jerusalem, Jesus frequently went to the temple to teach. There are many reasons that Jesus taught at the temple. These reasons can be grouped into two categories: spiritual and practical. On the spiritual side, Jesus chose to teach in a place that was holy, a place dedicated to God's purposes, a place of uplift, prayer, revelation, covenant, and renewal. By teaching in the temple, Jesus could associate His message with the things of God. He also demonstrated that His message was God's message, the message of His holy house.

There were practical reasons for teaching in the temple, reasons that we often miss because we may not be familiar with the physical layout of Jerusalem and the temple. Like most ancient cities, Jerusalem was cramped, over-crowded, and not designed for mass gatherings. When we consider other locations where Jesus taught, it was in open spaces, teaching on a mountain, or teaching a crowd gathered on the shore of the Sea of Galilee while He sat in a boat. If you want to reach the masses, large, unencumbered public places for teaching are required. Jerusalem had no such places, except for the temple. For practical purposes, the temple offered the largest, open-space gathering area in all of the city of Jerusalem.

The temple mount covered the equivalent of 27 football fields, much of it wide open plaza space suitable for teaching a large crowd. Consider this comparison: Put into your mind the size of Temple Square in Salt Lake City. That area comprises 10 acres. The ancient Jerusalem temple complex was three and a half times as large at 36 acres. That is an enormous amount of space by modern terms. That much space devoted to God was astounding in ancient times. The Temple complex was the crown jewel of the Jewish nation. Nothing gave them a greater sense of pride and reinforced identity, except, perhaps, the Torah (the Five Books of Moses). The Jewish Temple was renowned throughout the Roman world. It was an inspiration to Jews and Gentiles alike, much like beautifully magnificent structures are today for viewers of all persuasions. Incredibly, the Jerusalem temple complex was the largest religious structure in the Roman Empire.

The ancient Jerusalem temple was more than simply the temple building, which only occupied a small portion of the overall 36 acres of the temple platform. For comparison, the Salt Lake City Temple does not envelop the entire city block of temple square, occupying only a minor, though significant, footprint on the Temple Square plot. Within Temple Square are many open spaces and other buildings that collectively contribute to the purpose of, and possible experiences in, the Temple Square space. Similarly, the ancient Jerusalem temple was a larger complex with the temple proper only occupying a minor, though symbolically significant, portion of the total space. The ancient temple complex had colonnaded porticoes and large open plazas.

When we think of modern temples, we don't typically think of open-area places of enormous space and magnitude. We think of quiet, reverent, beautiful buildings where people gather in small numbers (perhaps not much more than many dozens at a time). In the days of Jesus, thousands of individuals could simultaneously be in the temple complex. On high holy days (such as Passover or the Festival of Tabernacles), tens of thousands of people would daily pass through the temple courts of Jerusalem. That is a scale we can only imagine when we compare to crowds at the Conference Center during general conference weekend or to the crowds drawn to a major sporting event.

We begin to see, also, that when such large crowds are accessible for teaching, chaos or rioting is a potentiality. The Jerusalem temple complex was designed to address such incidents. Herod commanded his builders to construct inside the temple complex the Roman Antonia Fortress. If any dispute or public disturbance broke out, the Roman soldiers could quickly pour out of their holds to quell uprisings and restore order. Imagine if we had a police brigade stationed in our modern temples. Anytime there was a disturbance (which are, thankfully, exceedingly rare in our modern temples), the secular police force came rushing out with their billy clubs to beat any offending (or perceived to be offending) individual. Tensions between Jewish worshippers and Roman imperial authorities were always raw, real, and close at hand. No wonder the Jews so regularly revolted, resorting to violence against their Roman overseers because of such pervasive, generational, long-standing grievances and injustices.

The temple building itself, at the time of Jesus, was surrounded by a low fence called by Paul the "middle wall of partition," marking the boundary of the court of the Gentiles, which separated the Jews from the Gentiles:

"For he is our peace, who hath made both one, and hath broken down the middle wall of partition between us; Having abolished in his flesh the enmity, even the law of commandments contained in ordinances; for to make in himself of twain one new man, so making peace; And that he might reconcile both unto God in one body by the cross, having slain the enmity thereby" (Ephesians 2:14–16).

This partition was meant to separate the holy people (the Jews) from the Gentiles. As Paul explained to the Ephesians, because of His sacrifice, Jesus Christ had metaphorically broken down the wall that separated the Gentiles from the presence of God at the temple. But before Jesus's atoning sacrifice, only the Jews could approach the temple. The Gentiles were to remain in the public areas of the temple complex. This short fence had various openings for Jews to pass through as they drew closer to the temple proper. Facing the pilgrims as they approached this short fence, on either side of the opening, was a warning written in Greek, to warn away Gentiles from passing too close to the holy temple. The warning words promised death upon any who dared violate the holy sanctuary. This fence and warning functioned a bit like our modern-day temple recommend desks. However, this analogy only goes so far since our modern-day temple desks and temple workers are not so wildly harsh as to promise death upon any who inappropriately enters past the temple recommend desk. In Jesus's day, religious fervor and fanaticism were rampant.

The temple was divided into several sections. The first area within the temple that Jews would enter was called the Court of the Women. All Jews, male and female, were allowed into this space. Within the Court of the Women, perhaps in the corners, though we are not certain where they were located, were four massive, golden, oil-fed lamps standing 86 feet tall. These were lit during the Feast of Tabernacles, the Jewish holy day commemorating ancient Israel's flight out of Egypt where they lived in temporary shelters made of palm branches and relied upon Jehovah who was their light in the wilderness. God was a cloud by day and a pillar of fire by night. As a pillar of fire, these stunning lamps symbolized God's ongoing presence with the people.

At the western end of the Court of the Women was a series of fifteen stairs that led to the Nicanor gate. On these stairs, Levitical priests would stand to sing temple hymns, typically drawn from the extensive repertoire of temple hymnody found in Psalms. At this gate, Jesus was presented as a baby (see Luke 2:22–40). It was near this gate where faithful and patient Simeon encountered Jesus, the Child of Salvation. Similarly, this is where the long-enduring prophetess Anna first saw Jesus and proclaimed that the Redeemer had come to Jerusalem (Luke 2:25–38).

Beyond the Nicanor gate was the Court of the Israelites. Only Israelite males were allowed into this space. At this spot, Israelite men would hand over their sacrificial animals or food to the priests, who were in the Court of the Priests. This latter area included the great altar of sacrifice. Only after passing through these four courts (court of the Gentiles, court of the women, court of the Israelites, court of the priests) did one enter into the holy temple itself. At 160 feet tall, the temple was about as tall as the Brigham Young University Kimball Tower. Within the temple was the holy place that held the candelabra, the shewbread, and the altar of incense. Dividing this inner space was a beautiful and large curtain, textured to represent the heavens.

Behind that curtain was the most holy spot, the holy of holies, which was only entered once a year by the high priest on the Day of Atonement. This was the space where the presence or Spirit of God resided. Up until the Babylonian destruction of the first temple (around 600 BC), the sacred tablets of covenant that God delivered to Moses at Sinai were carefully stored in the Ark of the Covenant that sat behind the heavenly imaged curtain. The Ark of the Covenant was imagined to be God's throne (or His footstool) where His presence would sit or hover. In the days of Jesus, the space behind the curtain was physically empty, besides the outcropping of rock that once served as the base for the Ark of the Covenant. By the time of Jesus, the temple treasures and the Ark of the Covenant had long before been looted by marauding Babylonian invaders.

Why did Jesus teach so often at the temple? Jesus would not pass up an opportunity to spread His message in the most holy spot possible to the most people possible. The temple at Jerusalem presented Him the perfect spot to fulfill His mission to teach the Father's message. This backdrop of the temple provides the visual and physical context for the episode of Jesus's encounter with the woman caught in adultery in John 8.

The Master Teacher

When confronted with a challenge and difficulty, instead of immediately answering, Jesus paused. As teachers, we may feel the need to have an answer to every question. And we may feel the need to give that answer immediately. Or, we may feel that the learners expect us to have every answer and that those answers are delivered as immediately and as fresh as they might experience had they gone to Google. However, Jesus demonstrates that a good teacher need not react to every situation. Taking a moment to think and consider can have powerful effects. First, it demonstrates thoughtfulness and care given to a response. Second, the teacher creates space and time to generate a thoughtful response appropriate to the situation, weighing and measuring the consequences of what will be said. How often have we spoken without thinking or seen others do the same? The risks of miscommunicating rise in correlation with how quickly we respond to a question or a situation. The book of Proverbs warns repeatedly, "A fool uttereth all his mind: but a wise man keepeth it in till afterwards" (Proverbs 29:11) and "Seest thou a man that is hasty in his words? there is more hope of a fool than of him" (Proverbs 29:20). There is no glory in a hasty response. Jesus demonstrated mastery in teaching when He paused under very stressful circumstances before responding. Third, when you pause before you respond, the questioners are also paused, giving them time to think of potential answers to their own questions. Sometimes they discover a solution without the teacher uttering a word. Or in a group, when there is a pause after a question, someone within the group might have an appropriate response that answers the need.

As learners, we too should take the time to pause, to not blurt out answers without thinking, to instead take time to compose our thoughts. When learning together with others, listening and pausing increases the likelihood that everyone is listened to and that what is shared is meaningful and positively contributes to the learning experience.

Did you notice that Jesus wrote on the ground? At first look, it may appear that Jesus is ignoring the crowd, or that He didn't hear them. As teachers, we have to be careful to not appear to be dismissive of learners because one of the most important laws of teaching is love, demonstrated by acknowledging the student. When people feel disrespected, love is broken, and the ties that bind teacher and learner together in a relationship of learning are frayed. Jesus was not ignoring the crowd. Instead, He was allowing time for reflection on the situation and what an appropriate response would be as the crowd persistently badgered Him to answer: "So when they continued asking him, he lifted up himself, and said unto them, He that is without sin among you, let him first cast a stone at her" (John 8:7). That was the most unexpected and appropriate response that could be imagined for this scenario.

But why did He write on the ground? We don't know for sure, but perhaps Jesus was symbolizing for those who had eyes to see that just as Jehovah had written the law on tablets of stone for Moses and the Israelites, Jesus was now writing the new law on stone for this generation of Israelites.

As teachers, we should plan in advance the types of symbols we employ to make our messages more memorable and engaging. Learners should be on the lookout for the higher meaning in learning experiences, always asking, "What symbols are at play in this teaching moment, and how do they support the purposes of this learning experience?"

Jesus was teaching an apparently peaceful group who had come to the temple early in the morning (John 8:2) when He was inappropriately and rudely interrupted with a very serious moral dilemma. What would you do as a teacher if you had a well-prepared lesson, had everyone's attention, and were in a quiet, peaceful, and reverent—even holy—spot, and suddenly a mob burst into your classroom with accusations of adultery against one in their midst? How would you handle such a viscerally sensitive matter, especially in front of a large group of learners, each who came to the lesson with different questions, burdens, and levels of willingness or ability, to be challenged in the gospel and helped by the gospel? You have, essentially, lost all control of the classroom. The class has been hijacked in the most painful and potentially disastrous way. Not only disastrous for the success of that class period, but perhaps also for the well-being of the testimony of the learners in the classroom. What do you do?

Jesus didn't raise His voice at the intruders, shouting, "Get out of my classroom!" Nor did He challenge them: "Who do you think you are to come into My teaching space demanding of Me an answer to your questions when I am in front of My class teaching them on a different topic?" He paused, considered His response, delivered simple yet profound truths that simultaneously taught and condemned, and then waited patiently for the intruding learners to learn. As they did, they slunk out one by one until only the woman was left of that crowd. He sent her on her way with no condemnation and the charge to sin no more.

Helps for Teachers

Instead of being angry at the interruption of His teaching, Jesus listens to the intruders. As teachers, we do not have perfect control of the learning environment. That fact is one of the challenges and demands of being a teacher that can cause any of us to feel nervous. How many of us have wondered when we teach, "What unexpected curve ball will be thrown at me from the learners and how will I appropriately respond?" Jesus, the Master Teacher, did not get "vexed if the game went wrong." He paused, collected His thoughts, sized up the situation, and responded with simple doctrinal truths that answered the need.

Questions that can encourage immediate involvement of students in class discussion and teaching are

- Did Jesus forgive the woman's sins immediately?
- Why do you think that Jesus did not immediately forgive the woman of her sins?
- How does Jesus use space and timing to make a point?
- How does Jesus use object lessons to make a point?
- What was so effective about the Master's lack of immediate verbal response to continued questioning by the scribes and Pharisees as He remained silent and stooped down and wrote on the ground with His finger? (See John 8:6.)

"I Am the Light of the World"

John 8:12

12 Then spake Jesus again unto them, saying, I am the light of the world: he that followeth me shall not walk in darkness [*spiritual darkness*], but shall have the light of life [*eternal life*].

Background, Culture, and Setting

Sometimes in the scriptures, two stories are told in a sandwich format. That is, one story begins and does not end, a second story begins and ends, and then the first story is concluded. For example, Matthew 9:18–26 contains two stories, with one story being enveloped or sandwiched between the other. In the first story, a synagogue leader petitions Jesus to heal his daughter. While on His way to the healing, a second story interrupts the first. Jesus is detained by a woman with an issue of blood. He heals the woman. With the second story completed, the first story resumes. Jesus moves on to heal the young girl who had been considered dead. In Matthew's telling, the story of the woman with the issue of blood is sandwiched or enveloped in the story of the young girl being healed. These two stories both deal with characters at the point of death being brought back from the brink. These two stories are told together to reinforce the shared ideas from each story. So, too, in John 8 there are two stories that are intertwined. Jesus enters the temple at morning to teach. Before He reaches the high point of His message, the story of the woman taken in adultery takes place. Only after that circumstance is handled, does Jesus return to His original plan for teaching. And, as readers, we may have already forgotten the context of when and where Jesus was teaching, because we (like Jesus) have been interrupted by the woman taken in adultery.

The Master Teacher

"I am the light of the world."

What time of day was it when Jesus pronounced these beautiful truths, and why does timing matter? Jesus used His physical surroundings to teach lessons. He also made use of festivals and holy days to help people see larger truths.

What we may miss, because of the disruption from the original context by the intruding scribes and Pharisees who throw the woman taken in adultery at the feet of Jesus, is this detail at the beginning of the chapter: "And early in the morning [Jesus] came again into the temple, and all the people came unto him; and he sat down, and taught them."

If we remove the episode of the woman taken in adultery and stitch the verses back together, we can listen in, without interruption, to the lesson that Jesus had planned to deliver. Here it is:

"And early in the morning [Jesus] came again into the temple, and all the people came unto him; and he sat down, and taught them . . . saying, I am the light of the world: he that followeth me shall not walk in darkness, but shall have the light of life."

Jesus came to the temple that day to teach the lesson that He is the light of the world. That was His teaching purpose that day. Because of the intruding story of the woman caught in adultery, we may miss the original purpose of Jesus's visit to the temple.

But let us pause and ask some questions. Why did Jesus choose to teach that principle then and there? Couldn't He have taught that principle in any location or at any time? Is the statement that Jesus is the light of the world true no matter where or when it is stated? Yes. So why did Jesus choose this moment and time to teach that principle?

Let's look again at the context. Notice what time of day it is and this little detail that is often overlooked but is extremely important: "And early in the morning [Jesus] came again into the temple . . . and taught them." What happens early in the morning? The sun rises! Why is Jesus teaching the principle that He is the light of the world at this time of day? As He stood in the holy temple, He very likely would have been bathed in glorious dawning morning light as He proclaimed, "I am the light of the world." What more dramatic cue could be used to reinforce this powerful truth about Jesus's characteristics?

And if the dawning sun was not a strong enough cue for capable learners to recognize, Jesus was likely teaching close to the four mighty 86-foot towers of burning flame inside the temple that were built to symbolize the flaming fire of Jehovah's light that guided the Israelites through the foreboding wilderness. Those with eyes to see and ears to hear must have certainly captured the power and truth of Jesus's statement that day: "I am the light of the world."

Possible Applications for Learners

As learners, are we looking for cues, watching for the larger context of the learning experience to see reinforcing bands of context, symbols, and learning textured together that mutually testify of the principles to be gained?

Helps for Teachers

As teachers, we too can use appropriate and powerful contextual cues, symbols, and object lessons to reinforce the principles we teach.

- How is Jesus the light of the world?
- How has Jesus provided light to your life?
- What does it mean to walk in the light of the Lord?

A Man, Blind from Birth, Is Healed on the Sabbath

John 9:1–11

At the end of John 8, Jesus is escaping from the temple from the angry Jews who were trying to stone Him. Then, in John 9, as He is escaping from the mob, Jesus sees a blind man, stops, and takes time to heal him.

1 AND as Jesus passed by, he saw a man which was blind from his birth.

> Some people have come to believe the false notion that physical illness in general is caused by sin. This was a common belief among the Jews in New Testament times. We see this reflected in verse 2, next.

2 And his disciples asked him, saying, Master, who did sin, this man, or his parents, that he was born blind?

> The Savior straightens out this mistaken idea in the case of the blind man, and then He bears witness that the Father sent Him to be the light of the world, just as He had testified in John 8.

3 Jesus answered, Neither hath this man sinned, nor his parents: but that the works of God should be made manifest [*be shown*] in him.

4 I must work the works of him that sent me, while it is day: the night cometh, when no man can work.

> JST John 9:4
>
> 4 I must work the works of him that sent me, while I am with you; the time cometh when I shall have finished my work, then I go unto the Father.

5 As long as I am in the world, I am the light of the world.

6 When he had thus spoken, he spat on the ground, and made clay of the spittle, and he anointed the eyes of the blind man with the clay.

> There is perhaps symbolism in the use of "clay" in verse 6 above. "Clay" is symbolic of this earth as well as of our mortal bodies. Touching the blind man's eyes with the clay so he could see can symbolize the fact that those who are faithful in this mortal experience will eventually be enabled to "see" as God sees as they enter into exaltation. (Compare also to the story in Moses 6:35–36 of Enoch who anointed his eyes with clay, washed, and came away seeing a grand vision of God's creation.)

7 And said unto him, Go, wash in the pool of Siloam, (which is by interpretation, Sent.) He went his way therefore, and washed, and came seeing [*could see*].

> Did you notice that the word "sent," in verse 7 above, is capitalized? It is capitalized because it refers to Christ. Thus, we see symbolism here. Among the possible symbolism is that if we "wash" our spiritual eyes in the "living water" from Christ, we will be able to see the things of eternity clearly.
>
> Watch now as people take the focus from a simple and beautiful miracle and ruin it by interrogating the once-blind man to the point of excommunicating him because of his simple, honest answers.

8 The neighbours therefore, and they which before had seen him that he was blind, said, Is not this he that sat and begged?

9 Some said, This is he: others said, He is like him [*he just looks like that blind* man]: but he said, I am he [*I am the one who was healed*].

10 Therefore said they unto him, How were thine eyes opened?

11 He answered and said, A man that is called Jesus made clay, and anointed mine eyes, and said unto me, Go to the pool of Siloam, and wash: and I went and washed, and I received sight.

Background, Culture, and Setting

The pool of Siloam was the southernmost pool within the walls of Jerusalem. It also was at the lowest point of elevation in the mountainous city. The pool was first conceived and constructed during the time of King Hezekiah and the prophet Isaiah, more than seven hundred years before the time of Jesus.

In ancient times, an invading army saved its soldiers' lives by surrounding cities and laying siege to them, hoping that the combined effects of thirst, lack of food, and demoralization would lead the city to surrender. Hezekiah knew all of this and had to prepare his people for the invading Assyrian army. Already Jerusalem had strong walls surrounding the city. However, the most important water source lay outside the city walls (the Gihon Spring). Any capable enemy would only have to occupy that water source and the city would fall within weeks, if not days. Executing brilliant engineering that was a marvel in the ancient world, Hezekiah commissioned his workers to tunnel through the limestone under the city to create a water channel from the Gihon Spring to a newly created catch basin, the pool of Siloam. Hezekiah simultaneously built fortifications around the Gihon Spring, denying the Assyrians access while he built the connecting tunnel to the pool of Siloam. The Gihon Spring was the lifeblood of Jerusalem and was the likely reason why Jerusalem was enticing to settlers in the first place. Survival at Jerusalem was primarily possible because of the miracle of the Gihon Spring.

Because of the marvels of Hezekiah's engineering, the citizens of Jerusalem would have a never-ending source of water. That tunnel is still there today, its water running constantly without pause, pure and clean, as it has for more than 2,700 years. These waters represent salvation, because they brought literal physical salvation to the people. Later, because of this physical preservation, the people of Jerusalem saw the waters as symbolically representing spiritual salvation brought by Jehovah who strengthens His people.

During the time of Jesus, the pool of Siloam was a major stopping point for Jewish pilgrims ascending to the temple for worship. Wearing white, a symbol of purity, the Jewish pilgrims would bathe in the cool and refreshing waters of the pool of Siloam, take palm branches in hand (symbolic of triumph and victory in that culture), and then ascend the royal road that led steeply up through the city until they reached the steps of the temple. Though there were other pools of immersion throughout the city of Jerusalem, the pool of Siloam was one of the most famous and most sought after.

Jesus uses opportune times to teach gospel messages. John 9 focuses on the story of a blind man but begins with Jesus who *saw* the blind man. In the ensuing conversation with His disciples about the origin of the blind man's physical condition, Jesus uses the right moment to teach truth, which fits snugly into the themes of the chapter: blindness versus sight; light versus darkness. Jesus declares (translating a bit) "this man is blind that I might show light to the world, for when the night is come and there is no light, no work can be done. But there is work to be done in the light, because 'I am the light of the world.'"

As we reflect on the conversation that Jesus and His disciples had about the cause of blindness, we may wonder why they would have ever imagined that a person or their parents would have brought blindness upon themselves because of sin. Today, we recognize that blindness is a physical condition that is typically unrelated to someone's level of spiritual purity. We have the benefit of understanding modern physiology, medicine, and the cause of diseases.

Those in the ancient world did not have the same benefit of understanding that we do. In the days of ancient Israel, there was no categorical distinction between the physical world and the spiritual world. They were all part of the same thread, gradations of the same essence or reality. The belief was that sin had not only a real spiritual effect in someone's life, but inherently also had a real physical effect. With such a worldview, ancient people believed the origin of blindness must be related to sin in some describable and identifiable way. There was no understanding that blindness is a natural condition, typically unrelated to someone's moral choices. The only conclusion that Jesus's disciples could make, given the worldview of those days, is that his sin caused the blindness or his parents' sin transferred the effects to him, resulting in blindness.

Jesus taught at a higher level. Instead of judging the man or his parents based on real or perceived sins, Jesus encouraged his disciples to ask, in essence, "Why not see this as opportunity for God's power to be manifest on earth?"

The Master Teacher

Jesus saw someone in need at an inopportune time for himself. We may miss the context for this healing moment because of the chapter break between John 8 and 9. At the end of John 8, Jesus was hiding, leaving the temple, avoiding an angry crowd that wanted to kill him. And as He passed through the midst of those who wanted to kill Him, He saw a man who was blind from birth. When Jesus was under such pressure for His own safety, and His time was not yet come for Him to give His life, it is instructive that He would be both observant enough to see the need and humble enough to forget Himself. He stopped to serve another who had been living in the valley of the shadow of darkness his entire life. Jesus "lost His life" in the service of others. Jesus was not so much concerned about His own life at this point, imperiled as it was by the frantic and raging crowds on temple mount, as He was concerned about the life of another—one who was a lowly, blind beggar. No one of consequence. No one, really, to be noticed. And yet, Jesus does see and notice. Jesus, who has eyes to see, is in contrast to the blind man who physically can't see but will eventually have his physical and spiritual eyes opened to see Jesus and the truth.

Did you notice how Jesus healed the man? Jesus used unexpected and surprising approaches for healing. If we turn to Matthew 8, we read stories of Jesus healing by touch or by a word. But here in John 9, we are surprised by the type of touch employed by Jesus and the lack of commands of healing. Jesus used words and touch to start the healing process, but the healing only occurred *after* the blind man left the presence of Jesus. Does it make sense for Jesus to send someone away who needs healing without completing the healing? Does it make sense that Jesus does not heal someone right there on the spot? It wasn't the blind man who requested the healing, though he surely must have been grateful for the offer that would allow him to behold his parents for the first time in his life or to see the warmth of the sun that he had so often felt on his weather-beaten face. Why did Jesus not simply say the divine words of healing to create an instant healing experience instead of sending the blind man off on his own to complete the healing process?

Have you ever wondered at the means Jesus used to effect this specific healing? Upon scrutiny, Jesus uses very unconventional methods. In fact, what Jesus does to heal the blind seems, on the face of it, to create the very blindness He seeks to heal. If you wanted to blind someone, wouldn't a cheaply effective approach be to shove your muddied fingers into their eyes? Could there be a more ineffective way to remove blindness than to add insult to injury by covering the blind's eyes with grime, gunk, dirt, and mud? Yet this is exactly what Jesus did, spitting into the dirt on the ground to make mud with which He could anoint (or cover) the blind man's eyes.

Again, we pause at the unexpected nature of this story.

There are reasons for all of it.

Yet, there is more to cause us pause from this story that is so familiar that we may be surprised at how unfamiliar it is upon closer inspection.

After Jesus covered the blind man's eyes with mud, He commanded the man to go to the pool of Siloam to wash. Our eyes take nearly no effort to continue along reading to see these words, "[The blind man] went his way therefore, and washed, and came seeing." Just like that, the miracle is complete. The healing has occurred. And because we can so quickly read the conclusion that we are all anticipating—Jesus is the Master Healer, after all, there is no question how this story is going to end—we may not see all the whys of this healing episode.

Why, for example, did Jesus send the blind man to the pool of Siloam? Jesus apparently saw the blind man right outside the great temple. Jesus was likely near the southern staircase of the temple that bordered the public plaza filled with numerous *mikva'ot*, ritual bathing pools used by faithful Jews to purify their bodies before they entered the temple. Why didn't Jesus send the blind man to one of these purifying pools? They would have been easily close at hand.

We are curious as to why Jesus sent the blind man about as far away as possible within the city of Jerusalem to wash. Jesus commanded the man to go to the pool of Siloam. Our reading of the text does not convey the scale of distance or the significant elevation that must be descended when a person walks from the Jewish temple to the pool of Siloam.

In essence, Jesus sent a blind man over a cliff—after sticking mud in his eyes.

Jesus plucks a blind man out of the crowd, sticks mud in his eyes, and then tells him to walk the long, descending path to the lowest pool within the city walls of Jerusalem, without even offering to hold his hand and offer assistance!

We authors have walked from the Jerusalem Temple mount down to the pool of Siloam. The hike down is significant. Every time we make the descent we wonder how much farther we have to descend before we finally arrive at the sought-after pool of Siloam. We have strong legs and eyes. If we had to make the walk all alone in the dark, we wouldn't do it. We wouldn't be able to make it!

Why would Jesus, the epitome of love itself, treat a blind man in such a way?"

Faith. Faith without works is dead. Jesus quietly inspired and empowered the faith of the blind man. Sure, Jesus could have instantly healed the blind man, as he had healed others. Or Jesus could have avoided smudging the man's eyes with dirt and spittle. He could have simply ordered the blind man down to the pool. Jesus could have held the man's hand and led him to the closest ritual bathing pool, probably only paces from where Jesus first saw the man. If Jesus was particularly interested that the man cleanse in a particular pool, in this case, the pool of Siloam, Jesus could have, at the very least, held the blind man's hand to guide him to the very spot Jesus desired him to wash.

Yet Jesus did none of these things. Instead of making the healing quick, easy, and painless, Jesus made the healing process more challenging, strenuous, and demanding.

A thing to love about this story is the humble obedience of the blind man.

He didn't protest Jesus's methods for healing. He didn't so much as question the assignment. The blind man was so humble and eager to be healed that he willingly endured whatever test Jesus put in front of him. Heaven knows he had already endured a lifetime of suffering. How much more suffering would it really be to descend the steep road, unaided, in the dark of his life, to the designated healing waters of Siloam?

Jesus tested the man's faith. He created a situation that let the man act for himself, to demonstrate his confidence in Jesus, his belief in Jesus, his love for Jesus, and his willingness to endure all things that he might win the prize, not just of light in this life, but also everlasting light in life eternal.

POSSIBLE APPLICATIONS FOR LEARNERS

What can we learn as teachers or students from this episode? We first have to ask ourselves, do we automatically cast judgment on the righteousness of others because of how they dress and speak, where they live, how many children they have (or do not have), whether they are married or not, what job they have (or do not have), or their resident status in the country, and so on? Even though we no longer occupy the ancient worldview that people's outward physical defects are a physical manifestation of inward moral defect, our society still shares the myth that someone's life circumstances must indicate something about that person's choices, diligence, willingness to work hard, etc. For example, if we see someone in poverty, the values of our modern day may tempt us to say, "They obviously are lazy and have made bad choices that led them to poverty." We may not understand that the father of the family died after a terribly long and costly battle with cancer. The family gave up every worldly belonging to save that beloved father and husband, but to no avail. And now they are living in squalor, the aftereffects of devastating loss. Perhaps we see someone who is overweight, and we judge them unfairly: "Well, they obviously have no ability to control themselves when an ice-cream bar walks by." But perhaps this individual suffers from a disease that attacks the body by adding unwanted pounds. We never know what someone is experiencing, or what their life journey is, unless we put ourselves, metaphorically in their shoes. But wearing their shoes with permission is always the best. That way, they feel respected and loved.

We can learn from Jesus that instead of judging or drawing conclusions, we should first ask, "How can the power of God be manifest in this circumstance?" Perhaps it is a loving word from us, inspired by the Holy Spirit. Perhaps we feel impressed to give a loving touch, or resources, or encouragement. Perhaps we simply recognize that God is in charge and is Father to all of His children, whom He loves with a perfect and endless love. Whatever the case, Jesus models for us that instead of judgment, act to spread the kingdom of God. And the kingdom of God is love, peace, joy, purpose, meaning, understanding, healing, forgiveness, kindness, and becoming as He is.

Are we willing to see? Are we willing to take the time, to make the effort to see? Do the cares of this world cloud or mud our eyes? This is the symbol that Jesus used in this story, to wipe the world from our eyes to see in the light of Jesus's love.

Learners, do we expect instant healing (or answers) to our questions? Are we willing to endure some privation, some effort, and even some apparently convoluted exercises that invite us to act on our volition? Are we willing to venture out on our own, unaided, not requiring the hand-holding of a teacher, to find our own pools of Siloam where we can wash away the filth of this world so we can return seeing anew and afresh?

There are so many lessons to taste in this story.

Perhaps the most important lesson is that the blind man represents all of us. Jesus is the one who came down from the temple, symbolizing His condescension from heaven into mortal life. Jesus is the one who loved us first, saw us first. We were symbolically blind from birth. Jesus asks us to exercise faith, to follow Him symbolically to the grave of resurrection, which we call baptism, and in the case of the blind man, the lowest spot of elevation in Jerusalem, the pool of Siloam. When we immerse ourselves in that faith-demanding experience, culminating in the washing of the purifying waters of Siloam or baptism, we come away seeing new through the eyes of salvation.

We can then testify, as Jesus testified, that He is the "light of the world," and we know that truth, because we "went and washed, and . . . received sight" as Jesus promised we would.

HELPS FOR TEACHERS

As teachers, do we give away all the answers without requiring any effort on the part of the learners? Teachers, do we create situations that make learners think and act? That make them purposely question? Do we provide symbols or stories to learners that are simultaneously readily accessible and enduringly applicable?

Here are some questions that can stimulate student involvement such that they help teach the class:

- What false tradition is evidenced by the disciples' question in verse 2? (The idea that illness and disabilities are caused by sin.)
- There are many examples of the Savior healing people immediately. What might be some reasons that, in this case, the man had to do more before he was finally healed?
- What are some examples of the "works of God" that are referred to in verse 3? (Answers can include miracles of healing, humbling, change of heart in others who decide to serve the sick and afflicted instead of avoiding them, etc.)
- What are some lessons we might learn from the information given in verse 3? (Possible answers can include that sometimes people get sick so that testimonies can be strengthened when they are healed by God's power, including through prayers of faith and priesthood blessings. Other answers could include that sometimes people are allowed to get sick so that those around them can learn to serve.)

Raising Lazarus from the Dead

John 11:1–45

As this chapter begins, Jesus and His disciples are staying in Perea (across the Jordan River, east of Jericho, roughly 30 miles from Jerusalem; see John 10:40), where there is relative safety from the Jews in Jerusalem who had recently attempted to stone Him. It is the Master's last winter during His mortal ministry.

1 NOW a certain man was sick, named Lazarus, of Bethany [*about two miles outside of Jerusalem on the east side of the Mount of Olives, on the road to Jericho*], the town of Mary and her sister Martha.

2 (It was that Mary which anointed the Lord with ointment, and wiped his feet with her hair [*Matthew 26:7, John 12:2–3*], whose brother Lazarus was sick.)

> JST John 11:2
>
> 2 And Mary, his sister, who anointed the Lord with ointment and wiped his feet with her hair, lived with her sister Martha, in whose house her brother Lazarus was sick.

3 Therefore his sisters sent unto him [*Jesus*], saying, Lord, behold, he [*Lazarus*] whom thou lovest is sick.

4 When Jesus heard that, he said, This sickness is not unto death, but for the glory of God, that the Son of God might be glorified thereby. [*In effect, He won't be dead very long. He will die (see verses 13–14), and this situation will help many believe in God and have a chance to be much more aware of who I am.*]

5 Now Jesus loved Martha, and her sister, and Lazarus.

6 When he had heard therefore that he was sick, he abode two days still in the same place [*Perea*] where he was.

7 Then after that saith he to his disciples, Let us go into Judæa [*to the Jerusalem area*] again.

8 His disciples say unto him, Master, the Jews of late [*just recently*] sought to stone thee; and goest thou thither again?

> His disciples are very worried about His safety and don't want Him going to Mary and Martha's house in Bethany, because it is only two miles from Jerusalem where the Jews are who have already tried to kill Him.

9 Jesus answered, Are there not twelve hours in the day? If any man walk in the day, he stumbleth not, because he seeth the light of this world. [*In effect, I must keep going right on with My work.*]

10 But if a man walk in the night, he stumbleth, because there is no light in him.

11 These things said he: and after that he saith unto them, Our friend Lazarus sleepeth; but I go, that I may awake him out of sleep.

12 Then said his disciples, Lord, if he sleep, he shall do well [*if he is just sleeping, he will be okay, implying again that they don't want Him going near Jerusalem*].

13 Howbeit [*however*] Jesus spake of his death: but they thought that he had spoken of taking of rest in sleep.

14 Then said Jesus unto them plainly, Lazarus is dead.

15 And I am glad for your sakes that I was not there, to the intent ye may believe [*in effect, I am glad he is dead, because what is going to happen will strengthen your testimonies*]; nevertheless let us go unto him.

16 Then said Thomas, which is called Didymus [*the twin*], unto his fellow disciples, Let us also go, that we may die with him.

> JST John 11:16
>
> 16 Then said Thomas, which is called Didymus, unto his fellow disciples, Let us also go, that we may die with him; for they feared lest the Jews should take Jesus and put him to death, for as yet they did not understand the power of God.
>
> This Apostle of Christ, Thomas, is usually known mainly as "doubting Thomas," because he refused to believe that Jesus had been resurrected unless he could see Him personally and feel the wounds in His hands and side (see John 20:25–28). Here we see Thomas in a much different light. He is a man of courage and conviction, and encourages the other disciples to join him in going to Jerusalem with Jesus so that they could all die with Him.

17 Then when Jesus came [*arrived in Bethany at Martha's house*], he found that he [*Lazarus*] had lain in the grave four days already.

> JST John 11:17
>
> 17 And when Jesus came to Bethany, to Martha's house, Lazarus had already been in the grave four days.
>
> Four days is significant because of Jewish beliefs about death. They had a false belief that the spirit must remain by a dead person's body for three days. After that, the person is for sure dead. The fact that Lazarus had been dead for four days, and in fact, had already begun to stink (verse 39) left no doubt in the minds of the mourners that he was very dead.

18 Now Bethany was nigh unto Jerusalem, about fifteen furlongs off [*two miles away*]:

19 And many of the Jews came to Martha and Mary, to comfort them concerning their brother.

20 Then Martha, as soon as she heard that Jesus was coming, went and met him: but Mary sat still in the house.

21 Then said Martha unto Jesus, Lord, if thou hadst been here, my brother had not died [*if You had come quickly, when I first sent word to You of Lazarus's illness, he would not have died*].

> Next, Martha expresses her great faith in Jesus. We see that she has been taught the doctrine of resurrection as she responds to the Master's assurance that Lazarus will be resurrected.

22 But I know, that even now, whatsoever thou wilt ask of God, God will give it thee. [*Martha had great faith. She believed that even though Lazarus was dead, Jesus could bring him back to life.*]

23 Jesus saith unto her, Thy brother shall rise again.

24 Martha saith unto him, I know that he shall rise again in the resurrection at the last day.

> Verse 25, next, is a well-known verse in the Bible. You may wish to mark it in your own scriptures. In a significant way, it is a brief summary of the Savior's purpose and mission. Through His Atonement, all will be resurrected, and eternal life (exaltation) is made available to all, contingent on repenting and living the gospel.

25 Jesus said unto her, I am the resurrection, and the life [*in effect, I have power over death and can give eternal life*]: he that believeth in me, though he were dead, yet shall he live:

26 And whosoever liveth [*is spiritually alive*] and believeth in me shall never die [*spiritually*]. Believest thou this?

27 She saith unto him, Yea, Lord: I believe that thou art the Christ, the Son of God, which should come into the world. [*I believe that You are the promised Messiah.*]

28 And when she had so said, she went her way, and called Mary her sister secretly, saying, The Master is come, and calleth for thee.

29 As soon as she heard that, she arose quickly, and came unto him [*Jesus*].

> JST John 11:29
>
> 29 As soon as Mary heard that Jesus was come, she arose quickly, and came unto him.

30 Now Jesus was not yet come into the town, but was in that place where Martha met him.

31 The Jews then which were with her in the house, and comforted her, when they saw Mary, that she rose up hastily and went out, followed her, saying, She goeth unto the grave [*to Lazarus's tomb*] to weep there.

32 Then when Mary was come where Jesus was, and saw him, she fell down at his feet, saying unto him, Lord, if thou hadst been here, my brother had not died.

33 When Jesus therefore saw her weeping, and the Jews also weeping which came with her, he groaned in the spirit, and was troubled [*this was a very emotional time for Jesus*],

34 And said, Where have ye laid him [*where have you buried him*]? They said unto him, Lord, come and see.

35 Jesus wept.

> Verse 35, above, is the shortest verse in the Bible. It is a reminder of the great kindness and compassion the Master has for us.

36 Then said the Jews, Behold how he loved him!

37 And some of them said, Could not this man, which opened the eyes of the blind, have caused that even this man should not have died? [*Couldn't Jesus have prevented Lazarus from dying if He had been here? Yes, and Jesus wanted to build their faith in His ability to save and resurrect.*]

38 Jesus therefore again groaning in himself cometh to the grave. It was a cave [*tomb*], and a stone lay upon it.

39 Jesus said, Take ye away the stone [*open the tomb*]. Martha, the sister of him that was dead, saith unto him, Lord, by this time he stinketh: for he hath been dead four days.

40 Jesus saith unto her, Said I not unto thee, that, if thou wouldest believe, thou shouldest see the glory of God [*you would see the power of God in action*]?

> Imagine the hush and the looks on people's faces as they watch with rapt attention as the stone is rolled away!

41 Then they took away the stone from the place where the dead was laid. And Jesus lifted up his eyes, and said, Father, I thank thee that thou hast heard me.

> As you have no doubt noticed, the Son humbly gives credit to the Father in all things, pointing our minds past Him and to the Father. Here we are seeing it again.

42 And I knew that thou hearest me always: but because of the people which stand by I said it [*I said it out loud for the benefit of the people who have gathered around*], that they may believe that thou hast sent me.

43 And when he thus had spoken, he cried with a loud voice, Lazarus, come forth.

44 And he that was dead came forth, bound hand and foot with graveclothes: and his face was bound about with a napkin. Jesus saith unto them, Loose him, and let him go.

45 Then many of the Jews which came to Mary, and had seen the things which Jesus did, believed on him.

BACKGROUND, CULTURE, AND SETTING

"Jesus wept."

This phrase constitutes the shortest verse in the KJV translation of the Bible. For being so brief, we might feel tempted to quickly pass this verse, driven by the flow of the story to continue our reading.

What will we miss if we don't pause to reflect?

This, the shortest, most brief verse in all of scripture, may be the most revelatory about the nature of Jesus.

Jesus is both divine and human. As God enfleshed, He shared our human passions, our pains, our joy. He even wept at the loss of His beloved friend.

But Jesus is God, too. Couldn't Jesus bring Lazarus back from the dead? In fact, isn't that what Jesus did a few verses following His recorded weeping? Why would Jesus weep if He knew that He was only moments away from bringing unbounded joy to Mary, Martha, their neighbors, and to Lazarus? Why didn't Jesus calm the tears of Mary and Martha with words like, "My dear friends, stop your crying and wipe your tears away. I am about to bring your brother back from the dead"? We know that Jesus chastised professional mourners at the house of Jairus. He told the weepers and wailers to leave the home so He could raise the little girl back from the dead (Mark 5:41). Why not repeat His performance here? We can suggest a few very compelling reasons.

First, in the story of Jairus's daughter, those who were making the racket of weeping and wailing were professional mourners. These individuals weren't even sincere in their emotional outbursts. They were paid to act as though they cared about the deceased. In contrast, in the story of raising Lazarus from the dead, Jesus did not verbally hush the tears of His friends. Their pain was real, authentic, and acute.

Second, and this may be the most telling aspect of this entire episode, as summarized by the phrase, "Jesus wept," because it declares the very nature of Jesus. Jesus demonstrated His divine, all-encompassing compassion for us and His willingness to *suffer* with us. Even though He knew that Lazarus was moments from taking his renewed breath, Jesus took the time to openly, empathetically, and sincerely weep together with His friends over the loss of their brother. Jesus loves us. He weeps with us. Even though He knows the stunning power of the Atonement to destroy the effects of death and sin, He feels for us and with us. He suffers for and with us. He does this all because He loves us. Never has there been a purer, more thorough love. And all of this is summarized in the achingly and beautifully succinct verse "Jesus wept."

The Master Teacher

Jesus did not immediately solve the need expressed by Mary, Martha, and others. In fact, Jesus *allowed* additional suffering to happen, beyond what they were already experiencing with Lazarus's illness. When the disciples shared the message of Lazarus's illness and of the request for Jesus's immediate presence, what did Jesus do? He delayed! How could it be that the God-man we worship as the source of our salvation, the very same Jesus who immediately reached out to save flailing Peter in storm-tossed seas when he cried out in fear and anguish "Lord, save me" (Matthew 14:31), would have purposely delayed visiting Lazarus *so that Lazarus would die*?

Jesus wanted to create a teaching and learning moment that would reverberate across the centuries. He is the Master who weeps with us in our pain, heartache, and loss, even though He knows with perfect certainty that there brighter days for us ahead. Jesus has a plan for all of us. If we are patient and trusting, He will realize our greatest dreams and aspirations.

Possible Applications for Learners

Learning, though typically a joyful experience, is fraught with challenge, difficulty, and faith-demanding experiences. Those who truly want to learn, especially to become more like God, recognize that pain is a necessity of mortality. Suffering is a reality. But in these moments of difficulties, faith must be the guiding star, providing perspective to continuously seek learning: we know that as we learn we become more like God.

Helps for Teachers

Teachers must allow learners to suffer and struggle a little in their learning. If teachers jump right in immediately to save learners, teachers may risk jeopardizing a learner's growth. Furthermore, teachers can express their love for their learners by *suffering* with them, even when the teacher knows that the answer is soon to arrive. Teachers who lead by example, who endure the difficulties of learning alongside the students, win the admiration, loyalty, and trust of learners.

At the same time, it may be appropriate to provide perspective and encouragement to struggling learners about how close they are to making a breakthrough, or to mastering a challenging idea.

Teachers should thoughtfully create learning experiences that help learners to feel, know, and experience the reality of God's love and the power of gospel principles. We are not Jesus. Of course, we should not delay so that someone physically or spiritually dies because we didn't teach what they needed. Still, teachers, following the guidance of the Spirit, should plan in advance to create specific learning experiences that the learners need.

Here are some involvement questions that can help inspire students to join in class discussion:

- What knowledge and testimony did Martha already have, according to verse 24?
- What is the value of that knowledge and testimony in your life?
- Who were the Savior's main students in this event? (Answers should include Mary and Martha, His disciples, friends and neighbors, and all of us.)
- In verse 25, Jesus said, "I am the resurrection and the life." How many doctrinal meanings can you come up with for this magnificent statement? (Answers should include that He provides resurrection for all and eternal life, meaning exaltation, for those who fully take the gospel into their lives.)
- Since Jesus knew He was going to bring Lazarus back to life, why do you think He wept?
- How would you respond to a friend who expressed the feeling, based on verse 15, that Jesus was being a little mean? (He is not being mean. Rather, He is using this intensely emotional situation as an incredible teaching opportunity to strengthen their testimonies.)

Jesus and Zacchaeus

Luke 19:1–10

As we begin this chapter, Jesus is on His way to Jerusalem for the last time and will be crucified in about ten days. We meet a delightful little man named Zacchaeus, who is despised by all but Him who is deeply good. Watch how the Master honors him.

1 AND Jesus entered and passed through Jericho.

2 And, behold, there was a man named Zacchæus, which was the chief among the pub-
licans [*the chief of the tax collectors*], and he was rich.

3 And he sought to see Jesus who he was [*tried to get where he could get a view of Jesus*];
and could not for the press [*because of the crowd*], because he was little of stature [*he was
a little, short man*].

4 And he ran before [*so he ran ahead*], and climbed up into a sycomore tree to see him:
for he [*Jesus*] was to pass that way.

5 And when Jesus came to the place, he looked up, and saw him, and said unto him,
Zacchæus, make haste, and come down; for to day I must abide at thy house.

> This is a rather tender scene. As mentioned in the note at the beginning of this chapter, the people hated tax collectors, considering them to be sinners, and Zacchaeus was the head tax collector. Jesus says, "I must stay at your house," implying that He himself, the Creator of heaven and earth, had a strong desire to stay with this humble man and reassure him of his worth to God. "I must stay at your house" can also convey the message that this action on the part of the Redeemer was essential for the well-being of Zacchaeus.

6 And he made haste, and came down [*out of the tree*], and received him [*Christ*] joyfully.

7 And when they saw it, they all murmured, saying, That he was gone to be guest with
a man that is a sinner.

> From the JST of verse 7, quoted next, we see that the disciples still had not finished learning the lesson that the Master judges by what is in the heart, rather than what others think.
>
> JST Luke 19:7
>
> 7 And when the disciples saw it, they all murmured, saying, That he was gone to be a guest with a man who is a sinner.

8 And Zacchæus stood, and said unto the Lord [*Jesus*]; Behold, Lord, the half of my
goods I give to the poor; and if I have taken any thing from any man by false accusation

[*if I have mistakenly collected more taxes than I should from anyone*], I restore him fourfold [*I pay him back four times what I took*].

> JST Luke 19:8
>
> 8 And Zaccheus stood, and said unto the Lord, Behold, Lord, the half of my goods I give to the poor; and if I have taken any thing from any man by unjust means, I restore fourfold.

9 And Jesus said unto him, This day is salvation come to this house [*I have come to this house*], forsomuch as [*because*] he also is a son of [*descendant of*] Abraham [*can also mean that Zacchaeus is righteous and honest like Abraham was, and thus will be saved*].

10 For the Son of man [*I, Christ*] is come to seek and to save that which was lost.

Background, Culture, and Setting

Today, not far from the ancient remains of Jericho, stands a large and solitary sycamore tree. Undoubtedly old, this sycamore tree is one of several in the area that have for centuries been a magnet for pilgrims seeking to experience the stories of Jesus. These religious tourists are seeking to experience something like what Zacchaeus did so many years ago when Jesus visited Jericho.

On the way to His last visit to Jerusalem, that ended with His death and resurrection, Jesus passed through Jericho, the last major city or town on the road from Galilee up to Jerusalem. This oasis city from ancient times has been fed by a never-ending flow of fresh water that bubbles up from the ground, bringing miraculous life and rich prosperity to the area.

Zacchaeus was one of the chief tax collectors, or publicans, of Jericho. During this period of Roman domination, enterprising individuals could receive contracts to collect taxes from the people on behalf of the Roman Empire. The contract allowed the tax collector to keep the excess taxes collected. Taxes and tax collectors are considered odious in all time periods, so, it is no surprise that the Jews of Jericho disliked their fellow Jew, Zacchaeus, who benefited from and supported the hated Roman occupation.

The Master Teacher

As Jesus entered the city, a crowd of people thronged the Miracle Worker. Zacchaeus was small in stature and wanted to see Jesus but could not because of the crowds. Ever the entrepreneur seeking for unexpected solutions, he climbed a nearby sycamore tree and waited for Jesus to pass beneath. From this vantage point, Zacchaeus saw Jesus, and Jesus saw Zacchaeus. Looking up, Jesus said, "Zacchaeus, make haste, and come down; for to day I must abide at thy house" (Luke 19:5). Surprised at Jesus's words and actions, the crowd, including the disciples, "all murmured, saying, That [Jesus] was gone to be guest with a man that is a sinner" (Luke 19:7).

Because Zacchaeus was a tax collector, the people judged him through a very narrow lens, but God sees people differently. He taught this lesson to the prophet Samuel when He said, "Look not on his countenance, or on the height of his stature . . . for the Lord seeth not as man seeth; for man looketh on the outward appearance, but the Lord looketh on the heart" (1 Samuel 16:7).

In Hebrew, the name *Zacchaeus* means "pure" or "innocent." Luke used a wordplay with Zacchaeus's name to highlight his inner qualities, which were overlooked by his countrymen. But Jesus saw the pure Zacchaeus, who sought to keep the commandments and live in love and faithfulness, and eagerly sought the coming of the Lord. In this story, we see the fulfillment of Jesus's promise delivered at the Sermon on the Mount: "Blessed are the pure in heart: for they shall see God" (Matthew 5:8). Zacchaeus in name and in reality was "the pure in heart" and was blessed accordingly to "see God." Jesus taught by word, by example, by deed, by parable, and by action. He found so many ways to teach principles. In the story of Zacchaeus, He taught that God loves all of His children, that everyone deserves the message of the gospel, and that they deserve to be treated with kindness, dignity, and respect. Jesus also taught using signs and symbols.

POSSIBLE APPLICATIONS FOR LEARNERS

Do we see others as God sees them? Or do we judge them based on limited labels of human construction? How do we see ourselves? Are we willing to see ourselves as God sees us? Or do we succumb to the temptation to believe the labels and trappings the fallen world places on us? Do we assume the identity that others give us or that our fallen natures seem to suggest for us? Or do we remember the truths that, as children of God, we are Gods in embryo, that our hearts can be pure before the Lord, and that we will see His face again as the temple promises confirm?

Zacchaeus didn't give up easily. He was proactive with his wish to see Jesus. What are we doing to actively seek God?

As Jesus testified at the end of this story, He will find the pure in heart, and they will see God. "For the Son of man is come to seek and to save that which was lost" (Luke 19:10)."[1]

HELPS FOR TEACHERS

As teachers, our personal example should model the principles we teach. We should also find ways to multiply the reinforcements to our message. Do we use analogies, symbols, metaphors, or unexpected connections to help learners see, hear, feel, and experience the message?

Some examples of questions that can lead class members to get involved in class discussion are

- What do you think it did to Zacchaeus's self-image when Jesus stopped, spoke to him, and said, "today I must abide at thy house (verse 5)"?
- According to verse 6, how did Zacchaeus feel about the Master's request?
- How did the crowd following Jesus feel about the Savior's attention to Zacchaeus? (See verse 7.)

1. The text in the sections "Background, Setting, and Culture," "The Master Teacher," and "Possible Applications" is modified from the *LDS Living* article "What We May Have Missed in Jesus's Loving Response to a Despised Man in the Bible," by Taylor Halverson and Scott Haines, originally published online November 4, 2017, at http://www.ldsliving.com/What-We-May-Have-Missed-in-Jesus-s-Loving-Response-to-a-Despised-Man-in-the-Bible/s/86841. Used with permission.

- How can we avoid being like the people in the crowd?
- If they were honest, how should those in the crowd have felt about Zacchaeus after hearing what Christ said to him in verse 9?
- What lessons do you see for yourself in these verses?

THE TRIUMPHAL ENTRY (PALM SUNDAY)

MATTHEW 21:1–11

These next verses lead up to what is known as "the Triumphal Entry," the day when Jesus rode into Jerusalem, accompanied by throngs of people shouting, "Hosanna to the Son of David," celebrating and cheering Jesus as the promised Messiah who would save them and free them from their enemies. The Passover was underway, and masses of Jewish pilgrims had arrived in Jerusalem from many lands to join in Passover celebration and worship. This begins the last week of the Savior's mortal life.

1 AND when they drew nigh unto Jerusalem, and were come to Bethphage [*on the east side of the Mount of Olives*], unto the mount of Olives, then sent Jesus two disciples,

2 Saying unto them, Go into the village over against you [*ahead of you*], and straightway ye shall find an ass tied, and a colt with her: loose [*untie*] them, and bring them unto me.

3 And if any man say ought unto you [*questions you about what you are doing*], ye shall say, The Lord hath need of them; and straightway he will send them.

4 All this was done, that it might be fulfilled which was spoken by the prophet [*Zechariah; see Zechariah 9:9*], saying,

5 Tell ye the daughter of Sion, Behold, thy King cometh unto thee, meek, and sitting upon an ass, and a colt the foal of an ass.

> In Hebrew symbolism, a donkey represents humility and submission. Thus, the Savior's riding into Jerusalem on a donkey is symbolic of his humility and submission to the coming suffering and crucifixion.

6 And the disciples went, and did as Jesus commanded them,

7 And brought the ass, and the colt, and put on them their clothes, and they set him thereon.

> JST Matthew 21:5
>
> 5 . . . brought the colt, and put on it their clothes; and Jesus took the colt and sat thereon; and they followed him." (See also Luke 19:30.)
>
> Have you ever noticed the miracle that just happened here? Luke 19:30 informs us that the colt had never been ridden before. Yet, the Master sat on it with no trouble from the colt, reminding us that Jesus has power over the animal kingdom too.

8 And a very great multitude spread their garments in the way [*along the path where Jesus rode*]; others cut down branches from the trees [*from palm trees: John 12:13*], and strawed [*spread*] them in the way.

9 And the multitudes that went before, and that followed, cried, saying, Hosanna to the Son of David: Blessed is he that cometh in the name of the Lord; Hosanna in the highest.

10 And when he was come into Jerusalem, all the city was moved [*everyone in the city was excited about him*], saying, Who is this?

11 And the multitude said, This is Jesus the prophet of Nazareth of Galilee.

BACKGROUND, CULTURE, AND SETTING

This majestic event preserved in Matthew 21 (as well as in Mark 11, Luke 19, and John 12) is now known as Palm Sunday, memorializing that on a Sunday Jesus rode triumphant into Jerusalem as the crowds hailed Him with palms. Palm fronds or palm branches held deep symbolic significance. In the ancient middle East, palm branches represented peace, victory, and eternal life. For Jews in particular, palm fronds reminded them of God's victory over the Egyptians and their deliverance from bondage. In Jewish symbolism, palm branches symbolized God's triumph and victory. Thus, in cutting palm branches and excitedly waving them and spreading them on the ground in front of the Savior, the crowd was enthusiastically expressing their belief that Jesus would bring them military triumph and victory over their Roman enemies. No more appropriate symbol could have been used by the people of Jerusalem than that of the palm branches to welcome Jesus, who will triumphantly make us victors over sin and death, if we have faith.

The shout of *Hosanna* comes from the ancient Hebrew word that means "Save us!" Significantly, the name *Jesus* is a variant of the Hebrew names Joshua and Hosea, which all mean "salvation." The people shouting "Hosanna" were simply using a variant of the name "Jesus" to praise the salvation that had come to their city.

Why did Jesus ride on a donkey? Arriving on a warhorse would represent that the king came in conquering anger. Arriving on a lowly donkey meant that the king came in peace. Jesus, the king of peace, came symbolically in peace to the proverbial city of peace. By tradition, ancient Israelite kings rode into Jerusalem to inaugurate their kingship. For example, when King David installed his son Solomon as the king, he had Solomon ride a donkey to the Gihon Spring at Jerusalem.

"And king David said, Call me Zadok the priest, and Nathan the prophet, and Benaiah the son of Jehoiada. And they came before the king. The king also said unto them, Take with you the servants of your lord, and cause Solomon my son to ride upon mine own mule, and bring him down to Gihon: And let Zadok the priest and Nathan the prophet anoint him there king over Israel: and blow ye with the trumpet, and say, God save king Solomon" (1 Kings 1:32–34).

This spring of water was a major source of life in Jerusalem. Without the flows of the Gihon Spring, Jerusalem could not exist.

If we read the JST version of Matthew 21:7 (JST Matthew 21:5), we notice a small, curious, but significant change. The Gospel writer Matthew was so anxious to demonstrate that Jesus was the promised Messiah, quoting Old Testament passages as evidence of Jesus as prophetic fulfillment, that in his drive to make the case for Jesus his narrative got slightly exaggerated.[2]

Matthew quoted Zechariah 9:9, which, following common ancient Hebrew literary style of parallelism or repetition, repeated twice the message that the king would ride a lowly animal. Below we've structured Zechariah 9:9 according to its Hebrew parallelistic literary pattern.

> "Rejoice greatly,
>   O daughter of Zion;
> shout,
>   O daughter of Jerusalem:
>
> behold, thy King cometh unto thee:
>   he is just,
>   and having salvation;
>   lowly,
>   and riding upon an ass,
>   and upon a colt the foal of an ass."

Zechariah didn't mean to say that the king would arrive both on an ass and a colt. He was instead using Hebrew literary structure to reinforce the idea that the king would ride upon a donkey. It appears that Matthew or later scribes missed this parallelism and took the quote at face value and then narrated that Jesus, to fulfill the scripture, rode in to Jerusalem on *two* animals at the same time. The JST appropriately corrects this minor, if humorous, scribal error.

Matthew (original)	Matthew (JST)
And the disciples went, and did as Jesus commanded them, And brought the ass, and the colt, and put on them [*both animals*] their clothes, and they set him [*Jesus*] thereon [*on both animals*].	. . . and brought the *colt*, and put on *it* their clothes; *and Jesus took the colt and sat* thereon; *and they [the disciples] followed him.*

Why did the crowds shout "thou son of David?" This phrase identified Jesus as the proper Davidic descendant who would rule and reign. The king was understood to have the power to establish his kingdom with might and justice, to bring harmony to where there was imbalance. That justice and harmony wielded by the true king included healing the sick. What did Jesus do immediately upon arriving in His city? He went to the temple and healed the blind and the lame. He demonstrated that He was king over His realm to bring harmony and justice.

2. Scholars have demonstrated this point through many forms of evidence. For example, when a reader compares the different Gospel writers' use of Old Testament quotes, the pattern that appears in Matthew is that he likes to say "and thus is fulfilled." Even inspired writers can show their humanity.

The Master Teacher

Jesus used scripture and symbolism to teach basic and important lessons. Jesus did not seek to complicate His message. Sure, He often taught in parables that were inscrutable for those who did not have "ears to hear" (Mark 4:9). But the purpose of His teaching was not to obscure, but to enlighten, to demonstrate what the kingdom of God is like. Jesus came in peace. His message will bring peace to all individuals who live His word and to societies in the measure that they follow His teachings.

Possible Applications for Learners

Learners can expand their understanding of scripture and Jesus's messages by learning about symbols and their meanings. Furthermore, when we read the scriptures through the lens of how they "talk of Christ . . . rejoice in Christ . . . preach of Christ . . . prophesy of Christ . . . that our children may know to what source they may look for a remission of their sins" (2 Nephi 25:26), we will find greater understanding, more joy, deeper love for Jesus, and the spiritual sustenance we need to endure to the end.

Helps for Teachers

Teachers should make use of the best resources to help learners understand scriptures. Sometimes there are confusing phrases or words, or obscure cultural background that make the scriptures harder to understand. One resource is the JST, which can clarify, correct, and enlarge our understanding. Teachers should teach learners about scriptural symbolism and how it points to Jesus (consider the book *The Language of Symbolism* by Alonzo Gaskill). Teachers should teach learners about the background and culture of the Bible (the Bible Dictionary comes in handy here). Teachers should show learners how Jesus is the fulfillment of scripture. And teachers should help learners apply the scriptures to their everyday needs following the sterling example of Nephi who "did liken all scriptures unto us, that it might be for our profit and learning" (1 Nephi 19:23).

Examples of questions that can lead to the involvement of class members in the discussion:

- How does the JST resolve some confusion that arises from verse 7? (See footnote 7a, which leads to a JST clarification.)
- What seldom-noticed miracle about Jesus riding the colt can you find, based on comparing verse 7 with Luke 19:30? (The colt had never been ridden before but allowed Jesus to ride him without trouble.)
- How does the Savior's entry into Jerusalem compare with His "entry" from heaven down to earth at the second coming? What differences can you point out?
- How would you account for the difference between the peoples' wild rejoicing and acceptance of Jesus as He rode into Jerusalem and their cries to "crucify Him" (Mark 15:13) about a week later?

AUTHORITY OF JESUS QUESTIONED

MATTHEW 21:23–27

23 And when he was come into the temple, the chief priests and the elders of the people [*the Jewish religious leaders who are trying to trap Him*] came unto him as he was teaching, and said, By what authority doest thou these things? and who gave thee this authority?

24 And Jesus answered and said unto them, I also will ask you one thing, which if ye tell me, I in like wise will tell you by what authority I do these things.

25 The baptism of John [*the Baptist*], whence was it? from heaven, or of men? [*Did John the Baptist have authority from heaven, or was he just another man?*] And they reasoned with themselves, saying, If we shall say, From heaven; he [*Jesus*] will say unto us, Why did ye not then believe him?

26 But if we shall say, Of men; we fear the people; for all hold John as a prophet. [*If we say John the Baptist was just an ordinary man, the people will mob us, because they consider him to be sent from God.*]

27 And they answered Jesus, and said, We cannot tell. And he said unto them, Neither tell I you by what authority I do these things.

BACKGROUND, CULTURE, AND SETTING

The temple in Jerusalem was tightly regulated, both by the interpretation of the Mosaic law that had been built up over the years, and by the temple authorities who saw it as their mandate to protect the holiness and the rituals that took place at the temple. As the largest open-air plaza area in all of Jerusalem, the temple precincts were a natural place to gather a crowd, preach, or even incite a riot. The temple authorities, worried about the safety of Jerusalem and worried about protecting their authority and their source of income derived from the ongoing flow of Jewish pilgrims buying sacrificial animals at the temple, kept a close watch on all the activities that occurred at the temple. They watched over the construction workers. The temple was under construction for decades, only being finished some miniscule number of years before the Romans destroyed the temple around AD 70 to quell a wild Jewish revolt. They watched over the money changers. Indeed, the temple authorities both set the price of the monetary exchange rate and benefited from the difference. The steady stream of wealth allowed the temple authorities to build great and spacious homes for themselves that overlooked both the temple and the poorer areas of Jerusalem. They watched over the procedures of temple sacrifices to ensure that they were conducted according to established protocols. They similarly kept watch over the seemingly never-ending flow of worshippers, watching out for insurrectionists, false prophets, and messiahs, and definitely keeping an eye out for anyone who would challenge the central and emblematic institution of Jewish life—the temple.

Jesus crossed many of the temple authorities' proverbial "lines in the sand," which is why they confronted him.

THE MASTER TEACHER

Jesus was not afraid of teaching and acting on truth, even when His actions were contrary to popular or authoritative culture. He knew that His enemies wanted to trap Him in His words so they could accuse Him and sentence Him to death. He therefore did not take the bait to answer as they expected. And He did not back down from teaching the truth, even when His opponents seemed to paint Him into a theological corner or conundrum. Most of us as teachers will not have to face such hostile crowds when teaching Sunday School or in other gospel-related settings (we hope!). We learn from Jesus that the truth can always win the day, no matter the opposition.

POSSIBLE APPLICATIONS FOR LEARNERS

Learners should strive to master understanding and living the gospel by study and by faith. The modern world prizes study instead of faith. Never forget the power of prayer, fasting, repentance, forgiveness, and love to bring insight and understanding of the scriptures. We are not advocating for the abandonment of scholarship. On the contrary, we would be fools if we were sick and expected to be healed if we only said, "I believe Jesus can heal me" and then *didn't* make use of the modern miracles of medicine inspired by God. So too, we should make use of the most thoughtful and careful scholarship about scripture (and Church history) so that our faith can be empowered and strengthened. But at the same time, we should not let the "learning of men" distract us from the learning that comes directly from God.

HELPS FOR TEACHERS

Though Jesus had authority from God to challenge the authorities of His day, it is not the role of teachers in the Church to launch any doctrinal or policy revolutions in the Church. Rather, our role is to teach the truths that bring revolutions in our personal lives. Who among us would not experience a personal revolution if we exercised faith unto repentance demonstrated by being baptized or partaking of the sacrament so that we have the power of the Spirit in our lives to help us endure to the end?

On the topic of authority: You are called of God to teach. You don't need a fancy theology or philosophy or biblical studies degree. You don't need any university degree, let alone a doctoral degree, to teach the word of God.

Yes, taking the time to study the words of living Latter-day prophets and learning from the best supplementary resources can go a long way in helping you avoid errors and misinterpreting scripture. But remember, as a teacher called of God you have been set apart and empowered to teach the truth, as found in the scriptures, as inspired by the Spirit of God, and as confirmed by modern-day prophets. Just as Jesus did not need the "authority of men" to teach in His day, so, too, you do not need the authority of men to teach.

Here are some questions that can help promote class discussion:

- How did Jesus skillfully avoid being pulled away from His goals as a teacher and minister by those who challenged His authority?
- Why do you suppose Jesus avoided being drawn into a contentious debate with these leaders of the Jews?
- Why is it generally best that we, personally, avoid being drawn into contentious debates by members of our own or other religions?

Parable of the Faithful Servant

Mark 13:34–37

34 For the Son of man is as a man taking a far journey, who left his house [*went to heaven*], and gave authority to his servants [*the Apostles, leaders of the Church*], and to every man his work [*to all members their responsibilities*], and commanded the porter to watch.

35 Watch ye therefore: for ye know not when the master of the house cometh [*symbolic of the Savior at his Second Coming*], at even [*evening*], or at midnight, or at the cockcrowing, or in the morning:

36 Lest coming suddenly he find you sleeping [*not living righteously*].

37 And what I say unto you I say unto all, Watch.

Background, Culture, and Setting

Two phrases in the New Testament actually mean the opposite of what we think they mean, which causes some confusion. The two phrases are "the Son of man" and "Son of God." Both these phrases are used to identify Jesus, but they identify different characteristics of Jesus.

First, "the Son of man" should not be confused with the very similar phrase "son of man." This latter phrase does not include the definite article "the" and, typically, is expressed all in the lowercase in the King James Bible. The phrase "son of man" means any human being. On the other hand, the phrase "the Son of man" does have the definite article at the beginning and typically has the word "Son" capitalized. This phrase primarily represents Jesus's heavenly qualities.

Second, the "Son of God" is a title of kinship. When used in the New Testament to refer to Jesus, "Son of God" identifies His earthly qualities *as the king*. Several Old Testament passages clarify how the king of Israel was understood to be God's son.

"I set my king upon my holy hill of Zion. I will declare the decree: the Lord hath said unto me, Thou art my Son; this day have I begotten thee" (Psalm 2:6–7).

"I will be his father, and he shall be my son. And thine house and thy kingdom shall be established for ever before thee: thy throne shall be established for ever" (1 Samuel 7:14, 16).

Interestingly, Jesus never calls himself the Messiah (a title of kingship with significant theological overtones) in the New Testament or the "Son of God" though others use these titles to identify Him, clearly pointing to His kingly role.

Jesus is far more likely to call himself "the Son of man."

So, it is likely significant that at the beginning of this parable Jesus uses the title "Son of man." As one who comes from heaven, where will He return to? To heaven. Where will His journey take Him that requires Him to put others in charge while He is away? To heaven. And what is this parable about? How those who have been empowered by Jesus to act as He would act and do as He would do if He were still here, break trust and build up their own power at the expense of saving God's children. As the heavenly "Son of man," He promises to come yet again from heaven to this earth. That is the day of reckoning when all the servants must give an accounting for how they managed their time and the Master's resources and authority.

THE MASTER TEACHER

Jesus came to make the comfortable uncomfortable and the uncomfortable comfortable. He kept His disciples and His listeners continuously learning, seeking, and growing. They were often confused, asked questions, and needed clarification. A good teacher does not simply hand over truth on a silver platter. We all know that we treasure most what we seek most diligently after. Jesus created learning situations that required diligent seeking, to the point that he emphatically reminded His disciples to be vigilant and "Watch"!

POSSIBLE APPLICATIONS FOR LEARNERS

Good learners are ever vigilant. They do not rest on their past successes. They do not believe that arriving at some learning plateaus signifies that they have "arrived," that there is nothing more of value, significance, or potential joy to gain from additional learning. Since we are in this life to improve ourselves as a test of our faithfulness to God, we have no excuse to stop learning. More learning does not necessarily mean more formal schooling (though it could). It does mean, however, to be open to new experiences, to take the time to reflect on your experiences, and to not be in such a rush that there is no time to consider where you are, how you arrived, and where you are going. When He comes, Jesus will find the best learners actively tending the gardens of their minds and hearts, constantly harvesting a bounty of new experiences, new insights, new applications, and treasured truths won through the labor of learning.

HELPS FOR TEACHERS

Teachers should challenge learners to never slack in their determination to develop and grow in their testimonies, to experience afresh the power of the spirit in their lives, to feel the love of God as they apply gospel truths to life's realities.

Here are some questions that can help promote student involvement in class discussion:

- How does verse 35 verify that no one knows exactly when the Second Coming will take place (Matthew 24:36)?
- According to this parable, why is it so important not to be "on again, off again" in your commitment to staying on the covenant path?
- What are some differences in thinking between members of the Church who strive to stay active and faithful in the Church and those who tend to be "on again, off again" in their Church activity?
- In verse 34, who are "his servants" and who is "every man"? (Apostles and leaders of the Church; all members of the Church.)

The Parable of the Talents

Matthew 25:14–30

14 For the kingdom of heaven is as a man [*symbolic of Christ, who will be crucified within three days at this point in Matthew's account*] travelling into a far country [*symbolic of heaven*], who called his own servants [*disciples, Apostles*], and delivered unto them his goods.

15 And unto one he gave five talents [*see Bible Dictionary under "Money"*], to another two, and to another one; to every man according to his several ability [*in other words, each is an individual and is given a stewardship according to personal capacities, talents and abilities*]; and straightway took his journey.

16 Then he that had received the five talents went and traded with the same, and made them other five talents. [*He developed and increased his God-given talents.*]

17 And likewise he that had received two, he also gained other two. [*He developed and increased his talents.*]

18 But he that had received one went and digged in the earth, and hid his lord's money. [*He did not develop and increase his talent.*]

19 After a long time the lord [*symbolic of Christ*] of those servants cometh, and reckoneth with them [*had them account for how they had used that which He gave them; symbolic of Judgment Day*].

20 And so he that had received five talents came and brought other five talents, saying, Lord, thou deliveredst unto me five talents: behold, I have gained beside them five talents more.

21 His lord said unto him, Well done, thou good and faithful servant: thou hast been faithful over a few things, I will make thee ruler over many things [*symbolic of exaltation*]: enter thou into the joy of thy lord.

22 He also that had received two talents came and said, Lord, thou deliveredst unto me two talents: behold, I have gained two other talents beside them.

23 His lord said unto him, Well done, good and faithful servant; thou hast been faithful over a few things, I will make thee ruler over many things [*symbolic of exaltation*]: enter thou into the joy of thy lord.

> Did you notice that the reward for both the servant who had received five talents and the servant who was given two talents, was exactly the same? Note the wording of the rewards in verses 21 and 23. It is comforting that those with fewer talents and abilities, who do their best, will receive the same reward (exaltation) as those who currently have higher abilities.

24 Then he which had received the one talent came and said [*made excuses for his lack of performance*], Lord, I knew thee that thou art an hard man [*that You expect a lot from Your employees*], reaping [*harvesting*] where thou hast not sown [*planted*], and gathering [*harvesting*] where thou hast not strawed [*thrown or scattered seeds*]:

25 And I was afraid, and went and hid thy talent in the earth: lo, there thou hast that is thine.

26 His lord answered and said unto him, Thou wicked and slothful servant, thou knewest that I reap where I sowed not, and gather where I have not strawed [*in other words, you knew that you would someday have to account to Me*]:

27 Thou oughtest therefore to have put my money to the exchangers, and then at my coming I should have received mine own with usury [*interest*].

28 Take therefore the talent from him, and give it unto him which hath ten talents.

29 For unto every one that hath [*symbolizing those who have done the best they can with what they were given*] shall be given, and he shall have abundance [*symbolic of exaltation*]: but from him that hath not [*symbolizing those who have not done their best with what the Lord gave them*] shall be taken away even that which he hath.

30 And cast ye the unprofitable servant [*symbolic of the wicked*] into outer darkness [*see Alma 40:13*]: there shall be weeping and gnashing of teeth [*among other things, symbolic of the fact that the wicked will have to suffer for their own sins since they were unwilling to repent and take advantage of the Atonement, see D&C 19:15–16*].

Background, Culture, and Setting

What type of parable of this? It is a three-point (or three character) parable, though a bit more complex than a typical three-point parable since there are four main characters: The Lord, two faithful servants (they both represent the character of a faithful servant, and so they express one lesson or one point), and an unfaithful servant. The Lord is obviously God. The faithful servants are those who know and act on God's will to increase His kingdom while He is away. The faithful servants do as God would do if He were here. He would grow and increase His kingdom. The contrasting character is the unfaithful servant who hides his talent so that when the Master of the Kingdom returns, no increase has been created by this slothful servant.

What do we learn from this parable about the kingdom of heaven? God will entrust His work to His servants. God trusts us to act as He would act if He were here. God will come at an undisclosed time, and we will all be held to account for how we made use of our time, talents, and resources in the service of the kingdom of heaven. Those who act in fear—who are too afraid to use their agency to act—will discover that their failure to act, unless they repent, will damn them from future action in the eternities.

The Master Teacher

Jesus wanted His people to understand what the kingdom of heaven (otherwise known as the kingdom of God) was like. How do you help people understand something new? Either give them a direct experience or relate the new thing to something they already know. Jesus often gave people direct experiences with what the kingdom of heaven is like. For example, His acts of healing were direct experiences and demonstrations of the nature of His kingdom. For those He didn't heal, He gave them indirect experiences with the kingdom of heaven by telling parables. Remember that "parable" means to lay two things side by side for comparative (or contrastive purposes). By telling a story using characters and characteristics familiar to listeners, Jesus could help them have indirect experience with a new concept or idea by building on what they already knew.

Possible Applications for Learners

One of the false traditions of our modern day is that we are all born with a certain set of fixed talents. We look at those around us who seem to have more success than we, and too many of us conclude that we have not been blessed with the same talents and so why even try. What do we learn from this parable on the kingdom of heaven? No matter the talents you start with, *you* have the capacity and the agency to grow and develop your talents. You are a child of God. That means you can accomplish anything with Him. If you don't currently have a talent that you desire to develop, have no fear. With work, effort, and sacrifice, you can develop your talents further. And as you do, you will feel the Spirit confirm in your heart the words from the Father, "Well done thou good and faithful servant." If you currently believe that your gifts and talents are fixed and static, look to God. No longer slouch in fear as the unfaithful servant in this parable. Instead, be like the faithful servants who faced their fears and concerns about failure, exerted effort, grew, developed, and eventually succeeded at increasing their talents regardless of how many talents they had to begin with.

Helps for Teachers

Are you encouraging your learners to increase their talents? To act in the face of fear and failure? Do you give your learners opportunities to develop their talents?

Do you give learners direct experiences with concepts and principles? Or, if direct experiences are not available, do you create memorable and meaningful indirect experiences to enhance learning, such as using parables, stories, similes, or analogies?

Here are some questions for helping class members get involved in class discussion:

- According to verses 21 and 23, what was the difference in rewards between the servant who started out with five talents and the servant who started out with two? (No difference at all.)
- What can we learn from the fact that both faithful servants gained the same reward?
- What are some possible ways that, if we are not careful, we could be like the servant who hid his talent?
- What phrase(s) in this parable can be symbolic of exaltation? ("I will make thee ruler over many things" in both verse 21 and verse 23.)
- How can this parable, properly understood, encourage members who think they can't really compare favorably with more talented members of the Church?

Parable of the Sheep and the Goats

Matthew 25:31–46

31 When the Son of man shall come in his glory [*the Second Coming*], and all the holy angels with him, then shall he sit upon the throne of his glory [*He will be our King during the Millennium*]:

32 And before him shall be gathered all nations: and he shall separate them one from another, as a shepherd divideth his sheep from the goats:

33 And he shall set the sheep on his right hand, but the goats on the left.

> Here, in this context, sheep symbolize the righteous and goats symbolize the wicked. The right hand, in Jewish symbolism, is the covenant hand. Thus, being on the Lord's right hand symbolizes those who have made and kept covenants.

34 Then shall the King say unto them on his right hand, Come, ye blessed of my Father, inherit the kingdom [*celestial kingdom*] prepared for you from the foundation of the world [*as planned in the premortal council*]:

> In the next verses, the Savior will beautifully detail more ways to be righteous and prepared for the Second Coming, as was the case with the five wise virgins. In other words, He is showing us how to have extra oil for our lamps.

35 For I was an hungred, and ye gave me meat: I was thirsty, and ye gave me drink: I was a stranger, and ye took me in:

36 Naked, and ye clothed me: I was sick, and ye visited me: I was in prison, and ye came unto me.

37 Then shall the righteous answer him, saying, Lord, when saw we thee an hungred, and fed thee? or thirsty, and gave thee drink?

38 When saw we thee a stranger, and took thee in? or naked, and clothed thee?

39 Or when saw we thee sick, or in prison, and came unto thee?

40 And the King [*Christ*] shall answer and say unto them, Verily [*listen carefully, this is the main point*] I say unto you, Inasmuch as ye have done it unto one of the least of these my brethren, ye have done it unto me. [*King Benjamin talked about this kind of service to others in Mosiah 2:17.*]

41 Then shall he say also unto them on the left hand [*in this context, being on the left hand of God symbolizes the wicked*], Depart from me, ye cursed, into everlasting fire [*hell*], prepared for the devil and his angels:

42 For I was an hungred, and ye gave me no meat: I was thirsty, and ye gave me no drink:

43 I was a stranger, and ye took me not in: naked, and ye clothed me not: sick, and in prison, and ye visited me not.

44 Then shall they also answer him, saying, Lord, when saw we thee an hungred, or athirst, or a stranger, or naked, or sick, or in prison, and did not minister unto thee [*take care of your needs*]?

45 Then shall he answer them, saying, Verily [*when He says "verily," it means "listen very carefully because this is the point I am trying to teach you."*] I say unto you, Inasmuch as ye did it not to one of the least of these, ye did it not to me.

46 And these shall go away into everlasting punishment: but the righteous into life eternal [*celestial glory and exaltation*].

BACKGROUND, CULTURE, AND SETTING

Matthew 25:31–46 may contain some of Jesus's most unexpected, revolutionary, and revelatory teachings for His listeners. Jesus taught that the world as they knew it should be turned upside down. The Jews in the times of Jesus lived in a social system that was the opposite of what He taught in this passage. To get ahead, one had to patronize the powerful and pay attention to those who had resources and serve their needs. If you wanted a life of success and luxury, especially if you were among the groveling masses of poor, the only real chance you had was to win the affection of a strong and powerful master or ruler. You had to put yourself under their authority and serve all their needs and whims: to work to feed them, clothe them, provide drink for them, and be with them at all times. It was veritable slavery all in the hope that your patron might allow some of his wealth to dribble down to you.

What does Jesus teach instead? The stunning reversal of the expected social conventions. Don't worry about the powerful, rich, well-placed, and self-important. Don't serve their needs. Rather, find those least likely to give you advantage in this life, those least likely to benefit you. Find those who will require the very most from you, for whom you'll have to give your very all. How? You'll be giving away your food and drink to the hungry, your clothes to the naked, your resources to the destitute, and your time and friendships to the stranger/immigrant and the incarcerated.

In Jesus's day, these people were considered the dregs of society. How could anyone wishing to make their mark in the world, to be a social climber or draw more resources to themselves, ever expect to achieve their wildly aspirational dreams if they squandered their time, talents, and resources on the least socially deserving and the least capable of returning the favor?

Jesus's words to serve those most in need could not have been more revelatory and stunning, and, most important, faith-demanding. Jesus promised that those who gave their lives away serving others would find themselves rewarded beyond imagination—eternal life at the right hand of God. No earthly ruler could offer even a glimmer of hope that would compare with such a supernal promise.

To this day, the basic message of Christianity could be summarized in Jesus's few well-chosen words of exhortation and promise uttered in Matthew 25: "Inasmuch as ye have done it unto one of the least of these my brethren, ye have done it unto me."

The Master Teacher

Jesus upended social conventions to teach the truth. He helped people see that though culture can follow truth or even be related to truth, culture in and of itself is not truth. For example, I may have a culture in my family to create positive experiences together around the gospel. I can live that truth by holding family home evening, and as I follow through with the truth of creating positive family experiences centered on the gospel, it becomes my habit or culture. However, if the culture of family home evening changes, that does not mean the truth of creating positive family experiences centered on the gospel is no longer valid. We are so enmeshed in our cultural circumstances that we often can be distracted. We may miss the truth, because we are distracted by culture. Jesus had no such illusions. The culture He taught was the truth that we are to love God and our neighbors. Jesus did not come to confirm our cultural ideals but to teach truth.

In summary, Jesus, as teacher, focused on the better part.

Possible Applications for Learners

When did you last reflect on the difference between true principles and cultural values? Is your testimony centered on truth or cultural expectations? Grounded learners recognize the underlying truths that animate their actions and are unperturbed if culture changes, such as when the policies for reporting home teaching are changed by God's prophet.

Helps for Teachers

Do you help learners see the truth even though we are all enmeshed in cultural expressions of our understanding of the truth and these cultural expressions or social systems may not be necessary for experiencing the truth?

Of course, as a teacher, it is also not your role to simply call into question practices and policies and cultural expectations. The best teachers are focused on helping learners understand and apply truth in their lives, not to create unnecessary confusion or controversy.

Remember that carefully constructed questions, which require thinking and active participation on the part of the class members, can be a key to encouraging interest and involvement in learning in class. Here are some example questions:

- What was it about what Jesus said in verses 35 and 36 that really got the people wondering? (They hadn't helped Jesus personally in the ways mentioned in these verses.)
- What was the Master's teaching technique in this parable that tipped the people off balance, so to speak, and immediately made them want to find out what He meant?
- What do the right hand of God and the left hand of God mean in this parable? ("Right hand" refers to the righteous, and "left hand" refers to the wicked.)

- In what ways could we be "sheep"? "Goats"?
- In what ways might this parable relate back to the previous Parable of the Talents? (Among possible answers, one would be that the Parable of the Sheep and the Goats would show us some examples of how to increase our talents, like the servants in Matthew 25:20 and 22, by doing good things for "the least of these my brethren." See Matthew 25:40, as described in verses 35 and 36.)
- What kind of thinking on our part could lead us to be included in the people described in verses 42–45?

The Anointing of Jesus

John 12:1–8

1 THEN Jesus six days before the passover [*this would probably be on Saturday, since Passover was on Thursday*] came to Bethany, where Lazarus was [*lived*] which had been dead, whom he raised from the dead.

2 There they made him a supper; and Martha served: but Lazarus was one of them that sat at the table with him.

3 Then took Mary [*the sister of Martha and Lazarus*] a pound of ointment of spikenard, very costly, and anointed [*poured it on*] the feet of Jesus, and wiped his feet with her hair: and the house was filled with the odour of the ointment.

4 Then saith one of his disciples, Judas Iscariot, Simon's son, which should betray him,

5 Why was not this ointment sold for three hundred pence [*about three hundred days' wages*], and given to the poor?

6 This he said, not that he cared for the poor; but because he was a thief, and had the bag [*the money purse*], and bare [*knew*] what was put therein. [*Judas Iscariot was apparently the treasurer of the Twelve.*]

7 Then said Jesus, Let her alone: against the day of my burying hath she kept this. [*She has anointed My body in preparation for My death and burial.*]

> JST John 12:7
>
> 7 Then said Jesus, Let her alone; for she hath preserved this ointment until now, that she might anoint me in token of my burial.
>
> It would appear here that Mary is more sensitive and aware of what is going to happen to Jesus than most of the others are at this time.

8 For the poor always ye have with you; but me ye have not always.

Background, Culture, and Setting

This chapter begins the last week of the Savior's mortal life. It is Passover time in Jerusalem and Jews from many countries have joined the huge crowds in Jerusalem in preparation for the festivities and worship. The Passover meal itself will be held on Thursday. It is eaten in celebration of the passing of the destroying angel over the homes of the children of Israel in Egypt when the firstborn sons of all the families of the Egyptians were slain to persuade Pharaoh to let the Israelite slaves go free.

There is much symbolism associated with the Passover. The children of Israel were held in bondage by the Egyptians, symbolizing the bondage of Satan and the accompanying abuse of agency. After repeated attempts by Moses to get Pharaoh to let the Israelite slaves go free, the children of Israel were instructed by Moses (Exodus 12:5) to select and sacrifice a male lamb (symbolizing Christ), without blemish (symbolizing that Christ was perfect), of the first year (symbolizing that Christ was in the prime of life when He accomplished the Atonement). They were to take hyssop (Exodus 12:22), a sponge-like plant, (associated with Christ on the cross, see John 19:29), dip it in the blood of the lamb and then put the blood on the lintel (top of the door frame) and on the door posts of the front door of their dwelling (Exodus 12:7 and 22). This blood of the lamb provided protection for their household. Incidentally, in the modern day, those who keep the Word of Wisdom have the promise "that the destroying angel shall pass by them, as the children of Israel, and not slay them" (D&C 89:21).

The ensuing death of the firstborn of Pharaoh and all other Egyptian families caused the Israelite slaves to be set free. The death of the firstborn is symbolic of the death of the Savior, the Firstborn of the Father in the spirit world (Colossians 1:15). The Savior is referred to as "the Lamb of God." It is through the blood of the Lamb of God that we are set free from the bondage of sin. During the Passover, at the very time the Jews were celebrating being set free from Egyptian bondage by the blood of lambs, the Lamb (Christ) would present Himself to be sacrificed in order that all of us might be set free from physical death and the bondage of sin.

Bethany is a Hebrew word that means "house of the poor," a fitting name that represents who Jesus devoted His ministry to. In this scene, Mary anoints Jesus with costly spikenard. John begins this chapter by informing us that Mary, Martha's sister, anointed the Savior's feet with very expensive ointment, and Judas Iscariot was irritated because he considered such use of expensive ointment to be a waste of money. Spikenard oil, also called nard, had high value and deep symbolism. It was exceedingly difficult to procure, since it only grows in a limited area of the eastern Himalayan mountains (think of where the land-locked country of Bhutan is today) between elevations of 10,000 to 17,000 feet. For any reader familiar with the Utah Wasatch mountains, made famous by the phrase "within the shadows of the everlasting hills," imagine cultivating spikenard on the top (or higher!) of any of the Wasatch mountain peaks. If you can locate Bhutan or India on a map and then trace your finger, as the crow flies to Israel, imagine how a pound of oil from that delicate plant would ever make its way over to the Middle East, to find itself in one of the poorest towns of Israel, so poor, in fact, its name is "the house of the poor."

How Mary came into possession of a pound of nard, the scriptures never dwell on, and for good reasons. The scriptures were written to testify of Jesus, not to answer questions of trade and commerce. Still, understanding the rarity of this oil and the difficulty in obtaining it gives us a greater appreciation for the learning moments that took place in the home of Lazarus that day over what would be the proper use of the nard. But Jesus closed down that conversation, "Let her alone: against the day of my burying hath she kept this. For the poor always ye have with you; but me ye have not always."

The value of the nard, as identified in this New Testament passage, was three hundred. That would be the estimated equivalent of an entire year's salary for a regular wage earner. The poor people in the household of Lazarus were unlikely to be regular wage earners, and so this sum would have been considerably more valuable to them than to a richer person. As an analogy, $1,000 is far more valuable to someone who has $20,000 to their name than to someone worth $2,000,000.

Nard held deep symbolic value. It was used in the temple rituals as incense. This masked the overwhelming stench that must have been ever-present in the temple (which was a place of animal slaughter and cooking). But more important, the incense symbolized prayers to God (see Revelation 5 footnote 8a).

Nard also was one of the representative oils God identified as a symbol of His covenantal relationship with His people in Song of Solomon 4:13–16.

"Thy plants are an orchard of pomegranates, with pleasant fruits; camphire [*resin*], with spikenard [*nard*] . . . and saffron; calamus [*aromatic reed*] and cinnamon, with all trees of frankincense; myrrh and aloes, with all the chief spices: A fountain of gardens, a well of living waters, and streams from Lebanon. Awake, O north wind; and come, thou south; blow upon my garden, that the spices thereof may flow out."

Speaking of gardens, the original garden, the Garden of Eden, contained the tree of life that had a connection to nard.

Adam and Eve lived blissfully in the paradise of Eden's garden. They could eat freely from all the trees in the garden, except the forbidden tree of knowledge of good and evil. The most important and central tree in the garden was the tree of life, and, according to ancient Jewish writings, its oil flowed like a fountain of youth providing vigor, healing, and eternal life to whoever consumed that precious oil. But the cunning serpent deceived Adam and Eve to eat the forbidden fruit, and they were banished from the garden of paradise. According to ancient Jewish tradition, when Adam lay on his death bed, he begged God for the healing oil from the tree of life so that he could be restored to life. God promised that at the end of time, all His children would have access to this restorative oil. But in the meantime, everyone would have to endure death. As an unexpected consolation, God gave to Adam and all humanity four essential oils and spices that served as replacements for and reminders of the oil from the tree of life. Nard was one of those special oils God provided humanity as a substitute for the oil of life that freely flowed from the tree of life. The other three were crocus (saffron), calamus (reed or resin), and cinnamon.

With this background, we can have an expanded appreciation for the monetary value and symbolic meaning that Jesus was anointed. Of course, we must not forget that *Jesus the Christ* literally means "Jesus the Anointed." Mary helped Jesus fulfill His preordained role to be the one anointed to die and rise again for our salvation.

The Master Teacher

Even as he contemplated His final mortal days with a few limited friends and loved ones—and certainly these were tender moments, for Jesus was aware, to some degree, about the unspeakable suffering He yet had to endure—He was not at all self-consumed. He made time to teach and let people serve and grow in their devotion. Jesus was in tune with the needs of friends and disciples (His learners). He knew why Mary wished to anoint Him. And when others expressed dissatisfaction with the circumstances, He offered a gentle rebuke, or course correction. Similarly, in our classrooms, great teachers are aware of their learners, their needs, and their preferences for how to participate and bring "gifts" to the learning experience. Great teachers, like Jesus, may need to offer gentle course correction when conflict arises because of different expectations among learners.

POSSIBLE APPLICATIONS FOR LEARNERS

Sometimes as learners we are impatient with or critical of teachers or learning experiences. We don't always understand the reasons for the learning invitations extended to us. We may feel, as did Judas, to complain: "Couldn't we have found a more effective, valuable, and efficient use of our time than what is currently going on?" The best learners are humble and willing to learn from *everyone*, even those who may not, on the surface, appear to have anything to teach. The best learners are patient. They are patient with developing teachers, they are patient with the learning experience, and they are patient with themselves recognizing that no plant can grow in a single day.

HELPS FOR TEACHERS

Teachers should remember that teaching is *not* about the teacher. It is all about the learner. Consider this: Learners can learn without teachers. But teachers cannot teach without learners. In the teacher and learner relationship, the one dispensable person is the teacher. Of course, why teachers matter is that they can catalyze learning, making it more accessible, powerful, attainable, effective, efficient, and useful for a learner. Too often, however, teachers find themselves, or place themselves, at the center of attention, of action and agency, even of learning. Some teachers actively crave and seek out the limelight. Not Jesus. He thought of others. He let others act and serve, such as Mary who made a costly choice to demonstrate her love and devotion to Jesus. The best teachers empower learners. The best teachers are windows to God.

Here are some examples of questions that can facilitate learner involvement:

- According to John, what were Judas Iscariot's true motives for protesting Mary's use of costly ointment to anoint Jesus? (Answer: See verse 6.)
- What symbolism can you see in the fact that Mary used very expensive ointment to anoint the Savior, as far as our lives and worship of God are concerned? (Answers might include that symbolically we put our very best efforts into worshipping the Lord, our best efforts into working toward exaltation, and our best efforts and materials into building temples and ministering to others, etc.)
- How do you think Lazarus felt about being at this dinner after having been raised from the dead a few days previously?
- What evidence do you see in these verses, including the JST footnote for verse 7, that Mary understood that Jesus's death was soon to be? (She anointed His body for burial.)

The Last Supper

Matthew 26:26–30

26 And as they were eating, Jesus took bread, and blessed it, and brake it, and gave it to the disciples, and said, Take, eat; this is my body [*this bread is symbolic of the Savior's body; when we partake of the sacrament bread, we are symbolically "internalizing" His gospel and making it a part of us*].

27 And he took the cup [*representing the blood which the Savior shed for our sins*], and gave thanks, and gave it to them, saying, Drink ye all of it [*not "part" of it, rather, "all" of it, symbolizing that we must fully accept Christ and His gospel and apply it in our lives*];

28 For this is my blood of the new testament [*"testament" means "covenant," in other words, the new covenant associated with the full gospel that Christ had restored*], which is shed for many for the remission of sins.

29 But I say unto you, I will not drink henceforth of this fruit of the vine, until that day when I drink it new with you in my Father's kingdom. [*This is the last time the Master will partake of the sacrament with His disciples during His mortal life.*]

30 And when they had sung an hymn, they went out into the mount of Olives [*about a 10–15 minute walk from the city wall of Jerusalem*].

Background, Culture, and Setting

What was the Last Supper and why was it so special? There are many reasons. First, this was the last earthly meal that Jesus had with His disciples before His death and resurrection. Second, Jesus taught beautiful truths that still resonate today. For example, His sacrifice constituted a "new" testament, in other words, a new covenant. Third, Jesus initiated the ritual of the sacrament whereby we partake of the tokens or symbols of His sacrifice (originally bread and wine representing His body and blood) to enter in to the New Testament. Fourth, as a good Jew, Jesus was celebrating the yearly Passover meal to commemorate God saving His people from Egyptian bondage at the expense of sacrificed lambs, or the first born in Egypt. What thoughts must have filled Jesus's mind as He partook of the sacrificial meat of the Passover lamb knowing that it represented His upcoming final and last sacrifice whereby the Lamb of God would be sacrificed once and for all to bring life to the relationship between God and His people?

Fifth, and perhaps often overlooked, even though it may be the most significant aspect of Jesus's last meal, Jesus identified Himself as the New Testament. Most of us are aware that one of the basic meanings of the word *testament* is "witness." For example, the Book of Mormon received a subtitle some decades ago, "Another Testament of Jesus Christ," to complement the existing Old Testament and New Testament. The Book of

Mormon subtitle means "another witness of Jesus Christ" to complement the witnesses that the Old Testament and the New Testament bear of Jesus Christ.

The word *testament* is the Latin translation of the ancient Hebrew word for "covenant." Jerome, the fourth-century priest who translated the Old and New Testament into Latin, decided that the Latin word *testament* (such as in "last will and testament") best represented the Hebrew word for "covenant." However, what we miss by using the word testament is the understanding that covenants are the animating force of God's plan of happiness. The scriptures are written to convey God's covenant with His people and the consequences of living or ignoring that covenant.

If "testament" is better translated as "covenant," what is the original old covenant as found in the Old Testament? That old covenant was the Mosaic law whereby God's people employed animal sacrifices (or other sacrifices) to access the atoning power of God's love so they could be in a close covenantal relationship with Him. God entered into a covenant with His people at Sinai because He wanted to be their God and He wanted them to be His people. The covenant established the terms and obligations for both parties. The ritually sacrificed animal enlivened the covenant and symbolically brought the force of the covenant to life. Without the animal sacrifice, the covenant was moot. And without the covenant, the people could not be in a close relationship to God. They would be barred from His presence.

If the old covenant was delivered to the Israelites at Mount Sinai at the time of Moses, and mediated through the sacrifices that endured for centuries afterward, then what is the New Testament, that is, what is the new covenant?

Jesus answered that during the Last Supper. He is the New Covenant.

The Master Teacher

Jesus is the sacrificial lamb that opens the door to relationship with God and atones and heals the breach that exists between God and His children. No longer are animal sacrifices and their attendant rituals required to maintain relationship with God. Instead, God is with Jesus, a relationship that will never be broken. We are invited into that relationship through the grace of Jesus Christ. If we are one with Jesus, we are then one with God. What is expected of us? To regularly witness of the new covenant by consuming Jesus, or symbolically participating in His broken flesh and blood.

Possible Applications for Learners

Jesus is the center of all that we should be doing. How is Jesus at the foundation of your learning? How do you remember Jesus in all you do, as you've promise to do at the sacrament table each week? How do you feel God's power and influence in your life, as promised at the sacrament table each week, guiding and directing you?

Helps for Teachers

Are you helping your learners draw nearer to Jesus? Are you helping them see how all truth points to Jesus? Are you helping them remember Him as we all covenant to do each week when we partake of the new covenant?

Examples of questions that can promote effective class discussion:

- What lessons or messages to us could you teach from the phrase "Drink ye all of it" in verse 27? (According to footnote 27b, everyone was invited to take advantage of the Savior's Atonement.)
- What does "the new testament" mean in verse 28? (See commentary on opposite page.)
- In verse 28, what possible reasons can you think of as to why Jesus used the word "many" rather than "all"? (Answers could include the fact that forgiveness of sin depends on if we repent. See 2 Nephi 9:21–24.)

The Promise to Send the Comforter

John 16:5–15

5 But now I go my way to him that sent me [*to the Father*]; and none of you asketh me, Whither goest thou?

6 But because I have said these things unto you, sorrow hath filled your heart.

7 Nevertheless I tell you the truth; It is expedient for you that I go away: for if I go not away, the Comforter [*the Holy Ghost*] will not come unto you; but if I depart, I will send him unto you.

8 And when he is come, he will reprove [*convict*] the world of sin, and of righteousness, and of judgment: [*in effect, after the full gift and power of the Holy Ghost has come upon you, it will inspire and direct you and bear witness through you such that your teachings and deeds will stand as a witness against the wicked of the world for rejecting righteousness and refusing to believe that the day of judgment will come.*]

9 Of sin, because they believe not on me; [*They will be accountable, convicted, of their sins because the Holy Ghost will bear witness to them as you preach.*]

10 Of righteousness [*your teaching of Me and My gospel*], because I go to my Father, and ye see me no more; [*They will be held accountable for your testimonies and teachings, because I am no longer here to teach them.*]

JST John 16:10

10 Of righteousness, because I go to my Father, and they see me no more;

11 Of judgment, because the prince of this world [*Satan, see John 12 footnote 31a*] is judged. [*They will reject the witness of the Holy Ghost which will accompany your testimonies and will thus be judged for their sins, like Satan, whom they choose to follow, is judged for his sins.*]

Apostle Bruce R. McConkie suggested some possibilities for interpreting verses 9–11, above. He said,

"These are difficult verses which have come to us in such a condensed and abridged form as to make interpretation difficult. The seeming meaning is: 'When you receive the companionship of the Spirit, so that you speak forth what he reveals to you, then your teachings will convict the world of sin, and of righteousness, and of judgment. The world will be convicted of sin for rejecting me, for not believing your Spirit-inspired testimony that I am the Son of God through whom salvation comes. They will be convicted for rejecting your testimony of my righteousness—for supposing I am a blasphemer, a deceiver, and an imposter—when in fact I

> have gone to my Father, a thing I could not do unless my works were true and righteous altogether. They will be convicted of false judgment for rejecting your testimony against the religions of the day, and for choosing instead to follow Satan, the prince of this world, who himself, with all his religious philosophies, will be judged and found wanting'" (McConkie, *Doctrinal New Testament Commentary, Vol. 1*, page 754).

12 I have yet many things to say unto you, but ye cannot bear them now [*you are not ready for them now*].

13 Howbeit [*however*] when he [*the Holy Ghost*], the Spirit of truth, is come [*when the gift of the Holy Ghost has come upon you in full power*], he will guide you into all truth: for he shall not speak of himself; but whatsoever he shall hear [*from Heavenly Father and Jesus*], that shall he speak: and he will shew [*show*] you things to come.

14 He shall glorify me [*bear witness of Christ*]: for he shall receive of mine [*He gets His instructions from Me and My Father; see verse 15*], and shall shew it unto you.

15 All things that the Father hath are mine: therefore said I, that he shall take of mine, and shall shew it unto you.

Background, Culture, and Setting

The pattern or thematic thrust of Jesus's final words in mortality is repeated in the final words of the Book of Mormon. Just as Jesus must leave His disciples but, in His leaving, they then receive the gift of the Holy Ghost, so too, in the Book of Mormon, Moroni must leave his readers. In so doing, Moroni exhorts us to invite the Spirit into our lives. Just as Jesus taught that the Spirit can "guide you into all truth" (John 16:13), similarly Moroni testifies that "by the power of the Holy Ghost ye may know the truth of all things" (Moroni 10:5).

The Master Teacher

Jesus loved His disciples and us too much to be here with us at all times, to give us every last insight, advice, or inspiration that we could pine for. Jesus knew that no one who wished to follow Him could ever become like God the Father unless they were left to choose for themselves after being taught the truth. "It must needs be that the devil should tempt the children of men, or they could not be agents unto themselves; for if they never should have bitter they could not know the sweet" (D&C 29:39). And "they taste the bitter, that they may know to prize the good" (Moses 6:55).

Possible Applications for Learners

Learners should be careful to not become too dependent upon a teacher. Sure, an engaging, passionate teacher can make learning feel like a walk in the park. Who among us wouldn't rather have the truth fed directly to us by a highly competent and capable teacher? Who among us really wants to endure the difficult effort required to learn for ourselves? Fallen human nature would rather take the easy road. And if we don't watch ourselves, we may become very comfortable with learning from the best teachers only to discover that when they are gone, we have not developed the skills, attributes, knowledge, behaviors, and attitudes that will sustain us as independent self-directed learners.

Helps for Teachers

Teachers should make sure to get out of the way of student learning as needed. Nothing is more detrimental to learning and growth than when a teacher makes learning too trivial, too easy, or, most problematic, does not allow learners to try for themselves. Some teachers are so controlling, so worried about their learners failing that they don't allow their learners to fail and thereby learn. If we remember, there was a war waged in heaven over our right to experience failure. On one side of the debate was Jesus advocating before the Father that He would sacrifice Himself so that we could all learn to be like God. On the other side, Lucifer was claiming that he would not allow anyone to fail. He would remove our agency so that failure was not an option. This truth is ironically simple: without failure we are damned. Learning requires failure. No one can attain perfection without practice. Practice requires failure. Failure separates us from God. *And the Atonement pays the price for all failure.* Therefore, we should rejoice that the Atonement empowers our practice as we practice becoming more like God.

Teachers should not get in the way of the Spirit, or the Comforter, coming to the learners. Notice how Jesus had to leave so that His disciples could receive the Spirit. He wanted the disciples to learn to act for themselves, to depend on their own wisdom *combined* with the inspiration that comes through the Spirit. Good teachers follow the example of Jesus and get out of the way, so to speak, of student learning.

Consider these questions for promoting class member involvement:

- Why, according to verse 7, did the Savior have to leave?
- What are some reasons you can think of as to why the Comforter wouldn't function fully while Jesus was still there? (Among possible answers is the fact that while Jesus was still with them, they would not feel the need to rely on and listen to the Holy Ghost.)
- According to these verses, what are some of the great blessings that come to us through the Holy Ghost?
- What experiences have you had when you knew the Holy Ghost was helping you?
- What do you think it would be like if you no longer had the Comforter?

Gethsemane

Luke 22:39–46

39 And he came out, and went, as he was wont [*as was His custom*], to the mount of Olives; and his disciples also followed him.

40 And when he was at the place [*the Garden of Gethsemane; see Matthew 26:36*], he said unto them, Pray that ye enter not into temptation.

41 And he was withdrawn from them about a stone's cast, and kneeled down, and prayed,

42 Saying, Father, if thou be willing, remove this cup from me: nevertheless not my will, but thine, be done.

43 And there appeared an angel unto him from heaven, strengthening him. [*Apostle Bruce R. McConkie suggested that this angel might be Michael (Adam); see April 1985 General Conference*].

44 And being in an agony he prayed more earnestly: and his sweat was as it were great drops of blood falling down to the ground.

> JST Luke 22:44
>
> 44 And being in an agony, he prayed more earnestly; and he sweat as it were great drops of blood falling down to the ground.
>
> Some Christians wonder if Jesus actually did sweat drops of blood or if it was figurative because of the wording in Luke. Mosiah 3:7 and D&C 19:18 clear up any doubt. He did bleed from every pore.

45 And when he rose up from prayer, and was come to [*returned to*] his disciples, he found them sleeping for sorrow [*exhausted by their worrying about Jesus and His safety*],

> JST Luke 22:45
>
> 45 And when he rose up from prayer, and was come to his disciples, he found them sleeping; for they were filled with sorrow;

46 And said unto them, Why sleep ye? rise and pray, lest ye enter into temptation.

Background, Culture, and Setting

The Garden of Gethsemane was so named because in Hebrew the word *Gethsemane* means "oil press." The garden was full of olive trees. As the olives were harvested, they were processed immediately on site into precious olive oil. Likely, there was a cave where the olives were crushed and pressed. In a cave, the temperature could be controlled year-round, preserving the harvest.

Olives, olive trees, and olive oil are some of the most significant symbols for Jesus and His Atonement. The Jews put olives into bags made of mesh fabric and placed them in a press to squeeze olive oil out of them. The first pressings yielded pure olive oil, which was prized for many uses, including healing and giving light in lanterns. In fact, we consecrate it and use it to administer to the sick. The last pressing of the olives, under the tremendous pressure of additional weights added to the press, yielded a bitter, red liquid which can remind us of the "bitter cup" which the Savior partook of. Symbolically, the Savior is going into the "oil press" (Gethsemane) to submit to the "pressure" of all our sins which will "squeeze" His blood out in order that we might have the healing "oil" of the Atonement to heal us from our sins.

If Jesus went into the cave in the Garden of Gethsemane, then He symbolically descended below all things. Moreover, our Fall occurred in a garden (that of Eden), our salvation was bought in a garden (that of Gethsemane) and thereby, according to our faithfulness, we are invited into the garden of paradise (the celestial kingdom of God).

Olive trees are evergreen trees. That is, they are green all year round. They never shed their leaves in the death of autumn. Olive trees can grow for hundreds if not thousands of years. If branches die, new shoots will grow out of the trunk. If the trunk dies, the roots will start new daughter trees. One can take a branch of a healthy olive tree, and under the right conditions, plant it and it will grow. Olives were used as food to sustain human life. Olive oil was used for cooking, adding flavor to foods, light, and medicinal purposes.

Olive oil was created by first crushing the olives and then applying extreme pressure to extract the oil. According to some accounts, the oil seeps out of the pores of the olives. Whatever the case for how the oil leaves the olive, the deeper the pressure, the purer the olive oil. Finally, and most strikingly, olive oil, when freshly pressed, can emerge blood red. As it is exposed to air, it eventually takes on its more familiar golden hue. Why do we use olive oil in significant rituals and healing ordinances? One reason is that it is a reminder that we must apply the atoning blood of Jesus for all healing and all salvation. Truly, olive oil is one of the most beautiful symbols of Jesus's atoning blood.

Jesus offers that salvation to all of us, because He willingly suffered and descended below all things: "And he shall go forth, suffering pains and afflictions and temptations of every kind; and this that the word might be fulfilled which saith he will take upon him the pains and the sicknesses of his people. And he will take upon him death, that he may loose the bands of death which bind his people; and he will take upon him their infirmities, that his bowels may be filled with mercy, according to the flesh, that he may know according to the flesh how to succor his people according to their infirmities" (Alma 7:11–12, emphasis added).

The word *succor* is significant, especially when paired with the word *suffer*. We all suffer. We all know the suffocating, drowning feeling of suffering. Will I survive? Will I endure to the end? These are achingly very real questions we may ask when we suffer. The word *suffer* comes from two Latin words: *sub* "under" and *ferre* (English: *ferry*) "to carry." The word *ferre* shows up in such words as Christopher, "bearer of Christ or one who carries Christ's name," and Lucifer, "bearer of light or one who carries light." The word *suffer* literally means "to be carried under" as though we are drowning in difficulty and see no way out.

That is why the word *succor* is so significant, especially as used by Alma to describe the saving Atonement of Jesus Christ. *Succor* also comes from two Latin words: *sub* "under" and *currere* (English: *course*) "to run." *Succor* literally means "to run underneath." Therefore, no matter how deep we've been pulled into our suffering, Jesus has descended below *all* things. He has descended further than us so that He might know how to succor us. Jesus *runs underneath us* to support us no matter how deep our suffering has pulled us down. Jesus is *always* there. The Atonement is infinite and eternal. We need never be alone in our suffering. Jesus came for us.

"And [Jesus] cometh into the world that he may save all men if they will hearken unto his voice; for behold, he suffereth the pains of all men, yea, the pains of every living creature, both men, women, and children, who belong to the family of Adam. And he suffereth this that the resurrection might pass upon all men, that all might stand before him at the great and judgment day. And he commandeth all men that they must repent, and be baptized in his name, having perfect faith in the Holy One of Israel, or they cannot be saved in the kingdom of God" (2 Nephi 9:21–23).

The Master Teacher

Perhaps this, the most poignant moment in all of scripture, is also the most telling and instructive. The Greatest Teacher of All was great because He served. He was willing to descend below all things. He was willing to suffer with and for us. He did not place Himself above us. He did not demand our service to Him. Rather, He enacted the greatest act of service of all time—all for us.

Possible Applications for Learners

Because Jesus was willing to suffer all things so that we might learn, the best learners embrace the Atonement and are willing to exert significant effort to learn *and they are willing to fail.* The best learners recognize that if they aren't learning, they are not participating in the Atonement. Remember, Jesus suffered all these things that we might find joy through learning. We should embrace our learning as thoroughly, deeply, and fully as Jesus embraced His suffering on our behalf.

Helps for Teachers

Great teachers serve their learners and are willing to suffer and endure difficulty and hardship on behalf of their learners. They are willing to suffer with their learners as the learners struggle and work to grow and develop. The best teachers are those who lead by example, who go with the troops, so to speak, at the head of the army instead of sitting back comfortably in the control and command center. What can you do as a teacher to demonstrate that you are willing to make sacrifices to learn? How can you model for your learners what a life-long learner is really like?

Healing the High Priest's Servant's Ear

Luke 22:49–51

49 When they which were about him [*Jesus's Apostles*] saw what would follow [*what was about to happen*], they said unto him, Lord, shall we smite with the sword?

50 And one of them [*Peter*] smote the servant of the high priest, and cut off his right ear.

51 And Jesus answered and said, Suffer ye thus far [*let them arrest Me*]. And he touched his ear [*the servant's ear*], and healed him.

John 18:10–11

10 Then Simon Peter having a sword drew it, and smote the high priest's servant, and cut off his right ear. The servant's name was Malchus. [*Malchus was a relative of the high priest. See John 18:26.*]

11 Then said Jesus unto Peter, Put up thy sword into the sheath: the cup which my Father hath given me, shall I not drink it? [*Should I not go ahead with the Atonement?*]

Background, Culture, and Setting

We all have the benefit of hindsight. We know that Jesus is the Lamb of God who went willingly and peacefully to His sacrifice. His disciples, at the time all these events happened, had no such understanding. They were regularly confused by what was happening, and they responded from the context of their misunderstanding. Peter, so passionate to do what was right, so desirous to follow, defend, and protect His Master, impetuously struck Malchus, the servant of the High priest, cutting off his right ear. Unexpectedly, Jesus reached out to heal the wound of one of His would-be captors.

The Master Teacher

Jesus always had others' needs in mind. In His moment of pending suffering and stress, Jesus did not lash out at others, did not turn and become self-focused. Instead, He healed. Great teachers contribute to the healing of others.

Jesus also taught His disciples to accept what was happening to Him, to let the Father's plan play out. And He taught how to care for the individual, even a supposed enemy. He taught that it is better to heal than to hurt, it is better to love than to hate. He had His soul focused on higher purposes and would not allow Himself to be distracted by the chaos around Him.

POSSIBLE APPLICATIONS FOR LEARNERS

If you can accept this analogy, as learners we are like the disciples of Jesus, and as teachers we are in the place of Jesus teaching us truth. Good learners help the teacher play their role well. Sometimes as learners, we don't understand the purposes of the lesson or why the teachers are teaching what they are. Sometimes we may feel to resist the instruction or to disrupt the learning experience. Sometimes we may feel justified to insert ourselves forcefully into a situation to change the direction of the lesson. As learners we should take care to understand the whole context instead of jumping in to take charge of the teaching situation. We do not want to interrupt what may be a very purposeful learning design, because, like Peter, we are both impetuous and unaware of the larger context.

HELPS FOR TEACHERS

Sometimes teachers have to deal with significant distractions or detractors. Remember Jesus. Loving, understanding, and helping to heal those around you can go a long way to diminishing the distractions. Staying focused on topic and on your purposes, unless otherwise prompted by the Spirit, can help keep you and the class from being derailed by inappropriate distractions. In some cases, a loving and candid private conversation before or after class with the individual or individuals that have distracted the learning environment can contribute to mutual understanding and appreciation that diminishes the likelihood of distractions.

Samples of questions that can further class discussion:

- Knowing that the high priest was a bitter enemy of Jesus and wanted Him killed, what can you teach based on the fact that the Savior healed the high priest's servant's ear after Peter cut it off?
- What does the phrase, "cup which my Father hath given me," in John 18:11, mean? (Answers should include the mission to carry out the Atonement.)
- What do Peter's actions here tell you about his courage and personality?
- What does the healing of the servant's ear tell you about the Savior?
- If there were additional verses here, telling about the servant's reaction to being healed, what would you want them to say?

Carrying the Cross

Matthew 27:31–32

31 And after that they [*the Roman Soldiers*] had mocked him, they took the robe off from
him, and put his own raiment on him, and led him away to crucify him.
32 And as they came out, they found a man of Cyrene [*a city in northern Africa*], Simon
by name: him they compelled to bear his cross. [*Jesus was too weak to carry His cross,
because of His suffering in the Garden of Gethsemane as well as the scourging.*]

Background, Culture, and Setting

Who is Simon? Where is Cyrene? And why is Simon in Jerusalem?

Simon was a Jew from the Roman province of Cyrenaica, where modern-day Libya is located on the Mediterranean coasts of North Africa. If one could get into a private jet and fly directly from Cyrene to Jerusalem, it would take a little less than two hours to cross the eight hundred miles distance between the two cities. Of course, Simon of Cyrene did not have access to a jet. He would have most likely traveled by boat (a journey of several weeks), hugging the coasts of the Mediterranean Sea as he headed east and then north. He likely ported in either Yafo (modern day Tel-Aviv), one of the most ancient ports on the Israelite coast, or a little further north at the shiny, new, cosmopolitan, provincial capital port city of Caesarea Maritima built by Herod the Great to patronize Caesar Augustus. Simon then would have walked the 40+ miles up into the Judean Hills, from an elevation at sea level to more than 2500 feet above sea level, to reach Jerusalem. A motivated hiker probably could make this hike in two days. But a typical ancient traveler, needing to travel in a group for safety and needing to stop for food, sleep, and other necessities would probably take three to five days to go from the coast to Jerusalem.

The Jews gathered several times a year for sacred religious celebrations. Passover may have been the most attended of the three major religious holidays (Feast of Passover, Feast of Pentecost, and the combined Feast of Tabernacles and Day of Atonement). Jews from around the world would make the trek back to their spiritual homeland. It was a journey that required considerable investment of time, money, and courage. Imagine if as a good Mormon you decided to be in attendance at general conference once a year, but it required a minimum of three weeks travel time one way to arrive, a week of religious festivities, and then three weeks to return home. Would you do it? Would your boss give you seven weeks off three times a year? Then imagine during the many weeks of travel time that you are under constant threat of robbers by land and death by shipwreck at sea. Are you still interested in attending general conference in person? Or might you opt to kick off your shoes, sink into your plush leather couch, and watch the general conference proceedings from the comfort of your own home? Listening to your kids fight over where to sit on the couch is infinitely more desirable than finding yourself in a raging Mediterranean storm in the middle of the night, clinging to what little remains of your once intrepid boat with the very real prospect of death by drowning staring you in the face.

So, Simon was a dedicated, deeply religious, and very courageous Jew to have come to Jerusalem to worship. He had come to Jerusalem to celebrate with other Jews from around the world God's salvation of Israel from Egyptian bondage. Simon would have brought money so he could purchase a lamb to slaughter in honorific and remembering sacrifice of God's saving deeds. The left-over remains of that sacrifice he would have consumed in a celebratory Passover meal with any friends and family that were with him in the city. Despite the personal discomfort of the overcrowding that was Jerusalem during times of celebration, Simon would have felt the joy of religious fervor, stirred by the memory of national salvation, and likely, also, buoyed by the knowledge of God's direct involvement in His life to bring personal blessings and salvation.

So, Simon was the "every man" Jew. He was an otherwise unknown and faceless worshipper, like the countless millions before and after him. Imagine his surprise. He was among the crush of people moving from one place to another in the narrow streets of Jerusalem, which was bursting with pilgrims, merchants hawking their wares, and soldiers bristling with weapons, barking orders in a language that may not be fully understood by everyone because of Jerusalem becoming a "Babel" for a short time, given the linguistic diversity that descended on it in the form of religious pilgrims from everywhere during these holidays. There is Simon, going about his religious duties to find a lamb to present to God in grateful sacrifice to acknowledge the Atonement, or covering, that protected him from the destroying angel. And without warning, he is thrust into the most momentous drama to unfold in human history. "You, dirty Jew! Yes, you!" Perhaps that is how the hated and overbearing Roman soldier got Simon's attention. Simon may have asked, "Me? Or are you talking to any one of the hundreds of other Jews with me here on this small, people-packed street?" "Yes, you! Take this cross and carry it." Who would refuse? The soldiers might be liable to crucify someone not willing to follow their orders. Unexpectedly, Simon came to carry the cross of the very Lamb of God who would hold back the destroying angel. This was the very purpose of the Passover celebration. Simon had come hundreds of miles and had endured untold ordeals to worship God with a lamb for God, and now, unexpectedly, he was part of the great drama, the great act, the culminating sacrifice of *the* Lamb of God that would permanently liberate everyone who looked to Jesus as their salvation.

Simon stands in our place as the "every man." We have all helped Jesus to His crucifixion. We all have contributed to the need for Jesus to be sacrificed. And simultaneously, we have all felt, to the smallest degree, comparatively, the burden of the cross of Jesus as He liberated us from our own crosses.

THE MASTER TEACHER

Though the ultimate sacrifice was Jesus's alone to make, He allowed, or empowered others to help Him. Only Jesus could sacrifice Himself for all of humanity and God's creation. But Jesus does not do all things at all times and in all places. He empowers His people to act on His behalf. And these actions are a blessing both to the One who is served (Jesus) and to the one who is serving (us). Teachers do not need to carry the entire load of learning for their learners. In fact, the more that instructors provide space and opportunity for learners to act for themselves, the more the learners can access the Atonement for growth.

POSSIBLE APPLICATIONS FOR LEARNERS

Obviously, our learning experiences will likely not be as dramatic and unexpected as Simon's. Still, as learners, we should be thoughtful about how we can help the teachers bear their cross of teaching. Do we show up prepared to learn? Are we appropriately participatory? Do we silently pray that we, the teacher, and others will have God's spirit to guide the learning and bring inspiration?

HELPS FOR TEACHERS

Teachers should not shy away from inviting others to share in the teaching experience. If the teacher is doing everything, then less learning is taking place. Invite others to share your cross. That does not mean that you abdicate your responsibilities to teach. Nor does it mean that you let the learners take over the learning experience. But thoughtfully preparing in advance the participation of learners will help them have God empower their shoulders to bear burdens, thereby growing by means of the experience.

Here are some samples of questions that may motivate class participation:

- What efforts did it probably take for Simon of Cyrene (a city in Northern Africa) to be in Jerusalem for Passover?
- What had the Savior already been through by the time He was compelled to carry His own cross (as was customary)?

The Crucifixion

Mark 15:22–39

22 And they bring [*brought*] him unto the place Golgotha, which is, being interpreted, The place of a skull.

23 And they gave him to drink wine mingled with myrrh: but he received it not.

> This mixture of wine and myrrh was designed to drug the victim of crucifixion to lessen the pain somewhat. See Talmage, *Jesus the Christ*, pages 654–55.

24 And when they had crucified him [*hung him on the cross*], they parted his garments, casting lots upon them, what every man should take [*gambling to see who got what item of clothing*].

25 And it was the third hour [*about 9 a.m.*], and they crucified him.

26 And the superscription of his accusation was written over [*above Him on the cross*], THE KING OF THE JEWS.

> The JST informs us that some of the Jewish chief priests were frustrated about the sign above the Savior's head, as mentioned in verse 26, above. They wanted Pilate to modify it to read that Jesus "claimed" to be the king of the Jews.
>
> JST Mark 15:29–31
>
> 29 And Pilate wrote his accusation and put it upon the cross, THE KING OF THE JEWS.
>
> 30 There were certain of the chief priests who stood by, that said unto Pilate, Write, that he said, I am the King of the Jews.
>
> 31 But Pilate said unto them, What I have written, I have written.

27 And with him they crucify two thieves; the one on his right hand, and the other on his left.

28 And the scripture was fulfilled [*Isaiah 53:12*], which saith, And he was numbered with the transgressors [*killed with criminals*].

29 And they that passed by railed on him [*shouted, mocked him*], wagging [*shaking*] their heads, and saying, Ah, thou that destroyest the temple, and buildest it in three days,

> These people obviously misunderstood what Jesus said regarding the temple. What He said is in John 2:19–21. He said that if they destroyed His body (the "temple of his body"), He would raise it up in three days (be resurrected in three days). By the time Jesus is on the cross, His statement has been misquoted and spread so that the

mockers claim that He said He would destroy their massive temple in Jerusalem and rebuild it in three days.

30 Save thyself, and come down from the cross.

31 Likewise also the chief priests mocking said among themselves with the scribes, He saved others; himself he cannot save.

32 Let Christ the King of Israel descend now from the cross, that we may see and believe. And they that were crucified with him reviled him [*mocked him*].

One of the thieves seems to have softened his attitude a bit later. The Savior said to him "Today shalt thou be with me in paradise."

33 And when the sixth hour [*about noon*] was come, there was darkness over the whole land until the ninth hour [*about 3 p.m.*].

34 And at the ninth hour [*about three in the afternoon*] Jesus cried with a loud voice, saying, Eloi, Eloi, lama sabachthani? which is, being interpreted, My God, my God, why hast thou forsaken me?

This had to have been a most difficult time for Jesus. Apparently, as part of the Atonement, Jesus had to experience what sinners do when they sin so much that the Spirit leaves them. At this point on the cross, we understand that all available help from the Father withdrew in order that Jesus might experience all things, including the withdrawal of the Spirit which sinners experience.

35 And some of them that stood by, when they heard it, said, Behold, he calleth Elias [*Elijah*].

36 And one ran and filled a spunge full of vinegar, and put it on a reed, and gave him to drink, saying, Let alone; let us see whether Elias will come to take him down.

37 And Jesus cried with a loud voice, and gave up the ghost [*left his body, died*].

38 And the veil of the temple was rent in twain from the top to the bottom.

39 And when the centurion [*Roman soldier*], which stood over against him [*across from Jesus*], saw that he so cried out [*had so much strength when he cried out*], and gave up the ghost, he said, Truly this man was the Son of God.

It was common for victims of crucifixion to live two or three days before dying. The soldier was startled because he was experienced in crucifying people, and it appeared to him that Jesus, who was still relatively strong, and after only six hours on the cross, had decided to leave His body and did so. That is exactly what happened, and the Roman soldier apparently received a witness of Christ at that moment.

Background, Culture, and Setting

There is so much beauty, anguish, and truth in this passage on the crucifixion of Jesus. Our purpose in this book is to not provide every possible insight or explain all things about the death of Jesus. Even the Gospel of John says, "And there are also many other things which Jesus did, the which, if they should be written every one, I suppose that even the world itself could not contain the books that should be written" (John 21:25). So, we'll limit ourselves to a few key ideas and highlights.

Though we do not have exact certainty of where in the vicinity of Jerusalem Jesus was crucified (although by long tradition and archaeological evidence it is likely at the site of the Church of the Holy Sepulcher), anciently it was called *Golgotha* (Aramaic) or *Calvary* (Latin), which both mean "the skull" or the place of execution. The soldiers would have placed Jesus on the cross on the major road leading out of the city so that hundreds, if not thousands of people arriving or leaving Jerusalem would see Him. Typical artwork about the crucifixion does not properly display the size of the cross. Artists often depict the cross as if it was a twenty-foot-tall beam with Jesus hanging near the top. Crucifixion was far more visceral and personal. Jesus, as was typical for crucifixions of that time, would have been nailed to the cross so that He was perhaps 6–12 inches above the ground. He would be, essentially, at eye level. Any passerby could nearly look straight into the eyes of the condemned, making it easy to verbally and physically assault the unfortunate soul attached to the cross. That is why people were able to get right in His face as He miserably hung suffering on the cross. "If you are the Christ, come down from this cross and save yourself!" And, "If you can't save yourself, how will you save anyone else?"

The Gospel writers tell us that Jesus was crucified between two thieves. The underlying Greek word for thieves could be better translated as "nationalistic revolutionary insurrectionists." The Roman centurion was one of the few who finally realized the truth of Jesus when he declared, "Truly this man was the Son of God." What did nearly everyone else think of Jesus? The fact that He was crucified between two nationalistic revolutionary insurrectionists meant that most people understood Jesus to be nothing more than a dangerous man of the same persuasion as those dying by His side.

Some have wondered why He was given vinegar. The Gospel record does not explicitly tell us the reason, but we could venture a possible connection with a symbol of death. In the ancient Biblical world, bitter vinegar was a symbol of death.

Another symbol that appears in the crucifixion story is the torn temple veil. Throughout Israelite history, only the high priest was allowed to enter the innermost sanctum of the temple, or "holy of holies," symbolic of heaven. He did so wearing the emblems of the twelve tribes of Israel, thereby representatively bringing everyone into the sacred temple with him. However, in practical reality, only the high priest was so honored to enter into this sacred place where, symbolically, God's presence resided. At the death of Jesus, the temple veil was torn in half, symbolizing that Jesus had opened the path to heaven for *everyone*.

The Master Teacher

Jesus's eternal sacrifice is the epitome of His role as a teacher. His Atonement ultimately empowers all of us to grow and develop, to learn to be like God. Without His Atonement, there would be no learning, no achieving, no growth, no possibilities, and no promise of eternal inheritance and increase with God. The Atonement is the foundation.

POSSIBLE APPLICATIONS FOR LEARNERS

What does the sacrifice of Jesus Christ mean to you personally? How has His sacrifice specifically blessed you? Empowered you? Changed you?

HELPS FOR TEACHERS

How can you help learners to embrace the love of Jesus more fully? How can you help learners see that all we do should be centered on Jesus? How can you help learners feel the joy of gratitude in recognizing our salvation in Jesus? How can you help learners remember that Jesus's sacrifice enlivens everything good we care about? How can you help learners act on the truth that because of Jesus's sacrifice, we can learn to be like Him and with Him?

Questions that can help increase class member involvement in the lesson:

- Why do you think Jesus refused the pain deadener offered Him in verse 23? (Answers could include that He had to go through all of the pain and suffering associated with His atoning sacrifice.)
- About how long was Jesus on the cross? (Using verse 25 together with verse 34, we see that it was about six hours.)
- Why was the Roman soldier, mentioned in verse 39, so startled? (Because it looked as if Jesus had left His body intentionally, which He did.)
- What evidence do you see in these verses that Jesus was not killed, rather, He left His body when this part of the Atonement was completed? (Verses 37 and 39 indicate that He was still relatively strong at that point and intentionally left His body when He had completed that part of His Atonement. See John 10:18.)
- Was the Savior's Atonement finished at the time He left His body? Explain. (No, He still had to be resurrected to finish His Atonement.)

THE EMPTY TOMB

LUKE 24:1–12

Luke gives us many details that are not included in the accounts of Matthew and Mark. It is Sunday morning, and one of the most glorious days on earth ever recorded.

1 Now upon the first day of the week [*Sunday*], very early in the morning, they [*the women named in verse 10, below*] came unto the sepulchre [*tomb*], bringing the spices which they had prepared, and certain others with them.

2 And they found the stone rolled away from the sepulchre.

3 And they entered in, and found not the body of the Lord Jesus.

4 And it came to pass, as they were much perplexed thereabout [*they were very concerned about this*], behold, two men [*angels*] stood by them in shining garments:

5 And as they [*the women*] were afraid, and bowed down their faces to the earth, they [*the angels*] said unto them, Why seek ye the living among the dead?

> JST Luke 24:2–4
>
> 2 And they found the stone rolled away from the sepulcher, and two angels standing by it in shining garments.
>
> 3 And they entered into the sepulcher, and not finding the body of the Lord Jesus, they were much perplexed thereabout;
>
> 4 And were affrighted, and bowed down their faces to the earth. But behold the angels said unto them, Why seek ye the living among the dead?
>
> Watch now as the two angels gently remind these faithful women about the Savior's prophecies of His crucifixion and resurrection. Imagine the look on these women's faces as they remembered and realization dawned that the Master was alive!

6 He is not here, but is risen: remember how he spake unto you when he was yet in Galilee,

7 Saying, The Son of man [*Jesus*] must be delivered into the hands of sinful men, and be crucified, and the third day rise again.

8 And they remembered his words,

9 And returned from the sepulchre, and told all these things unto the eleven [*the eleven Apostles—Judas was no longer among them*], and to all the rest.

10 It was Mary Magdalene, and Joanna, and Mary the mother of James, and other women that were with them, which told these things unto the apostles.

11 And their words seemed to them [*the Apostles*] as idle tales [*nonsense*], and they believed them not.

12 Then arose Peter, and ran unto the sepulchre; and stooping down, he beheld the linen clothes [*Jesus's burial clothing*] laid by themselves, and departed, wondering in himself at that which was come to pass.

Background, Culture, and Setting

Let's pay close attention to how Luke describes the scene. Women came to the tomb on the first day of the week (they didn't wait!), very early in the morning (they didn't wait!), and they *came prepared*, which means they had spent time in advance to be ready to visit the Savior's tomb. The women discover that Jesus's body is missing, only to learn from the angels that Jesus was resurrected. Yet, when they run to find the male disciples and declare the good tidings of joy, the male disciples do not believe these women. Why not? There are two relevant reasons. First, how rare is it for someone to be brought back to life? Most people hearing that someone dead has come back to life will immediately doubt or disbelieve the news. On that point, we can have empathy for the disciples' disbelief. Second, in the Jewish culture of the day, the testimony or witness of women was considered useless or suspect. For example, in a court of law, the witness of a woman was disallowed as evidence. The cultural tradition was that women could not be trusted to tell the truth, because too often (as the tradition suggested) they were telling idle tales. On this point, the disciples were creatures of their culture and time. Because of "false traditions" in their culture, the disciples were not disposed to believe the witness of a woman. Even on this point, we can empathize with the disciples, because we have the benefit of hindsight. We may wish that their ancient culture was different and that the disciples were not influenced at all by any negative cultural influences. But we are all wrapped up in the time periods and cultures in which we live. It takes effort to become self-aware and then work against the ingrained personal and cultural habits that have solidified over time. If we continue to feel frustrated that the ancient followers of Jesus were not as faithful, self-aware, and righteous as we might expect, it's helpful for us to remember the maxim "Forgiveness is to abandon all hope of a better past."

Though we've dwelt here on the inadequacies of Jesus's male disciples, we should be quick to remember, to their credit, that the male disciples tested the women's witness and went to find out for themselves the truth of their words.

The Master Teacher

Though this book is dedicated to learning from Jesus about how to be better teachers and learners, Jesus does not make an appearance in this episode. So why do we include it? Because sometimes our culture or our traditions hold us back from learning. Sometimes we are unaware of what impedes our listening, our learning. Yet, if we are like Jesus's disciples, we can act immediately to test truth for ourselves.

Possible Applications for Learners

Do you systematically not listen to certain people in your life who could be teaching you truth? Are you like Jesus's male disciples, who, living in a culture where the testimony of women was considered worthless, refused to believe their testimony? Do you seek to test truths immediately? Or do you go with the crowd, believing whatever your culture tells you to think?

Helps for Teachers

Do you favor certain classes or categories of people because of their race, gender, economic circumstances, or educational attainments, while excluding others? Or do you invite all voices to participate in the learning experience? Do you help learners, when appropriate, become aware of cultural traditions that may keep us from testing the truth ourselves? Remember, the role of the teacher is to not identify and correct every and all misconception, false tradition, erroneous cultural wisdom, or error that learners may have in their minds. There is not enough time in the teaching experience to do so. The best teachers know to stay focused on teaching the most important truths instead of being distracted by small and minor irritants of errors that float around in our society. And the best teachers appropriately involve each learner in the learning experience.

Samples of questions that might help draw class members into the discussion:

- What would you say to a person who is critical of the Apostles for not believing the women?
- How do you picture the angels' tone of voice as they spoke to these women?
- What do you think was in the hearts of these faithful women before they arrived at the tomb? (Answers might include deep sorrow, some confusion, wondering what was next for them now that Jesus was gone, and so forth.)
- How do you think these two angels felt about being the ones assigned to deliver this message to these women?
- What does it tell you about Peter, that he ran to the tomb to see for himself?

Resurrection of Jesus

John 20:11–17

11 But Mary [*Mary Magdalene; see verse 1*] stood without [*outside*] at the sepulchre weeping: and as she wept, she stooped down, and looked into the sepulchre,

12 And seeth two angels in white sitting, the one at the head, and the other at the feet, where the body of Jesus had lain.

13 And they say unto her, Woman, why weepest thou? She saith unto them, Because they have taken away my Lord, and I know not where they have laid him.

14 And when she had thus said, she turned herself back [*away from the angels*], and saw Jesus standing, and knew not that it was Jesus.

15 Jesus saith unto her, Woman, why weepest thou? whom seekest thou? She, supposing him to be the gardener, saith unto him, Sir, if thou have borne him hence [*if you have taken His body somewhere*], tell me where thou hast laid him, and I will take him away.

16 Jesus saith unto her, Mary. She turned herself, and saith unto him, Rabboni; which is to say, Master.

> This is a very tender moment. Mary is very concerned about where the Savior's body has been taken. After turning away from the tomb and the two angels therein, she sees a man whom she assumes is the caretaker. The question comes up as to why she did not immediately recognize Jesus. Several possibilities exist. One is that she had been crying and was so distraught that she didn't even take a good look at Jesus at first. Another possibility is that she hadn't turned all the way around from the tomb. She "turned herself back" from the tomb and the angels in verse 14, yet she "turned herself" in verse 16, implying that she had not turned completely toward where Jesus was standing when she first turned from the tomb. Whatever the explanation, when Jesus said "Mary," she recognized His voice, apparently looked again, and her sorrow was over.

17 Jesus saith unto her, Touch me not; for I am not yet ascended to my Father: but go to my brethren, and say unto them, I ascend unto my Father, and your Father; and to my God, and your God.

> JST John 20:17
>
> 17 Jesus saith unto her, Hold me not; for I am not yet ascended to my Father; but go to my brethren, and say unto them, I ascend unto my Father, and your Father; and to my God, and your God.

Background, Culture, and Setting

This beautiful scene at the garden tomb evokes in us all "the hopes and dreams of all the years" to borrow from a beloved Christmas hymn. We feel with Mary the longing for what has been lost. We can imagine being in that empty garden with her, distraught that our Beloved Master is dead and gone, the One who taught us to hope for a better future, to experience a greater present, to know pure love and truth as we have never before experienced.

The Master Teacher

The resurrected Lord, who knows all things, asks Mary a simple set of questions, "Woman, why weepest thou? whom seekest thou?" We might pause and wonder. Doesn't Jesus already know the answers to these questions? If so, why is He asking? Perhaps because He wanted Mary to discover, or to articulate her reality, her truth. He empowered her. If Jesus simply spoke what everyone was thinking, without inviting their involvement, where would be the agency? The discovery? The learning? The becoming?

Jesus does not compromise our agency. Instead, He empowers our learning, even if it requires asking questions that He already knows the answers to.

Possible Applications for Learners

In this passage, we hear the curious command from Jesus to Mary, "Touch me not; for I am not yet ascended to my Father." We've all wondered at the meaning of this phrase and likely have heard endless speculation about what it means. The JST change in verse 17, above, might solve a bit of a problem otherwise encountered when reading Matthew and then reading John. The common understanding of verse 17 is that the resurrected Lord told Mary not to touch Him. Yet, Matthew 28:8–9 informs us that some women were met by Jesus as they ran from the empty tomb to tell the disciples that the Master's body was gone. They were allowed to hold Him by the feet and worship Him. So why was Mary Magdalene not allowed to touch Him (John 20:17)? The answer may be that she was. The JST changes "touch me not" to "hold me not." The Greek word *harpazo*, which means "the continuous action of holding," was translated as "touch me not" in our New Testament but would be better rendered as "do not hold me" or "do not hold on to me." Thus, with the JST as reference, we glean that Jesus simply was explaining to Mary that He had other work to do. As much as He loved her and she loved Him and the sweet reunion of hugging could go on for hours, Jesus had a timetable of ministry and work He yet had to accomplish. This was Jesus's gentle way of letting Mary know, "Don't keep Me from moving on with My other work."

As learners, we may be so inspired by a teacher, or by an insight gained, that we want to spend more time with that teacher or dwell longer on that insight. We may, in so doing, hold up the teaching agenda that has been planned and designed in advance. Good teachers know when to spend more time on a topic. Yet, learning for ourselves and others may be disrupted if the learning experience does not move along. As learners, we should be sensitive to the learning agenda and contribute to a successful learning experience by not inappropriately or inadvertently holding everyone up because of our longing to hold on too long, metaphorically, to the teacher or to some new point that has been made.

HELPS FOR TEACHERS

Like Jesus, we can ask compelling questions of learners, even if we already know the answer. Allow space for learners to think, discover answers for themselves, articulate what they know, and become self-aware of what they feel.

Note that we are not recommending asking those bland questions that everyone already knows the answers to that limit learning instead of encouraging it. You know, those questions in Sunday School such as: "Why is prayer important?" or something similar. Instead of asking a bland question that everyone knows the answer to but is so embarrassed by how unengaging the question is that they don't respond, good teachers would change the question slightly, lighting a fire of engagement among learners, "When did prayer last work for you? What were the circumstances? Why did you use prayer? And what happened?" Or more simply, "When recently did prayer benefit your life?"

Here are some questions that might help quickly engage class members in a class discussion:

- What tone of voice do you imagine Jesus used as He addressed Mary in verses 15 and 16? (The answers should include "gentle," "friendly," "kind," and so forth.)
- How do you think Jesus felt as He spoke to Mary here?
- What might be some reasons that Mary did not act startled when she saw the two angels in the tomb?
- What evidence do you see in verses 11–15 that Mary, at this point, did not have confidence that Jesus had been resurrected?
- According to footnote 17a, what might be a better translation of "Touch me not" in verse 17? (Two possibilities might be "Don't keep hugging Me," or "You must let go of Me now.")

Road to Emmaus Appearance

Luke 24:13–32

13 And, behold, two of them [*two of Christ's disciples, not Apostles*] went that same day
to a village called Emmaus, which was from Jerusalem about threescore furlongs [*about
seven miles from Jerusalem*].

14 And they talked together of all these things which had happened.

15 And it came to pass, that, while they communed together and reasoned, Jesus himself
drew near, and went [*started walking*] with them.

16 But their eyes were holden that they should not know him. [*Jesus kept them from
recognizing Him yet.*]

17 And he said unto them, What manner of communications are these that ye have one
to another, as ye walk, and are sad [*what are you talking about that makes you so sad*]?

18 And the one of them, whose name was Cleopas, answering said unto him, Art thou
only a stranger in Jerusalem, and hast not known the things which are come to pass
therein these days? [*You must have just arrived or You would know the tragic things which
have happened here in recent days.*]

19 And he said unto them, What things? And they said unto him, Concerning Jesus of
Nazareth, which was a prophet mighty in deed and word before God and all the people:

20 And how the chief priests and our rulers delivered him to be condemned to death,
and have crucified him.

> As these two disciples of the Master continue chatting with this Stranger who has joined them, you can feel their disappointment as they express to Him their dashed hopes.

21 But we trusted that it had been he which should have redeemed Israel [*we were hoping
that He would turn out to be the promised Messiah who would free us from our enemies*]: and
beside all this, to day is the third day since these things were done [*and besides that, it has
been three days now since He was crucified*].

> We see from verses 22–24, next, that these two disciples were among "all the rest" in verse 9, above, when the breathless women excitedly told the eleven Apostles what the angels had told them.

22 Yea, and certain women also of our company [*of our group of followers of Jesus*] made
us astonished [*told us an amazing story*], which were early at the sepulchre [*who went to
the tomb early this morning*];

23 And when they found not his body, they came, saying, that they had also seen a vision of angels, which said that he was alive.

24 And certain of them [*Peter and John; see John 20:2–8*] which were with us went to the sepulchre, and found it even so as the women had said: but him they saw not.

> The implication here is that since Peter and John didn't see Jesus, and the women's account couldn't be trusted because of the emotional state they were in, the whole thing about Jesus has turned out to be a big disappointment for these two disciples on the road to Emmaus.
>
> Watch now as the resurrected Christ teaches a firm lesson on faith, reminding these disappointed disciples of the numerous prophecies in the Old Testament that fit what has just happened.

25 Then he said unto them, O fools, and slow of heart to believe all that the prophets [*such as Isaiah and Jeremiah*] have spoken:

26 Ought not Christ to have suffered these things, and to enter into his glory? [*In other words, why is it so hard to believe that Jesus was the Christ, that He suffered, died, was resurrected and has entered into His glory in heaven?*]

27 And beginning at Moses and all the prophets [*starting with the writings of Moses (Genesis, Exodus, Leviticus, Numbers, and Deuteronomy) and continuing with the other Old Testament prophets*], he expounded unto them in all the scriptures the things concerning himself [*prophesying of Him*].

28 And they drew nigh unto the village [*Emmaus*], whither they went [*which was their destination*]: and he made as though he would have gone further [*indicated that He was going farther*].

29 But they constrained him [*begged Him*], saying, Abide with us: for it is toward evening, and the day is far spent. And he went in to tarry with them.

30 And it came to pass, as he sat at meat with them, he took bread, and blessed it, and brake, and gave to them.

31 And their eyes were opened, and they knew him; and he vanished out of their sight.

32 And they said one to another, Did not our heart burn within us, while he talked with us by the way, and while he opened to us the scriptures?

Background, Culture, and Setting

We have the benefit of hindsight. When we read the New Testament Gospels (Matthew, Mark, Luke, and John), we know right away who Jesus is. We know His true identity. We also know how the story ends. So familiar are we with the most heroic and consequential story in human history that we may struggle to empathize with how little Jesus's disciples truly understood Him and His plan until *after* His resurrection. Yes, He taught them that He would die and rise again, but the disciples had so little understanding and experience with what He was teaching. It was all so new, and in their minds, bewildering. Remember, most of us have had our entire life to be familiar with the story of Jesus from beginning to end. The disciples didn't know the story from the end to the beginning, which is why in this New Testament passage Jesus reveals or teaches it all again.

Or, perhaps more accurately, He reviews everything from beginning to end with these disciples. This time, it sticks. They have enough experience and enough clarity from His explanations to finally connect all the dots and see the grand plan. If we can use a rough analogy for how their eyes were opened to finally understand, imagine a movie that, only at the end, provides a dramatic reveal where everything you thought you understood in the movie now has to be entirely rethought because of this new perspective, revelation, or information. In fact, only after this final big reveal of information does everything truly make much more sense. This was the experience the two disciples had on the road to Emmaus, as did eventually all of the other faithful disciples of Jesus.

THE MASTER TEACHER

Jesus reviewed with His disciples what He had previously taught. He reviewed the scriptures with them and helped them to more fully see the truths that pointed to Him. The eyes of the disciples were opened by this timely review that combined reflection on the disciples' recent experiences and their study of the scriptures.

In this book, we have focused nearly exclusively on Jesus when discussing "The Master Teacher." Jesus is part of the Godhead, which includes God the Father and the Holy Ghost. These two other members of the Godhead are also Master Teachers. In this scripture passage, the Spirit plays a quiet but very significant role. In this passage, the Spirit is also a Master Teacher, confirming in the hearts of these disciples the truth of what they learned. The most powerful learning is when the heart and mind are brought together in unity, sealed by the Spirit.

POSSIBLE APPLICATIONS FOR LEARNERS

Learners should not expect to have a single experience with an idea or concept, or whatever it might be, and think that they have "learned." Learning is an ongoing process that requires review and repetition. As our understanding grows, we gain new, deeper, and stronger insights that strengthen the existing foundation which allows for greater growth and learning. Learners should create a plan to regularly review and practice their learning, and then to expand their knowledge beyond the boundaries they've reached.

Additionally, the best learners let the Spirit guide. Like these diligent, if initially unaware, disciples, good learners reflect while they are learning, "Did not our heart burn within us?" They seek the confirmation of the Spirit, and they seek to recognize the Spirit.

HELPS FOR TEACHERS

Don't forget to identify the Spirit when it is present, to point it out to your students. The Spirit is a significant source of sustenance. We can never have too many experiences with the Spirit. Furthermore, though we should always stand ready to provide a logical and reasonable reason for the faith within us ("Be ready always to give an answer to every man that asketh you a reason of the hope that is in you"; see 1 Peter 3:15), it is ultimately the Spirit that converts. An intellectual conversion to Jesus is not the role of the Spirit. Nor is an intellectual conversion to Jesus the point and purpose of the gospel or gospel teaching. Just as we are fed drop by drop and day by day in our regular consumption of food and water to sustain our lives, so too it is with the Spirit in our lives. We need the daily and regular consumption of the Spirit to be sustained. Great teachers invite the Spirit into the classroom and do all in their power to help others recognize when they have felt the Spirit. This both sustains the listeners and helps them become self-aware of how the Spirit works in their lives so that when they are not in a Sunday School environment, where someone is available to help them recognize the Spirit, they can learn to recognize the Spirit for themselves.

Here are some sample questions for promoting the involvement of our students in class discussion:

- What evidence do you see in verse 32 that the Holy Ghost was present as Jesus taught them? (Their hearts "burned" within them.)
- What does the word *holden* mean as used in verse 16? (Prevented from recognizing.)
- How would you put verse 21 in your own words?
- Why do you think Jesus taught them what He did in verses 27, rather than simply letting them quickly recognize Him as the Resurrected Christ? (Answers can include that they apparently needed a better foundation in the scriptures testifying of Christ to better carry on the work after He was gone.)
- How do you think the Savior felt when these two disciples pled with Him to stay for supper?
- What hymn do we sing in church that comes from verse 29? ("Abide with Me; 'Tis Eventide," *Hymns*, no. 165.)

The Great Commission

Matthew 28:16–20

16 Then the eleven disciples [*Apostles*] went away into Galilee, into a mountain where Jesus had appointed them.

17 And when they saw him, they worshipped him: but some doubted.

> The statement "but some doubted" in verse 17, above, undoubtedly refers to people other than these Apostles who met the Savior as described in verses 18–20 and detailed in John 21. Some might think that this could refer to Thomas who is sometimes referred to as "doubting Thomas," but his doubt was done away with (see John 20:27–28) before they went to Galilee. Thus, "some doubted" is most likely a general comment of Matthew, contrasting the witness of the Apostles who "worshipped him" (verse 17) as opposed to some members who still doubted that He had been resurrected.
>
> As you will recall, up to now, the Savior had limited His mortal ministry to the Jews. Now, though, He instructs His Apostles to take the gospel to all nations. Not only is this a major change in policy, but it is a strong statement that all must have the opportunity to hear and understand the gospel of Jesus Christ.
>
> Remember that the Jews considered themselves to be superior in status to all other people in the sight of God, because they were direct descendants of Abraham (Matthew 3:9). What Jesus now instructs is a clear reminder to these Apostles that their cultural background must be discarded in favor of the true doctrine that all souls are of equal worth in the sight of God (D&C 18:10).

18 And Jesus came and spake unto them, saying, All power is given unto me in heaven and in earth.

19 Go ye therefore, and teach all nations, baptizing them in the name of the Father, and of the Son, and of the Holy Ghost:

20 Teaching them to observe all things whatsoever I have commanded you: and, lo, I am with you alway [*always*], even unto the end of the world. Amen.

Background, Culture, and Setting

Jesus often went to the mountains to pray and commune with God. There are probably several reasons for this. First, mountains are symbolic of temples. A person is spiritually and physically closer to God when on a mountain. Second, mountains are apart from civilization. In the mountains we can avoid the typical distractions that keep us focused on the here and now and instead focus on things of God. Third, effort is required to get to a mountain. Even more effort is required to ascend a mountain. We value what we put our time and effort into. Jesus signaled the value of His prayer and meditation time by ascending mountains to worship. That He asked His disciples to join Him on a mountaintop takes advantage of all these reasons listed above for why mountains can help us experience greater focus on, devotion to, and commitment to the things of God.

The Master Teacher

At this point, Jesus did not chastise any of His doubting disciples. Jesus recognized their humanity. He honored the fact that they were in the process of spiritual growth and development. He recognized that asking questions is as natural as being a child of God. We are inquisitive by nature. He knew that with experience *doing* the word of God—serving, sharing, teaching, and testifying—even the doubting disciples would come to experience the truth of His word and the reality of His resurrection.

In fact, so unperturbed was Jesus by the lack of 100 percent readiness of His disciples that He pressed ahead to commission and empower all of them to do what He would do if He were here. Did He know they would make mistakes? Yes. But more important, Jesus knew that nothing could stop the work of God. Jesus knew that if He didn't allow His disciples to act, try, experiment, exert themselves, ask questions, and fail, or, in other words, if He didn't allow them to learn by doing, then the kingdom of God could never roll forward.

Jesus commissioned the eleven Apostles to go forth to all the world, bearing the glad tidings of His life, death, and resurrection. The word *apostle* literally means "one who is sent." That commission is still in force today. The modern-day apostles and prophets are under responsibility from God to organize, direct, lead, and oversee all efforts throughout the world to spread the good news of Jesus. We can participate in that great commission, under the direction of God's modern-day authorized servants, by teaching the gospel to others and letting our lives exemplify the gospel.

Possible Applications for Learners

Learners may still have some doubt or questions, and that is expected and natural. We should work to find answers to our questions, to remove doubt through experiencing truth.

Learners should seek to become self-directed in their pursuit of truth, to become someone who is not wholly dependent upon the teacher. Some learners love the security of knowing that there is a teacher who potentially has all the answers. But what happens if that teacher is no longer available or accessible? If the learner has become so dependent upon the teacher, the learner's growth may be stunted. Their own hearts and minds might have atrophied from lack of direct action. Great learners appreciate capable and loving teachers but are not led away into the carnal security of an ever-present teacher. The best learners take control of their own learning and don't wait for the teacher to act.

Helps for Teachers

The purpose of a teacher is to *not* make learners dependent upon the teacher. The best teachers commission, authorize, embolden, and empower their learners. At some point, the teacher bows off the stage and allows the learners to act for themselves. Jesus did not stay forever. Yes, He left the Spirit to abundantly guide His disciples. But Jesus knew that He if stayed, if He did all things for them, answered all their questions without letting them work for their learning and learn from failure and success, they could never be with Him or become like Him. One of the hardest things for a teacher to do, especially for those who have loved their learners and loved teaching, is to let go. In some ways, it's like being a parent. Yes, once a parent, always a parent. But at some point, children grow up and need to become agents unto themselves. Good teachers will not get in the way of that natural process of learners no longer being dependent upon the teacher.

Questions that can facilitate involvement in class discussion:

- What symbolism can you see in the fact that Jesus had the remaining eleven Apostles go to a mountain to meet Him?
- What major change of policy do you see in verse 19 compared to the policy Jesus had during His mortal ministry of going only to the Jews? (Now take the gospel to everyone.)
- What are some examples of significant policy changes in the Church today? (Combining high priests and elders into one elder's quorum in each ward. Doing away with home teaching and visiting teaching, replacing it with ministering. Changing ages for young elders and sisters to serve missions.)
- What special assurance does the Savior give His Apostles in verse 20? (He will always be with them by way of supporting and sustaining them as they go forth to carry out His instruction to them.)

Catching 153 Fish

John 21:1–17

In Matthew 26:32, Jesus told His Apostles that He would meet them in Galilee after His resurrection. Matthew 28:9–10 informs us that He told the women to tell the brethren to go to Galilee and there they would see Him. And Matthew 28:16 records that before Jesus's crucifixion, He had "appointed them" to meet Him in Galilee after His death. In this beautiful chapter, John tells us that they followed those instructions, and he gives us details about what took place.

1 After these things [*after everything John has told us so far*] Jesus shewed himself again to the disciples at the sea of Tiberias [*the Sea of Galilee*]; and on this wise shewed he himself [*and this is how He showed himself to them*].

> As we get to verse 2, next, several of the disciples have already journeyed to Galilee in anticipation of meeting the Savior there. While waiting there, they have decided to go fishing.

2 There were together Simon Peter, and Thomas called Didymus, and Nathanael of Cana in Galilee, and the sons of Zebedee [*James and John*], and two other of his disciples.

3 Simon Peter saith unto them, I go a fishing. They say unto him, We also go with thee. They went forth, and entered into a ship immediately; and that night they caught nothing.

> In the days of Jesus, it was common for fishermen to fish at night on the Sea of Galilee, when the fishing was best. Peter, having been a professional fisherman on that lake before the Savior said, "Come follow me," now takes his fellow disciples, and they fish all night, with absolutely no success. The "sons of Zebedee," verse 2 above, were James and John, and they, too, had been professional fishermen before being called by Jesus to follow Him. It must have been extra frustrating for these professionals to have zero success fishing. Watch now as the Savior gets their attention. Perhaps it is appropriate to imagine a bit of a smile on His face and a twinkle in His eye.

4 But when the morning was now come, Jesus stood on the shore: but the disciples knew not that it was Jesus. [*He was apparently far enough away that they didn't recognize Him.*]

> Something quite wonderful is now going to happen. The tired disciples have had absolutely no success fishing throughout the night. In the morning, this stranger on the shore asks them if they have had any luck. He then tells them to simply cast their net overboard on the other side of the ship. Perhaps there are few things worse than a stranger telling professionals how to do their work. Nevertheless, they do

what He says, and suddenly the net fills with so many fish (153 big fish, see verse 11) that they could hardly pull it in.

This rings a bell. An almost identical thing had happened when He first called Peter, Andrew, James, and John (see Luke 5:1–11). Jesus had come by, and because of the crowd, had requested that Peter take Him a little way out from the shore in his ship. When He was through speaking to the crowd, He told Peter to go out farther into the lake and let down his nets. Peter replied that they had fished all night with no success, but since Jesus said to do it, he did. Their net filled with so many fish that the net began to break. James and John quickly brought their ship out to help, and the large number of fish almost sank both ships.

The same thing is happening again. Could it be the Master who is on the shore now?

5 Then Jesus saith unto them, Children, have ye any meat [*have you caught any fish*]? They answered him, No.

6 And he said unto them, Cast the net on the right side of the ship, and ye shall find. They cast therefore, and now they were not able to draw it for the multitude of fishes.

7 Therefore that disciple whom Jesus loved [*in other words, John, the Beloved Apostle*] saith unto Peter, It is the Lord. Now when Simon Peter heard that it was the Lord, he girt his fisher's coat unto him, (for he was naked [*stripped to the waist*],) and did cast himself into the sea [*Peter jumped in and swam to shore, a distance of about 300 feet; see verse 8*].

8 And the other disciples came in a little ship; (for they were not far from land, but as it were two hundred cubits [*about a hundred yards*],) dragging the net with fishes.

9 As soon then as they were come to land, they saw a fire of coals there, and fish laid thereon, and bread.

This is a very touching scene. No one in the universe could be busier than the Savior. Yet He had taken the time to cook breakfast for His weary, discouraged disciples who had fished all night with no success.

10 Jesus saith unto them, Bring of the fish which ye have now caught.

11 Simon Peter went up, and drew the net to land full of great fishes, an hundred and fifty and three: and for all there were so many, yet was not the net broken.

There is symbolism here. Jesus told the Apostles, when He called them, that He would make them "fishers of men" (Matthew 4:19). The fact that the Savior helped them have such success with actual fish is symbolic of the fact that He will help them have great success in bringing souls into the gospel net and unto the Father.

12 Jesus saith unto them, Come and dine. And none of the disciples durst ask him, Who art thou? knowing that it was the Lord.

13 Jesus then cometh, and taketh bread, and giveth them, and fish likewise.

14 This is now the third time that Jesus shewed himself to his disciples, after that he was risen from the dead.

Next, the Master Teacher creates a teaching moment and uses it to teach Peter, who will become the President of the Church. He repeats the main point of the lesson three times, in verses 15, 16, and 17.

15 So when they had dined, Jesus saith to Simon Peter, Simon, son of Jonas, lovest thou
me more than these [*do you love Me more than these fish*]? He saith unto him, Yea, Lord;
thou knowest that I love thee. He saith unto him, Feed my lambs.

16 He saith to him again the second time, Simon, son of Jonas, lovest thou me? He saith
unto him, Yea, Lord; thou knowest that I love thee. He saith unto him, Feed my sheep.

17 He saith unto him the third time, Simon, son of Jonas, lovest thou me? Peter was
grieved because he said unto him the third time, Lovest thou me? And he said unto him,
Lord, thou knowest all things; thou knowest that I love thee. Jesus saith unto him, Feed
my sheep.

Background, Culture, and Setting

Remember in Luke 5:2–8, when after a night of fruitless toiling on the Sea of Galilee, Jesus commanded His future disciples to cast out their nets yet again? And when they tried to bring in the mess of fish, the nets broke because of the abundance of fish?

At the beginning of Jesus's ministry, the disciples' nets broke. Now, at the end of His ministry, their nets did not break. After having followed the Master for such a long time, their nets brought in an overwhelming load of fish. The lesson that the disciples learned from heeding the words of Jesus, which led to the massive haul of fish, is that they now had overwhelming, if symbolic, evidence that they were ready to stand in Jesus's stead. They were ready to be fishers of men.

The Master Teacher

Why would Jesus ask His disciples to cast their nets into the sea when Jesus, as the creator of heaven and earth, could have caused a swarm of fish to jump into the boat? Jesus was testing His disciples yet again. Jesus knew that without tests and testing there would be no clear evidence of learning and growth. So Jesus tested His disciples. And what did they learn? They were reinforced in their faith to trust Jesus and follow His word, because when they did as He told them to do, they captured 153 fish. Incidentally, this must have been an unusually large catch for the Gospel writers to record such a specific number.

Jesus, as the Master Teacher, gave His disciples a test as evidence that they were ready.

Possible Applications for Learners

Learners should trust their teachers, especially when the teachers challenge them to demonstrate their learning. Learners should be willing and eager to be so challenged. Learners should seek for and expect opportunities to be tested. Without testing, we have no road signs to signal our progress. Tellingly, the word *testing* and *testimony* come from the same ancient word—*test*. What that means is that without a test, we have nothing of which we can later testify. In other words, we can only testify of what we have been tested on. That is why we should welcome testing so that our testimonies will grow.

Finally, the best learners show their love of Jesus by helping others to learn. Peter, the eager learner, was commissioned by Jesus to feed His sheep. Like faithful and devoted

Peter, great learners learn to become great teachers who empower others to be life-long learners.

HELPS FOR TEACHERS

Good teachers give opportunities for learners to see that they are capable. They give challenges to learners to demonstrate to everyone that the learners can or have achieved the expected and targeted abilities. They show the learners that they have succeeded or have arrived at the learning goals.

Involvement questions for discussing this block of scripture:

- Can you come up with any possible symbolism for casting their nets on the "right" side of the ship in verse 6? (Answers might include that in many scriptures, the "right" hand of God symbolizes being on the Lord's side, living righteously, and doing what is right, such as in the parable of the sheep and the goats (Matthew 25:31–34.)
- How did the miserable failure to catch any fish at all during the night help set the stage for meeting the Savior in the morning?
- What lesson do you see in the fact that Peter was first instructed to "feed my lambs" in verse 15 and then "feed my sheep" in verses 16 and 17? (Among other things, it can emphasize the importance of teaching and nurturing children in the gospel while they are young.)
- What tender truth about the Savior do you see in the fact that He had prepared breakfast for these tired, hungry disciples (verses 9–13)? (Answers could include that Jesus, the mighty Jehovah, the all-powerful resurrected Christ, has taken time out of His very busy schedule to cook breakfast for these humble disciples.)
- What does verse 7 show you about Peter's personality?

CONCLUSION

It is our hope that this book has demonstrated that there is always more we can learn about and from the Savior in the New Testament. We hope it has provided spiritual insights, teaching suggestions, and learning helps that bless your life and the lives of those you teach. This book was written to show how beautiful and compelling the gospel is and how tremendously amazing Jesus was at teaching it and helping people learn to live it for themselves. We hope you feel inspired, encouraged, and empowered to be a better teacher and learner because of Jesus.

This book has covered a lot of ground. We hope you do not feel the need to remember or master everything found here. Instead, use the index to return to pages that correlate with scriptures you are currently studying or preparing lessons on. Mark chapter entries that hold insights to inform your teaching and learning. Review applications and grow your ability to teach and apply the gospel.

In your drive to become a better teacher or learner, take the long view. Give yourself time to grow and develop. Find specific aspects of teaching and learning that you wish to improve upon. Make a deliberate plan to practice improving your teaching or learning. Any skill that matters takes time and practice to master. If we wish to be more like Jesus in our understanding, teaching, and application of the gospel, we need a lot of practice. The Atonement allows us to grow, change, make mistakes, and recover. Consider this: Without practice, we could never grow to be more like Jesus. Practice requires that we make mistakes. The Atonement, therefore, provides the conditions for us to practice without fear of permanent failure since it can heal all things as we strive to become more like Jesus.

BIBLIOGRAPHY

David Ridges, *Your Study of the New Testament Made Easier*, 2 vols. (Springville, UT: Cedar Fort, Inc., 2014).

New Testament Student Manual, *The Life and Teachings of Jesus and His Apostles*, Rel. 211–212, CES, Published by the Church of Jesus Christ of Latter-day Saints, 1979.

Bible Dictionary, Holy Bible, LDS Edition of King James Version of the English-Speaking Bible, 1979.

JST (Joseph Smith Translation of the Bible), taken from footnotes and longer JST quotes in the back of our LDS English Bible. JST passages not found in our Bible are taken from *Joseph Smith's "New Translation" of the Bible* (Independence, MO: Herald Publishing House, 1970).

James E. Talmage, *Jesus the Christ* (Salt Lake City: Deseret Book, 1977).

Teachings of the Prophet Joseph Smith (Salt Lake City: Deseret Book, 1977), 275–76.

Bruce R. McConkie, *Doctrinal New Testament Commentary*, vol. 1 (Salt Lake City: Bookcraft, 1977).

Webster's New World Dictionary, Second College Edition, 1980.

Rev. J. R. Dummelow, ed., *A Commentary on the Holy Bible* (New York: Macmillan, 1909).

Hymns of The Church of Jesus Christ of Latter-day Saints (Salt Lake City: Deseret Book, 1985).

Index

A

B

C

D

E

ACKNOWLEDGMENTS

As always, the marvelous folks at Cedar Fort have been incredible to work with, starting with Kathryn Watkins and continuing with the editors and all others involved in bringing this book to fruition. Also, this is the first time I have worked with a coauthor, and it has been a delightful privilege to work with Taylor Halverson. His teaching skill, enthusiasm, and tremendous insights and knowledge of the Holy Land have contributed immeasurably to the power and contributions of this book.

—David J. Ridges

Many thanks to Kathryn Watkins of Cedar Fort, who initiated this project and marshaled the support and resources to help bring it to fruition. And many thanks to my coauthor Dave Ridges, who, despite a very busy schedule, agreed to join this project. He brought perspective, humor, passion, key insights, and, significantly, encouragement. Finally, thank you to all the competent and dedicated professionals at Cedar Fort who bring forth goodness and light in this and so many other products they bring to the world.

—Taylor Halverson

About the Authors

David J. Ridges

David J. Ridges taught for the Church Educational System for thirty-five years. He taught adult religion and Know Your Religion classes for BYU Continuing Education and spoke at BYU Campus Education Week for many years. He has served as a curriculum writer for Sunday School, seminary, and institute of religion manuals. His callings in the Church include Gospel Doctrine teacher, bishop, stake president, and patriarch. He and his wife, Janette, have served two full-time Church Educational System missions. They are the parents of six children and are enjoying a growing number of grandchildren. They reside in Springville, Utah.

Taylor Halverson

Dr. Halverson is an aspiring master learner, seeking to learn from everyone he meets, everything he reads, and everything he experiences. His personal and professional passion is to empower learners to experience the joy of becoming. He fulfills his passion in a variety of ways: he is a Brigham Young University teaching and learning consultant, a prolific author of more than 200 articles and books, an educational travel leader to destinations worldwide, and an inspiring teacher. He holds a PhD in Judaism and Christianity in antiquity and another PhD in instructional systems technology.

Scan to visit	Scan to visit
www.davidjridges.com	www.taylorhalverson.com